FORTITUDE

AMERICAN RESILIENCE
IN THE ERA OF OUTRAGE

DAN CRENSHAW

TWELVE

New York

Twelve

Hachette Book Group

1290 Avenue of the Americas, New York, NY 10104

twelvebooks.com

twitter.com/twelvebooks

First Edition: April 2020

Twelve is an imprint of Grand Central Publishing. The Twelve name and logo are
trademarks of Hachette Book Group, Inc.

The publisher is not responsible for websites (or their content) that are not owned by the
publisher.

The Hachette Speakers Bureau provides a wide range of authors for speaking events. To
find out more, go to www.hachettespeakersbureau.com or call (866) 376-6591.

Library of Congress Cataloging-in-Publication Data has been applied for.

ISBNs: 978-1-5387-3330-1 (hardcover), 978-1-5387-3329-5 (ebook)

Printed in the United States of America

LSC-H

10 9 8 7 6 5 4 3 2 1

This book is for my mom, who taught me true grace and fortitude in the face of suffering.

And to my wife, Tara, who taught me love, loyalty, and strength.

I would not be here without you.

CONTENTS

Introduction: Stay Outraged   1

Chapter 1: Perspective from Darkness   11

Chapter 2: Who Is Your Hero?   35

Chapter 3: No Plan B   62

Chapter 4: Be Still   79

Chapter 5: Sweat the Small Stuff   108

Chapter 6: The Right Sense of Shame   127

Chapter 7: A Sense of Duty   158

Chapter 8: Do Something Hard   178

Chapter 9: The Stories We Tell Ourselves   197

Chapter 10: The Story of America   219

Acknowledgments   245

About the Author   249

INTRODUCTION

STAY OUTRAGED

I left my Washington, D.C., office in the Cannon building to go vote on the House floor of the Capitol, as I usually do multiple times a day while Congress is in session. It was spring of 2019, and I had just been sworn in to my first term a few months prior. It was sunny outside, barely above 70 degrees, the air pleasant and crisp, so I avoided the underground tunnels that connect the Capitol to the Congressional offices and crossed Independence Avenue above ground instead. It's a far more enjoyable experience to walk toward the Capitol with its majestic dome in full view, and hard not to be awestruck by the experience of entering the beating heart of our republic.

You never know who you will run into during that five-minute walk. Capitol Hill is teeming with journalists, activists, and tourists, most of whom are rather pleasant, most of the time. That particular day I noticed a group of protestors outside the Capitol. This was not an unusual scene; activists often gather at the steps of the Capitol. It is the People's House, after all. But this was an unusual group of protestors, because it wasn't clear what they were protesting *for*. There were no calls for the passage of a particular bill or attention to a certain issue. Instead, they wore shirts that simply read "stay outraged," along with a matching assortment of signs and buttons that appeared to be professionally crafted from an established vendor, not purchased hastily from some ragtag print shop.

I was puzzled. I wondered about the meaning of their slogan, *stay outraged*. Why this phrase? Why not instead rally around a slogan that more accurately depicted what they protested or advocated for (assuming there was one)? What drew these young people to the slogan and more importantly to the notion that *staying outraged* was the desired end goal? Perhaps I was simply too unenlightened to understand the value of perpetual outrage?

Perhaps. But unlikely. It was more likely that this small group of activists was born of a larger cultural paradigm, one that has permeated our media and national discourse as of late. It was far more likely that the antagonistic headlines of the last few years had finally succeeded in manipulating the behaviors and emotions of our citizens and directed these activists to the steps of the Capitol to encourage others along the same path of indignation and everlasting anger.

This aimless rage was deliberately designed, intended to produce this exact result.

"It's Important to Stay Outraged" implored the title of a 2019 op-ed, in the hope that their readers would not fall back into the complacency of their cheerful daily routines. "Get outraged and stay outraged" exclaimed another headline, equally desperate for sustained irritation. "Never lose your sense of outrage," tweeted Senator Bernie Sanders, knowing the most effective political manipulation is achieved by raw emotion. One recent op-ed acknowledged the psychological tax of outrage, giving more in-depth advice: "How to #StayOutraged without Losing Your Mind: Self-Care Lessons for the Resistance." Outrage is in vogue, they proclaim, and more than that, it is a *necessity*. But this story of unrelenting ire goes far beyond the abstract sloganeering of politicians and media: "Stay Outraged" is also sprawled on countless T-shirts and stickers and buttons for sale across the internet, as these young activists had clearly discovered.[1]

It's a peculiar thought, this notion that if only you were sufficiently informed, aware, and *woke*, that you would have a duty to exhibit an intense state of fury. The apocalyptic nature of our unjust reality must *surely* enrage you. It must! Not only that, but once you've achieved an enlightened state of madness, then you must *stay* that way. Perhaps forever.

Being a normal person with normal concerns, you may read those headlines with healthy skepticism if not outright confusion. Don't we live in the most prosperous nation on earth with a quality of life and freedoms that are the envy of the world? *But*, respond the outraged, *this is just proof you aren't paying attention!* If you *only knew* the true depths of disaster, despair, and injustice in our midst, you'd rush to join the mob in righteous cultural warfare, scream slogans in solidarity, march arm-in-arm to cancel those who disobey, destroy the careers of those who misspeak, and pile on those who dare to defend anything other than outrage orthodoxy.

A peculiar thought indeed. Let me suggest an alternative.

Outrage is weakness. It is the muting of rational thinking and the triumph of emotion. Despite what you've been hearing and seeing as of late, it is not a virtue. It is not something to be celebrated, nor praised, nor aspired to. It is a deeply human emotion—even understandable at times—but rarely is it productive, virtuous, or

---

1   https://medium.com/the-coffeelicious/how-to-stayoutraged-without-losing-your
-mind-fc0c41aa68f3
https://www.bostonglobe.com/metro/2019/04/10/important-stay-outraged/
TZbhVJVmQKvEtJJ4CsqcGJ/story.html
https://www.etsy.com/market/stay_outraged
https://townhall.com/columnists/michaelbrown/2019/06/29/get-outraged-and
-stay-outraged-n2549005
https://www.wisconsingazette.com/multimedia/stay-outraged-swing-left/video
_7fbc07d4-6036-5977-9501-bc160eb56447.html

useful. It is an emotion to overcome, not accept, and overcoming it requires mental strength. This book is about acquiring that necessary mental fortitude.

Let's define our terms. What do I mean by "outrage"? It is a specific term with a specific meaning. Not all forms of outrage are always unjustified—far from it. There is such a thing as righteous indignation. This book is not about "proper outrage," stemming from real tragedy or wrongdoing or injustice. This is not a book about overcoming true grief. It is about *outrage culture*, and the new-found tendency to reflexively assume the worst of intentions when reacting to news or commentary or political discourse, and default into an emotionally driven hatred of the "other," whoever that may be. It is the petty, weak-minded, and ultimately unproductive response to our neighbors, fellow citizens, and political opponents that has been normalized and even elevated in our culture.

It is about the hypersensitivity that has infected our society, where undesirable language is the equivalent of physical violence, where an old tweet or Facebook post can be grounds for ruination and public shame, and where an absence of reason or fact encourages public indictment, moral outrage, and mob rule. Outrage culture is the weaponization of emotion, and the elevation of emotion above reason. It is the new normal, where moral righteousness rises in proportion to your level of outrage. The more outraged one is, the more authentic one is perceived to be. And the more authentic one is, the greater one's moral standing. Reason, rationale, and evidence be damned.

My debut in the public eye was premised on an *avoidance* of outrage culture—a rare thing these days—when I was publicly expected to take *Saturday Night Live* and Pete Davidson to task for wronging me with an offensive joke. I didn't. More on that later. For now, it suffices to say that mere words could not hurt me, a statement that is becoming less and less prevalent or even desirable to many these days. It was my first personal encounter with modern-day outrage culture, but I am certainly not the first to notice this new and troubling trend.

Jonathan Haidt and Greg Lukianoff dissect this new phenomenon in *The Coddling of the American Mind*. Focusing on college students in particular, the authors find that a culture of "safetyism" has become widespread, wherein students actually feel that opposing views are a literal danger to their *physical* well-being. The mantra of "sticks and stones" is being turned on its head. This false sense of danger leads to extreme reactions to that perceived danger. Students and activists feel justified shouting down others, vandalizing property, and even assaulting political opponents. This sort of emotional reasoning has been promoted instead of discouraged, leading students to see microaggressions everywhere they look. Instead of seeking understanding, people are increasingly interpreting the actions of others in the least generous way possible and assuming the worst of intentions.

While Haidt and Lukianoff write about this phenomenon in terms of recent history and the modern terminology that accompanies it, it is not entirely new. I first encountered irrational microaggression interpretations when I was in third grade, growing up in Katy, Texas, just outside of Houston. We were discussing food chains in class, a fairly simple subject for a third-grader. Big animals eat small animals. Small animals eat plants or insects. But being a kid, this explanation was not really sufficient to hold my attention. I built out my own explanation of food chains, using the reality and experiences around me. After all, you master a subject faster if you put it into your own words. And so I went on to describe food chains in the context of our classroom. I pointed to my classmates, one by one, and said, "John ate Lindsey. Merril ate John." And so on. And then I ended my lecture with the final apex predator in my food chain: my teacher. For the sake of anonymity, I'll call her Miss

Smith. I said, in perfect earshot of said apex predator, that "Miss Smith ate Merril."

It did not go over well. My teacher, Miss Smith, was unable to imagine the audacity of a nine-year-old suggesting she might eat a student, even in the context of discussing food chains. It was clear that she thought I was referencing her weight, despite the fact that I had listed everyone in the class as part of my food chain exercise. She was decidedly outraged, lacking in facts and context with which to address the situation, and unable to assume anything but the most malevolent of intentions.

She dragged me to the vice-principal's office, my classmates looking on in terror as I left the classroom. "Shame, shame," they must have thought. Merril was in shock, but perhaps he was also re-lieved that Miss Smith had no intention of eating him. Into the VP's office we went, where a serious woman sat and listened intently as a flustered Miss Smith explained the extent of my misdeeds. The red-haired professional administrator gave no indication that she thought this was a frivolous accusation. In fact, as she nodded along to Miss Smith's frantic story, she brought out a book to show me. In it were the disciplinary codes and potential punishments for "profanity." I had not learned this word, "profanity," yet, and given my vocabularic disadvantage I was in no position to argue.

This is where the whole episode really went off the rails. The VP pointed to a section where it said that law enforcement could be called in serious cases of profanity. They were dead serious. They were threatening to call the police on a nine-year-old for saying Miss Smith ate Merril. I was scared to death as they discussed going easier on me with mere in-school suspension. My mom was eventu-ally called into the office to be informed that I would be punished with in-school suspension. She was terminally ill with cancer and would pass away a year later. We had real struggles, not perceived ones. Life-and-death circumstances, not microaggressions. She was undergoing another round of chemotherapy, and she couldn't care less about the hypersensitive, outrage-prone Miss Smith. At home, I was not in trouble. We had more important things to worry about.

Since that day in 1993, things have only gotten worse. It is anyone's guess as to why—many other authors have examined this trend—but I think the internet, social media, and transformed incentives within mainstream media reporting are a good place to start. What used to be rare instances of political correctness, microaggressions, and irrational anger have metastasized into the outrage culture we see today—characterized not just by outrage and political correctness but also by identity politics and an increasingly polarizing media and digital environment. Haidt and Lukianoff note, "Common-enemy identity politics, when combined with microaggression theory, produces a call-out culture in which almost anything one says or does could result in a public shaming." Add in the element of anonymization inherent in social media comments, and you have the ingredients for a toxic mob-politics culture.

This mob, unshackled by the interpersonal limitations of good manners, won't even let progressive leaders like President Barack Obama off the hook. The *New York Times* Opinion section pounced on the former president after he made this all-too-sensible observation on cancel culture: "I can sit and feel pretty good about myself because, man, you see how woke I was, I called you out. That's not activism. That's not bringing about change. If all you're doing is casting stones, you're probably not going to get that far. That's easy to do." The young columnist at the *Times* dismissed Obama as an out-of-touch boomer for his comments. It was a foolish, emotional reaction to sensible remarks by the former president.

It isn't just millennials and Gen Z, of course. The entire US political system seems to be infected by these problematic cultural trends, cheered on by our media and opinion journalists who thrive on drama, conflict, and strife. Knowing that the most salacious headlines will get the most clicks, journalists are all too happy to oblige. As Jeffrey Berry and Sarah Sobieraj of Tufts University note in *The Outrage Industry*, headlines and commentary are deliberately misleading and infused with "outrage speech," designed not for substance but for emotional response. In *Hate Inc.*, Matt Taibbi notes that this is partly because the financial incentives for incendiary opinion journalism are so strong: "There is a financial pull toward research-free stories. Writing 1,200 words of jokes about a Trump tweet costs less than sending a reporter undercover into a Mexican *maquiladora*."

It has grown terribly difficult to separate objective journalism from opinion journalism. Back in the days when evening news anchor Walter Cronkite was considered "the most trusted man in America," there was a well-defined separation between news and opinion. Today they have bled into each other. This exacerbates division and resentment. Whereas we have long understood that Fox News leans right and MSNBC leans left, the rest of the news networks still try to pass themselves off as objective nonpartisans. This frustrates conservatives the most, since networks like CNN still proclaim to be "just the facts" or "news analysis," when in fact most hosts persistently engage in left-leaning opinion journalism. It is no wonder that trust in mass media has been edging lower and lower over the past twenty years, down to 41 percent in September 2019, according to Gallup.

This has deeper consequences than just heightened societal tensions. These problematic cultural trends and misleading media practices are changing the actual values that we deem *good*. Our culture has come to view heroes—the figures or attributes that we should emulate—differently, and that's a problem.

A classic view of the hero archetype would be a person who is calm, collected, and self-assured. A person raised on the mantra of "sticks and stones," or the great Rudyard Kipling line "If you can keep your head when all about you are losing theirs and blaming it on you." Of course, few people have an honest claim to such virtue—we are all prone to overreaction and emotional reasoning—but the point is that we *strive* to be better. We want to be that hero, the one who has a cool head, a calm soul, and a sharp tongue.

It seems that that archetype has lost standing to its own antithesis: righteous outrage, emotional reaction, and moral grandstanding. The new hero is the one who "speaks truth to power" (a tired cliché with an elusive definition) and signals their oppression loudly, ready to bravely point out how others have wronged them. Where the bravery is in this scenario is lost on me, but people believe it nonetheless. It's an indication that certain *versions* of heroic attributes, like being brave and outspoken, are still valued—though their meaning has been twisted to accommodate what is clearly a victimhood mentality. And why not? In this day and age, victimhood is power.

That is the setup for this book. As a society we may have finally reached a point where we realize something is a little off. The pathos has grown out of control, often at the expense of logic, decency, and virtue. We aren't acting the way we are supposed to. We mock virtue, without considering how its abandonment accelerates our moral decay. We aren't acting as a culture that is mature or enlightened or educated, we aren't acting worthy of this beautiful country and political system that we inherited from our revolutionary ancestors. Rather, we don a mantle of fragility, of anger, of childishness, and are utterly shameless in doing so.

The consequences of this decay are many, but ultimately it's a question of sustainability. How long can our society endure when we are at each other's throats? We don't want to know the answer to that question. We want to know how to fix it.

These lessons will make you mentally stronger, better equipped to face life's challenges, and as impervious as possible to the outrage culture all around us. The basic message is this: If you're losing your cool, you are losing. If you are triggered, it is because you allowed someone else to dictate your emotional state. If you are outraged, it is because you lack discipline and self-control. These are personal defeats, not the fault of anyone else. And each defeat shapes who you are as a person, and in the collective sense, who we are as a people.

This book is about actively hardening your mind so that you can be the person you think you should be. It is about identifying who that person is in the first place, and taking responsibility for the self-improvement required to become them. It is about learning what it means to never quit. It is about learning to take a joke and giving others some charity when they make a bad one. It is about the importance of building a society of iron-tough individuals who can think for themselves, take care of themselves, and recognize that a culture characterized by grit, discipline, and self-reliance is a culture that survives. A culture characterized by self-pity, indulgence, outrage, and resentment is a culture that falls apart. It really is that simple, and it is a truly existential choice.

We must make that choice. And it must be a choice to be more disciplined, mentally tougher, and convinced of the fact that we control our own destiny. The next chapter of our American story depends on it.

CHAPTER I

PERSPECTIVE FROM DARKNESS

The bomb—a homemade fertilizer-based compound wrapped in plastic—was mere feet away, buried about a foot below the hard surface. A rudimentary pressure plate—two panels of wood and some wire and a battery—was all it needed to detonate right in my face. We, Americans, spend millions of dollars trying to blow up our enemies. Smart bombs aren't cheap, and national security is an expensive pursuit. The Taliban spent about ten bucks, including the cost of labor and medical benefits.[1]

The blast felt like a truck hitting me head on—and in the truck were a dozen angry men with shotguns, all shooting at me simultaneously. My world went dark. I suffered through the pain for about forty-five minutes until I got myself up and walked to the helicopter, able to hear the soothing rattle of the Mk 46 machine guns laying down cover fire around me. But I could not see them. When I slipped into unconsciousness on the medevac helicopter, I was in Afghanistan. When I woke up, I was in Germany.

Getting blown up by an IED, and enduring what came after, was not an experience I am eager to repeat. But that day in Afghanistan was something I had come to expect. I had sought leadership and

---

1 Note to the Fact Checkers: THIS IS A JOKE. Taliban don't have health insurance.

combat from an early age—most SEALs do—and I knew death and wounds were possibilities. They were what we signed up for. Hell, I had known it ever since my dad gave me a copy of Dick Marcinko's first book, *Rogue Warrior.*

"Read this," he said.

"Sure, whatever," I said. I was only thirteen and therefore incapable of showing excitement to a parent. But secretly, I was psyched.

Rogue Warrior—a gritty, rough-hewn, half-true book series written by the founder of SEAL Team Six—is not fine literature, but it might as well have been Hemingway and Shakespeare combined for a kid seeking adventure and glory. I hadn't just found an entertaining book about the SEAL teams. I had found my purpose. At that young age, I decided I was going to become a Navy SEAL. I was going to join the teams and relish in the risk-taking bravado that made these guys superhuman.

But here's the thing: Romanticized, hypothetical thrill-seeking eventually becomes pretty damn real.

On that fateful 2012 deployment, we found ways to deal with the threat of injury and death. For one, we painstakingly planned our missions so as to mitigate risk. Just as importantly, we used humor to dilute the seriousness of our circumstances. Some of the guys had a shirt made for the deployment with "Keep Your Feet 2012" inscribed on the front—in reference to the high likelihood that one of us would get our legs blown off. Dark humor really is the best humor.

And it is terribly necessary in a place as unfunny as Afghanistan, with its long history of destructive conflict. Kandahar Province has been a seat of war for the past three thousand years. The eponymous city of Kandahar itself was an Iron Age fortress. Centuries later it served as a garrison town of Alexander the Great, who named it after himself. If you list the nations that have fought in, around, and over Kandahar, you get a list of many of the great powers of

Europe and Asia across the ages. Greeks, Macedonians, Afghans of all stripes, Persians, Sikhs, Russians, Britons, and Americans: We've all come, fought, and bled in this place where an infinite number of tribal afflictions and familial conflicts spread across the region. Within these small subgroups, loyalty runs deep. In this culture, the slightest insult is met with fatal retribution, and enmities are passed down through generations, never forgotten. Behind the eyes of every Afghan live thousands of years of blood feuds and tragedy. Their history resides deep within.

I noticed, especially in the rural outskirts, that the Afghan gaze was never bright and optimistic, but piercing and unsurprised, as if they had witnessed history a hundred times over. Their knowledge of the modern world was practically nonexistent, and yet their eyes revealed a sort of hardened wisdom. Their movements were slow and even careless, as if they understood that their existence was but a fleeting moment in the dustbin of history. Laughter was rare, and our American joviality was popular only with the children.

Perhaps it was nihilism they exhibited. It would be understandable, given that their circumstances could be described by Western standards as utterly hopeless. But that wasn't quite the right explanation for what I saw. What I saw felt more like *perspective*. And it struck me how fundamentally different, down to the bone, the Afghan perspective was. These people were *hard*. Able to endure suffering that a typical American would never dream of. I recall on various operations—conducted in the deep cold of January—that Afghans we encountered would look relatively comfortable in sandals and a thick blanket thrown over their shoulders. Not much different from their wardrobe in the spring or summer. The biting cold didn't faze them. Punishment was part of their routine.

Being a sixth-generation Texan, I can relate to this sentiment that history lives within you. My ancestors' history gives me perspective when I want to complain about the Wi-Fi on a passenger jet being too slow or intermittent. I need only recall that Sarah Howard, my first ancestor to settle in Texas, at age sixteen, had to walk across the frontier for weeks. Drinking water had to be discovered daily. During her travels, she had a run-in with Comanches that resulted in the death of her first husband. She remarried, and her new husband was killed in similar circumstances, as was her infant. She was held captive and miraculously escaped. She remarried again.[2] And here I am, complaining about the Wi-Fi.

Perspective is a revealing thing. It's perhaps a lesson we could learn from Afghans and the first Texas settlers. The men we met in Afghanistan, aged in warfare and hardship, never uttered the word "microaggression." I believe the women were equally steely-eyed—maybe more so—but their customs prevented us from ever finding out. Only family members are allowed to see women in the rural, deeply traditional areas of Afghanistan where we operated. The children, having not yet come to terms with their hopeless reality, brightened when they spoke of coming to America one day. Frankly, it was heartbreaking. While our own citizens burn our flag or sneer at our pledge of allegiance, millions of people around the world would do anything to be here. America is a place of opportunity for individuals willing to seize it, and that fact is still well known around the world, even if our own population is increasingly ignorant of it. Our country consistently ranks as the number one destination for all immigrants, when asked where they would go if given a choice. Germany, at second place, isn't even close.[3]

---

2 Handbook of Texas Online, Susan Orr and H. D. Orr, "HOWARD, SARAH CREATH," accessed November 18, 2019, http://www.tshaonline.org/handbook/online/articles/fhoat.

3 The US ranks as the top destination for 21% of immigrants surveyed, and Germany ranks second at 6%. https://www.weforum.org/agenda/2017/11/these-are-the-countries-migrants-want-to-move-to/

The Afghan perspective changed our tactics in combat as well. Fighting in Kandahar required unlearning so much of what we learned, and thought we knew, about action in combat. The transformative agent of it all was the improvised explosive device, or IED. In my prior deployments to Iraq I had of course encountered IEDs. They are the ubiquitous tool of the insurgent and the terrorist: bombs, traps, explosives set off by command or activation, placing time and distance between the act and the man. An IED, well hidden and well built, maximizes the insurgent's advantages of concealment, surprise, and terrorization—and minimizes our advantages of firepower, communication, and action. It generates stress and fear in unaccustomed and untrained men—and dread in even the most experienced soldiers, sailors, and Marines. Those who have seen combat understand that there is something qualitatively different between a stand-up fight, where a man may be shot but may also shoot back, and an IED, where death comes in an explosion and there is no defense.

The roads and byways of Kandahar Province were riddled with IEDs in ways I'd never before seen. The bombs, improved by the Taliban with more than a decade of experience plus the expertise of Pakistani and Iranian trainers, were everywhere. And, we came to understand, they were the enemy's main effort.

This changed our tactics dramatically. When you take fire on a battlefield, the traditional course of action is to seek cover, and do it fast. Bullets are troubling things, and they have the unique ability to force a 200-pound man into as tiny a profile as possible behind the nearest rock or other small object. In the movies, incoming fire sounds like a buzzing mosquito shooting past your ear. But this isn't the right sound. An actual bullet is breaking the sound barrier when it goes past you, creating a physical and audible conical waveform, which sounds like *snap! crack!* It is an unmistakable sound that requires immediate reaction. If you have air support overhead, call 'em up. AC-130 gunships are deadly accurate with their 30 mm cannons and they aren't stingy with ammo. But barring overpowering air superiority, a proper response to incoming gunfire typically means returning fire and maneuvering against the enemy. Hold a base of fire to keep their heads down, and send a squad around to the enemy's flank. Run from cover to cover, never staying up more than a few seconds. Know the difference between cover and concealment. A thick mud wall is cover, because it stops bullets. A thick bush in the mud is concealment, and does not stop bullets. See the difference? This isn't your weekend warrior airsoft match. We practice these maneuvers ad nauseum in the SEAL teams, so that when the time comes, we are taking action instead of contemplating a response.

In Kandahar Province, here's what you did when the snaps came: nothing. Well, not *nothing*—we would fire back when appropriate—but we wouldn't take cover, we wouldn't move off our route, we wouldn't seek refuge in an unscouted location, even if mere feet away.

We had learned the hard way that nearly all those alternatives were riddled with IEDs.

IEDs buried in the street. IEDs concealed in doorways. IEDs along garden walls. IEDs in sheds. IEDs in canals. IEDs in culverts. IEDs in homes. IEDs in houses of worship. IEDs in random hilltops that made no sense at all.

On one particular mission, three of our guys hiked up a small hilltop to establish an overwatch position while the platoon cleared through the village below. The hilltop was impossibly remote, even by Afghan standards: a mountainous waste in the middle of nowhere, where neither we nor the Taliban reasonably expected the other to conduct operations. The village was quiet, and we never encountered the enemy. My teammates dug in, and as they prepared their position, a loud bang pierced the air.

They had set up atop a large IED—and the blasting cap went off without detonating the main explosive charge. They should have died but, thanks to Providence and a hasty bomb emplacement, did not.

The damn things were *everywhere*. It was possible to predict, to an extent, the placement of IEDs by professionals or informed amateurs. But the freelancers—locals looking for revenge or just some extra pay—were just anarchic. You didn't know where they would decide a good bomb location would be. A vegetable garden. A bicycle. A window. A garbage pile. A courtyard. All these could be the grotesque welcome mats known as IEDs. On more than one occasion I watched our Afghan partner force, the "Afghan Commandos" as they were known, fall victim to such horrors.

This meant that ordinary tactics went by the wayside. We traveled in single file—which is a crappy tactical formation in normal circumstances—because stepping outside of that could mean death, or at best *not* "Keep Your Feet 2012." Our whole world shrank to what was cleared—and what was not. We worked, patrolled, and fought in this landscape—ranging from Mars-like deserts to pristine river valleys to snow-covered peaks—strewn with bombs hidden at the whim and direction of uncompromising Taliban, fanatical students, and vengeful grape farmers.

On June 15, 2012, they got me.

During a last-minute emergency mission, we flew out to support a United States Marine Corps special-operations (better known as "MARSOC") operation underway in neighboring Helmand Province. Helmand was every bit as bad at Kandahar: Two years earlier, a major offensive there in and around the town of Marjah had sputtered out with a putative coalition victory but no lasting gains. The MARSOC platoon had already sustained casualties, and was running out of ammo and radio batteries after two days of fighting. They needed to be tagged out, and higher-ups wanted to maintain a presence in the area. So they volunteered us (also known as "voluntold," in military jargon). We were happy to join the fight, as I recall. I didn't have any obligation to go on that mission, but I asked to go anyway. Thus, how the small decisions change your life forever.

We flew in under cover of darkness. We liked to do that for reasons beyond ordinary nighttime surprise. After a decade-plus of war, we understood IEDs fairly well. One thing an IED generally needs is power. They require batteries to detonate them if they aren't manned—and most of them weren't. Batteries aren't hard to get out in the world, but in remote rural Afghanistan they, like most manufactured products, are not to be squandered. When an IED was not imminently needed, the Taliban would disconnect or even remove the battery powering it. If they didn't—if it was kept connected with a bit of current sapping its potency over time— eventually it would run down. Fresh batteries meant functional bombs.

Swooping in before dawn meant the enemy would not have the chance to reconnect those disconnected batteries. That was the theory.

On June 15, 2012, it was wrong. The Marines had been fighting there for days, which meant all the IEDs were connected to their power sources, a sickening array of deadly welcome mats meant to maim their victims, not kill them.

We were clearing a mud-walled compound just as daylight appeared above the horizon. There is a beauty to the early morn- ing that most don't get to see. The deep green countryside, with patches of poppy fields throughout, is blanketed with a thick morning mist. The intense humidity permeates your clothing. The smell of fire in the village reminds you of its ancient quality, where not a single modern appliance can be found. Goats and roosters begin stirring as the sun rises. Locals brew strong chai and cook shakshuka, an egg-and-tomato-puree dish. Even in the intensity of a combat operation it is impossible to miss the undeniable charm of these places, untouched by modern civilization, captured by ancient tradition and the conflict that accompanies it.

In this former home, abandoned after years of warfare by the family who lived there, we poured into the inner courtyard. Our explosive ordinance specialists were still clearing it as best they could with metal detectors, and in hindsight that clearance should have been more methodical and deliberate. But there is a fine balance between thoroughly clearing a compound for IEDs and forcing the platoon to wait outside, exposed, for extended periods of time.

Someone called for my Afghan interpreter, Raqman, a good man with whom we had worked for some time. These interpreters are the unsung heroes of the wars in Iraq and Afghanistan. They often suffer threats and ostracism for their willingness to endure the battlefield alongside us. Their motivation isn't money; there isn't enough money to make it worthwhile facing down insurgents who know where you and your family live. They are idealists. They work and risk death because they believe in our common cause of freedom.

Raqman responded to the call immediately. Running before me, his foot fell on a particular spot just two feet away from where I stood. I was looking right at him. As I later discovered, he instantly lost all his limbs in the explosion. Even though I was staring right at him, I never actually saw it happen. My experience was a series of tremendous blows and subsequent realizations.

A train hit me. Ears ringing. What the fuck was that.
Darkness. Something is wrong. Got hit.
My legs—reach down and see if they're still there.
They're there. I feel them.

Pain everywhere. Mostly my abdomen. Something shot
through it, I think.

My eyes must be caked with mud. I can barely see anything.

I hear groaning and screaming—someone hit an IED.

Pain everywhere *but* my eyes.

I crawl around a little bit. Mostly to see if my body still functions.

My teammates make their way to me.

I ask someone to pour water on my eyes to remove the dirt,
so I can see.

It doesn't work. I can only see light and some shapes. Must be
a lot of dirt.

I recognize my corpsman's voice, as he works on my wounds.

I say, "Dude, don't get blown up. It sucks."

He laughs and tells me to shut up.

I was conscious throughout. Our corpsman stopped my
bleeding—the worst of which was from my knees—and wrapped
up my eyes. It still did not occur to me that there was anything
wrong with them. I could only hear the situation around me: my
teammates calling to each other, communicating the situation with
tense voices. I later found out that a foot—wearing the typical
Solomon boot that we all wore—hit one of my teammates in the
chest about fifty yards away.

Raqman was groaning in pain. Deep, deep pain.

Most people's experience of combat wounds is from the movies.
A soldier gets hit, his guts spilling out, and he looks down at them
screaming in horror. But this is not the way it is. In reality, truly bad
injuries sap your energy and prevent you from screaming. Instead,
the sound a wounded man makes is much deeper, more visceral,
emanating from the depths of his being. It is a groan, a cry, a moaning that reeks of utter desperation. It is far worse than a scream. It
is true pain manifested into sound.

This was the sound that Raqman made. It is unforgettable.

As the corpsman tended to me, and we waited for the medevac helicopter, a thought entered my head: We may be in a firefight any second now. Raqman was barely alive, and he would later die in the hospital. Our EOD (explosives ordinance disposal) chief petty officer took a little frag also and would be evacuated with us. All hands were needed to fight. I could hear the medevac helo coming in low. This was no time to ask someone to carry me. Blown up and blind, I stood up and walked myself to it. Dave Warsen, who would be killed two months later, heroically laid down cover fire for me as I boarded the helo. It was my last memory of him.

Medics on board the helicopter took one look at me, laid me down, and eased me into unconsciousness. I woke up, days later, far away from Helmand, far away from Kandahar, far away from my brothers in arms, far away from the war and dust of central Asia. I was brought back into consciousness in Germany, at the American hospital at Landstuhl. A breathing tube was being unceremoniously ripped from my throat. Rather unpleasant.

I opened my eyes—or thought I did—and saw nothing.

A physician came to see me and told me the truth. My right eye was gone. My left eye was so heavily damaged that there was virtually no chance I would see with it again. My future was a future of blindness, of darkness—of no sight, no color, no visual beauty. I would never see a sunset, a friend, a loved one again. In one instant, in a fatal footfall, all that was ripped away. I would never read a book again. I would never see a movie again. I thought about Tara, my fiancée, and the chance that I might not see her when we finally got married. Would I be able to remember my loved ones' faces?

I thought back to another time in my life, two decades earlier. The first time I ever witnessed the kind of inescapable pain that I was now feeling—and the grit to overcome it—was with my mother. She fought a battle that so many other modern women fight: breast cancer. And she did so with endurance, grace, and optimism. Her example has never left me, and I wasn't about to let some cheap-ass IED in the ancient killing fields of Afghanistan render me unworthy of her memory.

She was only thirty-five years old when she was diagnosed; same age as me as I write these words. When she got the news, it was one day before my little brother's first birthday. I was five years old. The doctors told her she might have five years to live, and they were right. Soon after, she would be feeling the pain I was feeling now, as the cancer and chemotherapy ripped apart her body in battle.

She fought it for five years, and when I was ten, she died. If you've ever cared for a loved one in terminal decline, you know what that's like. There is an intensity of loss that is immeasurable. Words don't do it justice. The hole deep down in your gut feels like it will never go away. As a child, the intensity of the experience is made worse as grief is amplified by incomprehension. Going from kindergarten to fourth grade knowing that your mother is dying—that the center of a small boy's world is collapsing—is an experience I wouldn't wish on anyone.

But from this grief came learning. I got to experience the nature of a true hero, and the example she set was the most powerful, fortifying, and selfless thing I have ever seen—including in combat. Lying helpless in a hospital bed, I had to wonder whether my mother had asked the same desperate question I was currently asking: Would I ever see my family again? I figured that if she could suffer through that question and the unknowable answer, so could I.

My mother spent half a decade staring death in the face, burdened with caring for two small boys whom she would not live to see grow up. She lived day to day in ever-increasing pain. The cancer afflicted her—and the cancer treatments afflicted her, too. Six rounds of chemotherapy on top of radiation treatments are a brutal experience for even the strongest constitution. Self-pity is never a useful state. But if anyone had reason to feel sorry for herself, and to complain a bit, it was my mom.

She never did.

In terminal decline and in pain, across five years, I never heard her complain once. I never heard her bemoan her fate. I never saw her express self-pity. Every day she woke up was a day she was still alive, and she *lived*. She was dying, and she was grateful to not be dead yet. Every extra day was a gift where she could look her boys in the face. Every next evening was another night she could tell us she loved us before bed. Even during her last days, when the hospital delivered her deathbed and hospice nurse to our dining room, her demeanor did not change. We played Clue every night. We played with my G.I. Joes. She laughed through the pain and the anguish, knowing she had just a few days left.

Susan Carol Crenshaw was exactly the opposite of what she had every right to be. Instead of wallowing in victimhood and despair, she was an optimist with a genuine heart and a goofy sense of humor. She told my dad before she died, "You bring any floozy women around my boys and I'll scare the shit out of them." Dark humor is the best kind of humor. Maybe that's where I got it from.

A little perspective can be the difference between spiraling into dark despair and clawing your way back to the light. A brave young woman fought through despair twenty years before, which meant I could do it now, suffering in darkness in a sterile hospital room in Germany. So when the doctors told me I had virtually no chance of seeing ever again, I just heard one thing:

Virtually.

Self-deception and optimism are sometimes indistinguishable. I decided right then that I was going to see again. I still had one eye. I used to have two, but that was twice the number I needed. Whatever it took, I was going to *see*.

But if I was going to see, I needed surgery immediately. I have never been one to believe that you can simply will yourself to miraculous healing. Buried in my ravaged left eye was a sliver of copper, an artifact of the bomb, and it was slowly, surely, inexorably burning out what remained of my retina. Metal is toxic when inside the eye, unsurprisingly. It needed to go. To do that, I would have to be transported again—this time to Walter Reed hospital in Bethesda, Maryland.

It took a couple of days to make it happen. This was where some of the misery set in. I'd been through a serious physical trauma. Awake now in Landstuhl, I could not move. I was beaten and, for the moment, physically broken. I was riddled with shards and debris, under the skin and deep within. I was swollen badly, suffering from a thousand small cuts. Everything burned and itched. Though oddly enough I don't recall any pain in my eyes. Go figure.

The physicians and I fought a lot. I wanted to go to Walter Reed *now*. Their timelines for action were informed by medical and logistical realities. My timeline was not. I wanted to be stateside in hours, not days. I had an eye to save, dammit. Resignation is not in my nature, much like it was not in my mother's.

Two other SEALs, Joe and Rey, had flown with me to Germany to be by my side, and thank God they did. They understood me better than anyone in a hospital could and they managed my tumultuous relationship with the doctors. They made sure I wasn't going through it alone.

And what was *it* exactly? I said before that I woke up unable to see. But this was not entirely true. I could not see my surroundings, true, but I was certainly *seeing*. I was surrounded by constant hallucinations, the result of my optic nerve still communicating erratically with my brain. The hallucinations were lucid, and all followed a pattern:

I was in Afghanistan.

I was with the guys.

I was in an Afghan village. Mud walls and compounds.

There was an Afghan man sitting next to me.

There were piles of weapons in the corner.

I lived my previous experiences over and over again. I knew it wasn't real. I was hallucinating but not delusional. If I was awake, I was seeing these images. If I was lucky enough to fall asleep and dream (never more than thirty minutes), then I would wake up still inside the visual reality of the dream. This literal living nightmare would continue unabated for another week.

Tara was there when I finally arrived in Bethesda and never left my side from that moment on. Most of my family came up to see me, as did many friends. They were far more worried than I was, and their spirits were low. This was most likely due to the fact that they were mentally coherent enough to sense the pessimistic expectations of my surgeons. The doctors did not think I would see again. They said so many times, and I simply didn't believe them. My optimism, my self-deception, my belief that the coming surgery on my left eye would work and that I would see, was nothing less than a delusional gift that allowed me to keep my sanity.

Though I am not one for overt expressions of faith, I will say this: I genuinely believe God's strength was working through me then. He was allowing me to believe something impossible. I prayed, and my family prayed, and we *believed*. We believed that military surgeons would pick through a pierced and shrapnel-ridden eye, remove the most minuscule shards and debris, and *restore my sight*. We did not have good reason to believe it. But we did.

Often, now, someone will ask me, "What was it like knowing you might never see again?" I tell them I don't know. It's true. I don't. I never believed it. I was in a lot of pain and anguish in that period. But I never believed *that*. I never believed I was blind for life. I believed I would see again and fully recover, minus one eye. I believed I would return to my platoon and serve a full career as a one-eyed Navy SEAL.

The physicians and the surgeons didn't believe it. Yet they did their work and did their best—and as they did, miracles happened there in the operating room. They told me up front what they expected. My lens was destroyed. (It still is. I have no lens.) My retina was likely to detach. My iris was ruptured. (It still is. I can't dilate my pupil as a result. It's why you'll never see me outside without sunglasses.) My eye was a mess. My best-case scenario was a patch over the right eye and glasses thick as a Coke bottle over the left (which I still wear when not wearing a special contact). Maybe, they thought, I would live a reasonably happy life with vestigial vision: shapes, colors, shadows, that kind of thing.

I thought otherwise. I thought I was going to see. The best-case scenario was the only scenario. I went into my first surgery with some degree of confidence and an upbeat spirit, despite the fact that I hadn't slept in days and my hallucinations were in full nightmarish swing. Every night Tara slept by my side. I needed her there for comfort and peace of mind, but also because the hallucinations were so disorienting. They were driving me mad. I was convinced, for instance, that my bed was in the shape of an X. I could only lie diagonally, and because I could never see the bed, I couldn't get reoriented. I remember waking up one night (or day?) from a dream where I was in a sort of third-world department store—full of fluorescent lights and cheap clothing—pushing through racks of disorganized musty clothes. In the dream, someone might have been chasing me. I had a sense of anxiety but wasn't sure why. When I woke up, I couldn't escape the dusty, decidedly unfashionable shirts, jackets, and dresses that were all around me. The nightmare was literally inescapable.

I was on edge, and Tara was one of the few people I wanted around to dull the pain. I was too irritable to handle small talk, which meant I was too irritable for most people. A couple of my best friends from the teams, Joe and Dave, were also there around the clock to provide support and much-needed comedic relief. One of the first questions they asked me when I arrived in Bethesda was, "So, Dan, we can start making fun of you for looking like a pirate for the rest of your life, right?" Never too early for the dark humor of the teams.

Two great things happened after my first surgery. They removed the broken lens (the cataract) along with the copper wire and other debris in my eye, and my hallucinations stopped. As I was being wheeled back to my room for recovery, an astutely observant nurse finally asked the question, "How long have these hallucinations been going on?"

"The whole time," answered Tara, exhausted from caring for me and watching someone she loved suffer for the past week.

"Oh my God," she replied. "He will have irreparable PTSD if we don't stop them." She requested a heavy dose of Ativan, a strong antianxiety medication, in the hopes it would make the hallucinations disappear. It worked. But it didn't work immediately. Oddly enough, I still had hallucinations, but they were *Christmas-themed* hallucinations. Christmas trees, presents, candy canes. It was downright bizarre, and just as crazy as it sounds. After a few hours on the potent drug, everything faded to black. I was finally blind. And it was a relief like you wouldn't imagine. I slept.

Within the next few days, I began to recover from surgery and see the shapes and colors around me. I remember the complete and utter relief from my friends and family. We were on the verge of a miracle.

And then, a few days later, it all came crashing down again. During a checkup with ophthalmology, they discovered a small hole in my retina, a "macular degeneration" in doctor-speak. Now, a small hole isn't a big deal since it just creates a small blind spot in your vision. The problem is that the hole will keep expanding, because of the natural anatomy of your eye, until you are totally blind.

The surgerical fix for this is actually quite simple, but given the fragile state of my eye, doctors were reluctant to open it back up. We were faced with two simple options. One: Don't do the surgery and enjoy the limited sight I had for a period of time. See Tara again, see my family again, and then say good-bye as the vision slowly deteriorated to blackness. Or two: Do the surgery and risk going blind right away, since there was such a high chance of my retina detaching during surgery. There was virtually no chance I would have a successful surgery.

But I have some family history in last-ditch pursuits of medical miracles. My mom died in 1994, after volunteering to be a patient in a clinical trial for an anticancer drug known as Taxotere. She didn't qualify for the trial at first, but the lead physician was so impressed with her vitality, positivity, and *fight* that he sought an exception— and she became patient number one. A local TV station in San Antonio interviewed her about the treatment, and she looked up-beat. "It's been wonderful," she said. "Before, I had no hope. I had gone through all the stages of treatments and there wasn't really anything left. I had no options." She is seen in the news report laughing and relaxed as she undergoes the therapy. There was real risk in this unknown new drug. The side effects and correct dosage were not yet known. But fear and hesitation were not an option. She went for it.

The Taxotere worked too well. Rapid remission of tumors in her right lung led to its collapse and several surgeries, during which time the Taxotere was discontinued and the cancer returned, more aggressive than before. She kept fighting as she always had, and she was fighting when she passed.

And so the option seemed obvious to all of us. Risk blindness? Yes. Blindness was coming either way. Best to confront it head on, like the image of that old farmer hurling a bottle of cheap whiskey at the incoming tornado. We went for it, and my second miracle happened. But there's a downside to this surgery even when it is successful: My world went dark again for six weeks.

This six-week recovery period was far from ideal, but bearable. I was accustomed to being blind at this point, but I do admit that the trauma of being blind would have been far greater if it was a permanent condition. It is one thing to deal with blindness as a possibility, with some hope that you will see again in a matter of weeks; it is quite another to adapt to blindness knowing that it is your permanent state. I know other veterans who have suffered similar injuries to mine, but lost both eyes. My story pales in comparison to theirs. My story pales in comparison to *many* other acts of sacrifice and heroism.

The great danger for me postsurgery was a detached retina. If that happened, all else would be for naught. It would be blindness, whole and permanent, with no recourse. My eye needed to heal and my retina needed to stay firmly in place. So here is what the doctors do: They place a gas bubble in your eye. The bubble fixes the retina firmly in place—but only if you stay facedown.

For six weeks.

Facedown for six weeks, blind and waiting, takes a bit of adaptation. No one is particularly built for it, and I am less so than most. The fact that the whole front side of my body was still sore and riddled with shrapnel wounds didn't make lying facedown any more pleasant. It was an enforced helplessness. Even if I could have moved, and I could by then, I didn't dare. Just straightening my neck up or rolling over could be a fatal moment, plunging me into darkness forever. I made certain to heed the doctor's orders and always face the ground. I even borrowed a massage chair—the kind where you place your face down for a back massage—which I sat in all day, listening to audiobook after audiobook (my favorite was *77 Shadow Street* by Dean Koontz). I sat with my thoughts, my family, a very patient and loving Tara, and my white chocolate mocha from Starbucks (don't judge me, I had a craving for them—couldn't help it).

I thought about a lot of things. Some of them pleasant—mostly seeing and getting back to my platoon—and some not so pleasant. I was irritable. I probably lashed out way too many times. I sometimes partook in some of the petty outrage that this book indicts. Tara stuck by me anyway.

But I never thought about being blind. I took issue with the small stuff—the menial annoyances of daily life were highly amplified for me. Perhaps because they were things that I could control. But when it came to the truly frightening possibility of blindness or even just permanent visual problems—the thing I could not control— I was silent on the issue. The assumption of eventually recovering my sight in my left eye was unwavering. It was fact. Nonnegotiable. In a sense, I was able to handle the hard stuff because I let off steam on the small stuff.

When the six weeks were over, I sat up—and I was not blind. Moreover, with the help of a truly remarkable contact lens from BostonSight, to which the Navy referred me years later, I was eventually returned to 20/20-correctable vision with my left eye. Without my contact in, I still use Coke-bottle lenses to see. I do still have a cataract that can't be totally fixed. But the fact that I can correct my vision to 20/20 is nothing short of a miracle.

That's my story of being blown up. I can't say I recommend the experience. Yet even as it was happening—even in the moment after the blast, I had to admit: It could have been worse. I still had my legs. I had my arms. I had ten fingers and ten toes. My brain worked, even after the severe concussion. I was still alive. It is impossible not to constantly think of the many veterans who have sacrificed so much more. Impossible not to think of SEAL Petty Officer Second Class Mike Monsoor, who threw himself on a grenade while on a rooftop in Ramadi, Iraq, in 2006, saving his teammates. Impossible not to think of Air Force Master Sergeant John Chapman, who fought all night against the Taliban, coming in and out of consciousness from his wounds, eventually succumbing to them on that Afghan ridgeline, but only after earning the Medal of Honor for saving twenty-three servicemembers. Impossible not to think of my platoon members and dear friends, Dave Warsen and Pat Feeks, who were killed just two months after I was evacuated from Helmand. Impossible not to think of their loved ones who had been expecting them home a month later. Impossible not to think of the eight men whose initials are tattooed on my chest in remembrance: Charles Keating IV, Patrick Feeks, Dave Warsen, Brad Cavner, Brett Marihugh, Kevin Ebbert, Brendan Looney, and Tom Fouke. This is the simple reality: Others have had it harder than me. Many, many others.

From that darkness comes realism. From that realism comes gratitude. From gratitude comes perspective.

A healthy sense of perspective is an antidote to outrage. It is an antidote to self-pity, despair, and weakness. It is not a cure-all for your mental state when faced with adversity, but it is sure to dull the edges of your worst tendencies toward mental breakdown. It is an appreciation of context with which to approach your experience. A sense of perspective is imbued into BUD/S[4] students from the very beginning, when instructors say to a class full of shivering, tired, and sore students, "Thousands have come before you and they did just fine. So quit your complaining." The fact is that *if someone else can do it, so can you.*

---

4 BUD/S stands for Basic Underwater Demolition/SEAL, and it is the six-month crucible to become a SEAL. More on BUD/S later.

Perspective doesn't necessarily have to be gained through experience, though it certainly helps. It can be self-taught. You can open your mind to the obvious truth that your experience, your hardship, your inclination to outrage, can be overcome because others have done so. Perspective, and the benefits of it, can be a simple choice you make.

A short review of recent human history may help. By every measurable metric, this is the best time to be alive, period. We have more equality and respect for human rights than at any other time in history. Diseases that used to wipe out millions are now easily treatable. Poverty, crime, and illiteracy are down. Violent crime is down. Society has grown safer. Life expectancy is up. Having multiple children die of disease or violence used to be commonplace, especially on the frontier. Now it is mercifully rare. Today, child and infant mortality is a fraction of what it was just a century ago. Our lives, particularly here in America, are blessed with comforts that never could have been imagined a generation prior, let alone imagined in other modern-day countries. Because of my father's work as a petroleum engineer, I spent all four years of high school in Bogotá, Colombia, then a war-torn country where the rule of law was a mere suggestion and kidnappings were the norm. If there's a people who know a bit about perspective and perseverance, it is the Colombian people. Their country today is a model of what can be accomplished when people choose to rise from the ashes of war, not fall victim to it.

Despite living in what is by any reasonable definition a Golden Age of civilization, people are anxious, unhappy, and outraged, seeking moral purpose from activism and politics instead of church or community or social fabric. With many big problems cured, reduced, or eliminated, our small problems have been elevated remarkably in our public discourse. Now that society is immensely safer, kinder, and better for children's aggregate survival, we complain vehemently about proper pronoun usage and disrespect-ful remarks on Twitter. In New York City, the size of chairs at a private school was deemed a microaggression to overweight people.[5] The City of Berkeley felt it a priority that the word "manhole" be changed to "maintenance hole," lest we be worried about the patriarchal nature of "manhole" or its lack of "non-binary gender inclusivity."[6] The students at Oxford University voted to replace clapping with "jazz hands" because clapping could, in their words, "trigger anxiety."[7]

You don't need to live in the 1800s or an impoverished war-torn country to gain perspective and gratitude, but you *can* simply learn about them. And maybe that's all you need to adjust the lens through which you view your current situation.

I had many defensible reasons for bitterness and grievance after getting blown up and losing an eye. I *chose* not to be bitter. It was not an easy choice, and there were many times when I failed to act with the grace that my mother taught me. But it was the right choice, and the right standard to aspire to. I knew, on a very basic level, that the difference between choosing to be optimistic and choosing to be embittered would be the difference between choosing to live and choosing to die. The right perspective made that choice easy.

Aristotle wrote that *habit* defines us. Before we pursue our higher purpose, before we have quality of character, we have habit. My habit was to never quit. My habit was to avoid self-pity and believe in a better future, albeit with a bit less vision. My habit was to strive for self-improvement and learn to adapt. Lose an eye? Turn your

---

5   https://www.nationalreview.com/2018/01/pc-culture-2017s-most-ridiculous-moments/

6   https://www.foxnews.com/politics/berkeley-will-remove-gender-terms-including-manhole-and-manmade-from-city-code

7   https://www.nationalreview.com/corner/oxford-students-vote-to-ban-clapping/

head more so you don't run into doorjambs. Adaptation is built upon good habits, after all.

Those habits were forged by lessons from a dying mother; her grit, her humor, her grace. They were shaped in lessons from a loving father who gave us a decent life and refused to be beaten by the loss of the woman he had planned to spend his life with. They were informed by travels around the world, growing up in places like Colombia. They were hardened in the crucible of BUD/S. And I was reminded of them by Tara, now my wife, as she stood with me through the worst of times. If ever I was close to an embittered and self-pitying existence, only she saw it, and brought me back from it.

All that prepared me to survive this. Not physically survive it, but mentally survive it.

My *mental* outcomes were a consequence of my habits—and my habits were a consequence of my choices. It is true that character is to some extent innate. Our genetic makeup imbues in us certain proclivities. But it is as true that character is mostly a consequence of choices. We all make them. And we should make them *deliberately*, with the knowledge that these choices are part of our *responsibility* toward a purpose other than our own selfish aims. That responsibility is to your family, friends, community, and country.

Perspective from darkness, perseverance in the face of adversity, purpose through action, and optimism in the face of failure are foundational antidotes to outrage and victim culture. But more than that, they're a prescription for a happier life.

CHAPTER 2

WHO IS YOUR HERO?

As a teenager I spent my summers working on a ranch just outside San Antonio. The pay was crap, but my dad said it would "build character," so there I was. I don't remember resisting the idea any. I listened to my parents, generally speaking. My father emphasized the importance of a traditional upbringing: Earn your own money, learn the value of hard work, get good grades, and be respectful. You can talk about these values all you want, but experience tends to be the best teacher. And so that was how I ended up on a ranch in the blistering Texas heat, clearing rocks and brush, cleaning out stables, and repairing fences. On a good day I got to sit on a John Deere mower and cruise around for a few hours cutting the grass. But that was rare, and the rocks needed moving. Manure needed shoveling.

The rancher I worked for was a family friend named Steve. He was a man straight out of Central Casting: When God needed a straight-up Texas rancher, He designed this guy. Before becoming a rancher in his later years, he was a collegiate football player, a US Air Force Academy graduate, and in time a US Air Force colonel. He owned his own consultancy firm. He worked as an engineer. He held multiple advanced degrees. This was a man who had seen and done it all—and as a boy, I took him seriously.

One day, sitting in the passenger side of Colonel Steve's F-350 truck, we had a simple conversation that I'll never forget. On our way to a section of the ranch that needed some maintenance, he turned and fixed his gaze on me. "Dan, you have to figure out who you want to be in this world. It's a question we have to answer...who we want to be. Do you know who you want to be?"

I looked a little confused, and he could tell.

"I don't mean what you want to do when you grow up. I mean who you want to *be*."

"I don't know, sir," I said.

He shared his own story. "When I was young, I wanted to be a tough guy. Then I grew up and wanted to be a smart guy. Then I retired, and now I want to be a fun guy."

Then he kicked me out of the car and pointed to the field full of rocks that needed to be cleared. In that moment, I was a rock-clearing guy.

I thought about that conversation for years afterward. At the time the meaning wasn't apparent to me. The deeper lesson of that question was not yet obvious. Being a young teenager, I conflated "who we want to be" with "what we want to do." But this was not the meaning implied by the retired colonel.

When we ask ourselves who we want to be, we are defining the character traits that we aspire to. Those character traits don't just appear out of nowhere; they are observed and then adopted. We identify them in others, and we make those people our "heroes." This implies certain questions: When we look to the future and envision ourselves ten years from now, what does it look like? And how will we be different, new, and improved? What new attributes and character traits will we have, and whom can we look to in our present life to derive such character traits?

When I graduated from high school, I wasn't anything close to being a SEAL. But I knew I had to start believing I was someone who *could* be a SEAL. I had to be a tough guy. I had to be an athlete. I had to be a humble leader. More than that, I had to be a smart guy. My goal was to become a SEAL officer, and to do that I would need a college degree and good grades. I was mapping out what psychologists call the "ego identity," which is an enduring sense of who a person is. Coined by Dr. Erik Erikson, the term merges all of the different versions of oneself: the SEAL-self, the academic-self, the social-self, and so on. And for me, there were different heroes that I sought out for every category of self.

When I say that heroes are important, I don't necessarily mean that you should have a specific hero in mind, like a particular person. People are flawed and imperfect, and idolizing a particular person as *the* person you want to emulate inevitably leads to eventual disappointment or disenchantment. My heroes are more abstract. They are archetypes—symbols or stories that project a set of ideas, values, and collective knowledge. In another sense, heroes are the visualization for a set of goals that you are setting for yourself. Our culture is rife with these kinds of archetypes, as all cultures are. It's a very human thing to tell stories of the people, often mythical characters, whom we should learn from. Sometimes these people, or in some cases gods, are in fact not good at all. We learn those lessons, too.

Last year I visited the new Star Wars theme park at Disney World. My wife is a big Disney fan, so I have been to the Disney parks more often than most guys. The stories of Disney are deeply imbued with hero archetypes and the narratives that accompany them. These heroes are faced with uncommon adversity that they overcome, learn from, and inspire the rest of the world with.

On that day in the newly opened Star Wars park, we stopped to watch a fairly entertaining exhibit: Jedi training. Kids could sign up for a short class on how to handle a lightsaber, led by real-life Jedis. It was thoroughly entertaining to watch, and it looked like a lot of fun for the kids. Each kid was given a small circle on the stage to train inside of, and issued a Jedi cloak and lightsaber. Before their epic battle began with Darth Vader (who eventually entered the stage from a very cool smoky cave) the Jedis trained the kids in various fighting moves—"Saber ready! Cut right! Cut left!" Interspersed between lightsaber movements were lessons about the Jedi mind-set—"Do or do not, there is no try." In classic Disney fashion, the attention to detail was impressive and the execution flawless.

One thing stood out to me. At one point, while quizzing the kids, the Jedi teachers asked, "Do we let hate and anger drive our actions?" (The younger kids initially screamed "Yes!" prompting a quick correction from the Jedis, and a good laugh from me.) But in that moment, the kids were being taught an important lesson in behavior and mental toughness. And they were being taught that lesson by a respected hero archetype, the Jedi.

These broader and deeply entrenched archetypes provide a culture like ours with some basic heroes. And there are lessons to be learned within each one of those characters, real or imagined. Superman's actions spin a positive narrative for attributes like chivalry and humble service. The stories of Jesus teach us love and forgiveness as they encourage us to be more like Him. Rosa Parks teaches us courage in the face of oppression. The lessons of the gods in Greek mythology often teach us what *not* to do, as their actions are punished accordingly. The stories and myths that make up the collective understanding of our cultural values are vital to our development.

Imagine that you grow up in solitude without any real human interaction, raised by robot caretakers, but you have access to a variety of stories and cultural hero archetypes. Though deprived of human relationships, you are given a whole database of classic stories, the Bible, and movies. There is a decent chance you would come out knowing the basics of moral reasoning and social norms. The reason is that those social norms and moral truths are interwoven throughout the stories that you would hear. The heroes of those stories become successful because of certain attributes: kindness, generosity, bravery, charisma. Fictional heroes influence our real lives. It's no surprise that Christopher Reeve, the actor who played Superman and suffered his own serious paralyzing injury, said: "A hero is an ordinary individual who finds the strength to persevere and endure in spite of overwhelming obstacles."

Hollywood often relies on certain hero archetypes to build the most likable characters. The main characters of romcoms always seem too good to be true—funny, gracious, humble, quirky but in a cute way—basically figments of our imagination. They aren't real, of course, and they aren't meant to be. They are meant to be idealized versions of ourselves. They are meant to be something we attempt to aspire to, because there is something about these role models that makes them likable and successful.

In psychological terms, our heroes would score well on the Big Five personality traits. These traits, first described in academia in the 1960s and reaching general acceptance over the following twenty years, are a means to encompass the scope and themes of personality and engagement with the world. They are:

1. Openness to experience[1]—receptivity to new ideas and new experiences
2. Conscientiousness[2]—tendency to be responsible, organized, and hardworking; to be goal directed; and to adhere to norms and rules

---

1   "Openness," *Psychology Today*, https://www.psychologytoday.com/us/basics/openness.

2   "Conscientiousness," *Psychology Today*, https://www.psychologytoday.com/us/basics/conscientiousness.

3. Extroversion[3]—tendency to search for novel experiences and social connections that allow them to interact with other humans as much as possible

4. Agreeableness[4]—tendency to be cooperative, polite, kind, and friendly

5. Neuroticism[5]—tendency toward anxiety, depression, self-doubt, and other negative feelings

A person's success is often tied directly to their score on certain traits. Research confirms this,[6] but I think we also know this intuitively. Taking this concept further, Dr. Scott T. Allison and Dr. George R. Goethals write extensively about heroic personality traits in their book *Heroes: What They Do and Why We Need Them*.[7] They identify the Great Eight Traits of heroes—smart, strong, selfless, caring, charismatic, resilient, reliable, and inspiring.

Throughout your life, you have people you look up to. You have noticed the way a teacher, parent, coworker, mentor, or friend interacts with others, and you come away thinking, "That behavior simply works better." They are respected, admired, and successful, and you find yourself wondering why that is. You are

---

3 "Extroversion," *Psychology Today*, https://www.psychologytoday.com/us/basics/extroversion.

4 "Agreeableness," *Psychology Today*, https://www.psychologytoday.com/us/basics/agreeableness.

5 "Neuroticism," *Psychology Today*, https://www.psychologytoday.com/us/basics/neuroticism.

6 Brent W. Roberts et al., "The Power of Personality," *Perspectives on Psychological Science* 2, no. 4 (December 1, 2007), https://journals.sagepub.com/doi/full/10.1111/j.1745-6916.2007.00047.x; Arthur E. Poropat, "A Meta-analysis of the Five-Factor Model of Personality and Academic Performance," *Psychological Bulletin* 135, no. 2 (March 2009), https://psycnet.apa.org/buy/2009-02580-011; Murray R. Barrick and Michael K. Mount, "The Big Five Personality Dimensions and Job Performance: A Meta-analysis," *Personnel Psychology* 44, no. 1 (March 1991), https://onlinelibrary.wiley.com/doi/abs/10.1111/j.1744-6570.1991.tb00688.x.

7 https://global.oup.com/academic/product/heroes-9780199739745?cc=us&lang=en&#.

noticing attributes and character traits that are good and worth aspiring to. You are noticing attributes that make certain people more successful than others. You are noticing what a hero looks like. And in the process you are discovering a path, made up of desirable personality traits, that helps you ascend in human social hierarchies.

The word "hierarchy" can be confusing to people. But it is important to understand, because the whole point of establishing personality goals is to move beyond your current self. You move beyond your current self by ascending in a hierarchy, and one way you do that is by absorbing superior character traits. Whether we like it or not, our entire society is based on a multitude of hierarchies. Some people are better at sports and move up the ladder of athletics. Some people have exceptionally high emotional intelligence and gain success from their social connections and positive interactions. They excel in a social hierarchy, given their high aptitude for empathy and conscientiousness. Some people are gifted in a given subject and thrive in that particular academic hierarchy. Some people are best suited for entrepreneurship. I am of the firm belief that everyone is perfectly capable of thriving within at least one hierarchy. It is your duty to find the one that best speaks to your strengths (or doesn't), and then identify the traits that made others before you successful. In this context, the word "hierarchy" could also be used to define your *purpose*. Any goal you set for yourself, by definition, requires you to excel within a competitive hierarchy, whether that be academics, sports, management, politics, or social networking. The fact is, there are people who have excelled in these hierarchies before you. All you need to do is observe the behavioral traits that made them successful.

This was how I started out. My first interpretation of what it meant to be a Navy SEAL came from Dick Marcinko and his winner-take-all attitude. When I entered the actual world of the SEALs separated from the romantic version in Marcinko's books, my examples to observe and emulate multiplied. I was in the company of good men and great Americans, and so I observed what made them great in my eyes. SEALs who reacted decisively and aggressively in tense situations were respected, and the guys who barked orders frantically were given less responsibility the next time, so I worked on my tone and decibel level. Guys who took criticism to heart were forgiven, and guys who became defensive were deemed to be thin-skinned. I learned to humbly accept criticism as a result, a skill which gets plenty of practice as a member of Congress.

The SEAL teams, like many military units, are relentless in the pursuit of establishing hero archetypes. Doing so is extremely important when the goal is to create a monoculture that operates as a mission-oriented team. This is a community with a very deep sense of who we want to be. We talk about it all the time, and we beat it into our trainees:

You will be someone who is never late.

You will be someone who takes care of his men, gets to know them, and puts their needs before yours.

You will be someone who does not quit in the face of adversity.

You will be someone who takes charge and leads when no one else will.

You will be detail oriented, always vigilant.

You will be aggressive in your actions but never lose your cool.

You will have a sense of humor because sometimes that is all that can get you through the darkest hours.

You will work hard and perform even when no one is watching.

You will be creative and think outside the box, even if it gets you in trouble.

You are a rebel, but not a mutineer.

You are a jack of all trades and master of none.

We have an official ethos that describes this set of goals. It reads like hypermasculine attitude shaped by a deeper sense of chivalry, virtue, and integrity. It is strength and honor, courage and commitment. It's a vision statement. But make no mistake, it is not the corporate version your company has: anodyne, boring, and unlikely to excite their employees to higher virtue and purpose. A typical corporate vision statement usually goes something like "We want to be the number one service provider on the West Coast. We want to put customers first." Fine. It says what your company does. But it doesn't speak to the core of a community's character. It doesn't encourage them to be anything more than what they already are and what they already do. The SEAL ethos goes much further than just goals; it is a statement of *who* we want to be. It describes the SEAL Hero archetype, and your fellow SEALS hold you accountable to that archetype on a daily basis.

In times of war or uncertainty there is a special breed of warrior ready to answer our Nation's call. A common man with uncommon desire to succeed. Forged by adversity, he stands alongside America's finest special operations forces to serve his country, the American people, and protect their way of life. I am that man.

My Trident is a symbol of honor and heritage. Bestowed upon me by the heroes that have gone before, it embodies the trust of those I have sworn to protect. By wearing the Trident I accept the responsibility of my chosen profession and way of life. It is a privilege that I must earn every day.

My loyalty to Country and Team is beyond reproach. I humbly serve as a guardian to my fellow Americans always ready to defend those who are unable to defend themselves. I do not advertise the nature of my work, nor seek recognition for my actions. I voluntarily accept the inherent hazards of my profession, placing the welfare and security of others before my own.

I serve with honor on and off the battlefield. The ability to control my emotions and my actions, regardless of circumstance, sets me apart from other men. Uncompromising integrity is my standard. My character and honor are steadfast. My word is my bond.

We expect to lead and be led. In the absence of orders I will take charge, lead my teammates and accomplish the mission. I lead by example in all situations.

I will never quit. I persevere and thrive on adversity. My Nation expects me to be physically harder and mentally stronger than my enemies. If knocked down, I will get back up, every time. I will draw on every remaining ounce of strength to protect my teammates and to accomplish our mission. I am never out of the fight.

We demand discipline. We expect innovation. The lives of my teammates and the success of our mission depend on me—my technical skill, tactical proficiency, and attention to detail. My training is never complete.

We train for war and fight to win. I stand ready to bring the full spectrum of combat power to bear in order to achieve my mission and the goals established by my country. The execution of my duties will be swift and violent when required yet guided by the very principles that I serve to defend.

Brave men have fought and died building the proud tradition and feared reputation that I am bound to uphold. In the worst of conditions, the legacy of my teammates steadies my resolve and silently guides my every deed. I will not fail.

Sometimes we will illustrate our hero archetype in the form of a short story that we often tell ourselves. It goes something like this: A SEAL can engage in a horrific firefight, and then turn around and calmly and politely help an old lady cross the street. Be aggressive enough to kill the enemy, but immediately calm enough to not scare the little old lady. You will be that man who is mentally tough enough to operate in horrific chaos, then immediately transition to tranquility, all without mentally breaking. He can effectively transition from a hypermasculine aggressor to a gentle caretaker. He is both a warrior and a gentleman. The story is representing the mentality of a warrior, and what we should aspire to in terms of a mental state. We don't claim we are all *good* at this, or live up to those archetypes perfectly, but we know that we *are supposed to try*, and that is a critical first step.

We develop this ethos—this goal of who we want to be—because our community wouldn't survive without it. Without those deep and intrinsic cultural qualities, we would have to rely purely on standard operating procedures from a field manual, authoritative chains of command, and clear and detailed orders to achieve our missions. These are obviously important aspects of a functioning and effective military, don't get me wrong. But without the human spirit they are just superficial structures. That spirit is developed through shared culture, and the gauntlets of training and combat that we share together. Even if I have never met another SEAL, I know him. We can immediately connect. The collective unconscious that we share is clear as day, and it makes the teams a formidable force to reckon with. You can't be the best in the world with just an instruction manual. You need a culture of elitism. The ethos is what moves us beyond mediocrity.

So I began to choose my heroes. I read the books, the history, the ethos, and I started to think of myself as that man. Envisioning yourself as the hero you want to be is always the first step. Just like Colonel Steve, I wanted to be a tough guy. I wanted to be someone who wouldn't quit, even after my bones broke. (I was lucky enough to put that particular claim to the test, after my leg quite literally broke in the middle of Hell Week.[8]) I wanted to be that man who would be respected by his men.

As my career progressed, I took note of the leaders I respected. I thought about their actions, their manner of speaking, their habits. I noticed the way they incorporated humor to give a successful briefing, interacted gracefully with their subordinates, and thought creatively about tactical situations. I observed how some leaders would react too emotionally in tense situations, and how the team reacted as a result. Calm breeds calm, and panic breeds panic. Were these great leaders the fastest or the strongest? The best shooters? Not always. The qualities that made SEAL leaders great were rarely physical in nature. They listened. They empowered their team to be successful, carefully entrusting individuals with additional responsibility. They highlighted good performance publicly and criticized bad performance privately. They didn't waste their men's time. They were prepared and thoughtful with mission planning. They were articulate but also genuine. They came across as real people with humor and emotions instead of just robotic military men.

I was always taking mental notes of the traits that earned respect in the SEAL teams and the ones that didn't. I noticed how some guys reacted to pain and hardship with humor and style, while others engaged in self-pity. This is why, minutes after being blown up, I jokingly told my friend and medic, "Dude, don't get blown up, it sucks." Some guys fell out of shape, forcing the platoon to carry their ruck up a mountain on a training exercise. Others made sure they were always in better shape than everyone else. Which guys do you think gained more respect from their peers? The 140-pound SEAL who carried two 60-pound rucks up that mountain in Utah in the middle of the night during a training op? Or the guy who

---

8   Hell Week is the most infamous crucible during SEAL training. More on this later.

carried nothing, because someone else had to carry it for him? Yes, this really happened. As to who gained more respect, the answer is obvious.

Heroes matter. And as it pertains to mental toughness, there are certain character traits that we should aspire to. Those character traits are demonstrated by the heroes we look up to. The goal is not to make you SEAL ready. The goal is to make you life ready. Life is nasty, brutish, and short, as Thomas Hobbes had it in *Leviathan*. It is unfair. It is offensive. It is hard. It is riddled with unexpected obstacles and inconveniences. Oftentimes those inconveniences are perceived as actual problems, when in fact they are just inconveniences or temporary setbacks. The hero you aspire to be knows the difference and reacts accordingly.

What might some of those traits look like? Here are some ideas:

You want to be someone who can take a joke. A strong sense of humor is a gateway to fortitude. You don't want to be easily offended. And if the joke sucks (or is *actually offensive*), you calmly say "Not funny" and move on.

You want to be productive. You want to be someone who makes progress every single day. Admiral McRaven, the senior Navy SEAL who planned the Bin Laden mission, said this starts with the mundane: making your bed. "If you make your bed every morning you will have accomplished the first task of the day. It will give you a small sense of pride and it will encourage you to do another task and another and another. By the end of the day, that one task completed will have turned into many tasks completed. Making your bed will also reinforce the fact that little things in life matter."

You want to be someone who identifies a goal and sticks with it. You want to be seen as reliable. You want people to ask things of you because you have a reputation for getting it done. Reliability is an element of fortitude.

You want to have the ability to delay gratification. A mentally tough person can avoid that next cupcake and save it for later, after earning it with some exercise. They save money for rent instead of recreation. This also relates to overindulgence. You can still be the life of the party without being sloppy. Be disciplined.

You want to be even-tempered. When an uncomfortable or difficult situation arises, you want to be the rock that everyone else leans on. You never want to "lose it." Emotions do not drive your actions.

You want to be humble. This can mean a lot of things, so let's be a little specific. You say "please" and "thank you" often, and practice the good manners that are a timeless doctrine of civil society. You do not expect people to do things for you that you can do yourself. You put your shopping cart away instead of leaving it in the parking lot, for instance. You have confidence but it isn't overbearing.

Be someone who actually listens and internalizes someone else's point of view before speaking at them. Have at least the decency to be polite in your response. Fully and reasonably rebuke their argument, avoiding the accusatory habit of saying, "You just don't care" or "You aren't listening." The dismissive and insulting tone of today's political debate is a reflection of mental weakness.

This isn't a complete list, but it's a good start, especially as it relates to being a resilient and tough-minded individual. The next trick is figuring out how to get there. Each subsequent chapter attempts to provide a lesson to become mentally tougher, but we start with this one because it is so important to visualize your goal first. It is quite difficult to work toward a goal that you do not fully visualize or understand. As you begin each chapter, you should start reading with the thought, "I will decide to be this way."

In a sense, what I wrote above is your own version of a SEAL ethos (and by all means, continue to add to it). If we all lived with at least some of these attributes, our society would be healthier, happier, and more pleasant. People would be tougher and more successful. And to be fair, my list isn't all that different from any other typical self-help book's. The question is: How do we become the heroes we want to be?

My answer: Sanctioned intellectual property theft, that's how. No one has a patent on good habits. You can steal them. Identify your heroes, and emulate the character traits that make that person more successful than you currently are.

This has probably occurred throughout your life without you being fully aware of it. As kids and teens, we often look to peers or pop-culture icons for our behavioral traits. We grew up observing the popular kids and what they did to be popular. Maybe we tried to imitate them. In high school, I wanted to be a SEAL. I also wanted a social life. To be a SEAL, I needed to perform well in the hierarchy of physical and academic achievement. To make friends in a foreign country, I had to figure out how to fit in with my Colombian classmates, and I adopted some of their music and social habits. The traits that I identified as a means to success evolved—albeit in an unevolved teenage reality—and my personal hero archetype evolved with it.

We should of course be careful not to steal *all* habits from someone we admire. For instance, many of us emulated celebrities in our younger years. Some adults still do. But there is some risk in overstepping here. Celebrities are incredibly successful at some things—singing, acting, dancing, etc. But we often fail to distinguish their success on *different* hierarchies, and assume that authority in one category means authority in all categories. For instance, should we be taking political advice from pop music stars? Or just singing advice? In the pop music hierarchy, they have been successful in moving up. In the political hierarchy, not so much. Aren't we making a mistake by assuming their words and actions should be emulated in all things, when in fact they are successful only at a select few? Our choice of heroic attributes must be tied to the success those attributes deliver, otherwise the adulation is inherently nonobjective.

There is a deadpan joke among professional novelists and screenwriters that "good writers borrow material; great writers steal it outright." Plagiarism is wrong, but good imitation of desirable traits is healthy and advisable. The idealized version of yourself always acts correctly, in the way best suited to achieve your goals and move up whatever hierarchy you choose. Your hero is a mix of fictional or historical characters—like Superman or Jesus or Rosa Parks, respectively—and people you know personally. As you identify the traits that make those people successful, you'll get to know your hypothetical hero, and you'll be able to compare your actions to theirs. You will begin to ask yourself: If my hero archetype had been the one in that situation, what would they have done? And how did it differ from my own actions? Am I living up to the vision that I set out for myself?

Every time the answer is no, do better.

THE WRONG HEROES

Not all heroes are created equal. The problem with today's society is that it is swelling with the wrong role models. Sometimes we mistakenly look up to and emulate the wrong hero attributes entirely, abandoning traditional heroes for new and exciting villains who represent self-indulgence, loudmouthed commentary, angry fist-shaking activism, or insulting spitfire politics.

The predicament we find ourselves in now is that these hero

attributes I discussed are not universally agreed upon anymore. And that's a problem. There is diminishing consensus on what constitutes a good character trait. Nothing I have stated in this chapter has traditionally been up for debate. The Jedi lesson—do not let hate or anger drive our emotions—has long been undisputed. Tough-minded grit has always been a virtue. Overcoming adversity with grace and humor has been a tried-and-true trait to be emulated and aspired to. And for many people, they still are. But to a growing and ever-louder segment of our culture, they are being shunned in favor of far less heroic attributes. I find myself watching public debates and observing the national discourse, and wondering with frustration: Does our society still value the deep sense of personal responsibility that comes from our American pioneer spirit? Do we still value the mental toughness that empowers us to be personally responsible in the first place? Are we looking up to those who exhibit these qualities, or are we casting them aside in favor of the loud, angry, and ignorant?

At the risk of understatement, this has been a disheartening trend. Instead of discouraging outrage, members of Congress actually *encourage* it, like when three of my freshmen Congressional colleagues held aloft a T-shirt that said, IF YOU'RE NOT OUTRAGED THEN YOU'RE NOT PAYING ATTENTION.[9] Such a message doesn't just dismiss a more tempered and level-headed demeanor, but outright indicts it. More and more, we are putting a preference on victimhood, glorifying weakness instead of strength, and outright shaming anyone with more traditional characteristics. We are teaching our young men not to look up to classical masculine archetypes, but instead to feminize themselves lest they be accused

---

9   Representatives Katie Hill, Ilhan Omar, and Ayanna Pressley held up this T-shirt in a picture.

of "toxic masculinity." Chivalrous acts like holding a door open are considered by a growing number of people to be patronizing, for instance. We are teaching young women to feel oppressed instead of empowered by their own will and determination. And this is the theme that is oft repeated: one group oppressing another. The groups often change—usually based on some kind of association or identity—but the story remains the same. Life is a power struggle, and the heroes we value are no longer those who gracefully over-come adversity, but those who complain the loudest about their story of injustice.

I'm trying to thread a needle here. I don't want anyone to read, "Injustice isn't real." Of course injustice is real, tangible, and occurring daily. But there is a rational definition of injustice, and victimhood culture has put that rationale to the test. If you define "injustice" as an infringement on another person's life, liberty, and property, unfair due process, or outcomes based on something other than merit, then yes, that is an injustice. The question isn't about the existence of injustice, but whether our reaction to said injustice is productive—or strewn with self-pity. The former reaction allows for growth beyond the injustice, and the latter imprisons you in victimhood. Not only that, victimhood culture also seeks to alter the definition of injustice entirely, where all disparities become discriminations, even when the evidence suggests otherwise.

Let's illustrate both ends of the spectrum. In the movie *Cinderella Man*, set in the Great Depression era, hardscrabble former boxer James Braddock begins the movie by accepting a welfare check in depression-ravaged New Jersey. By the end of the movie he returns the check. He found himself in dire straits, worked hard to overcome them, and proudly returned the welfare after getting back on his feet. His triumphant return to boxing and escape from poverty were based on a true story. But more important than that,

Braddock's was a deeply American story. We have long felt a burning desire to be responsible for ourselves and our prosperity. Americans pride themselves on individual achievement. It's in our blood. But we are also a good and compassionate people. We institute welfare programs because we believe that everyone deserves a safety net and a little help when times are tough. But we have, across our history, been proudest when we stand on our own two feet. This story in *Cinderella Man* is a healthy mix of government-sponsored compassion and individual responsibility, and that healthy mix is held together by cultural norms. Those cultural norms are held together by the heroes we admire.

To cite another example, I recall my own experience with government assistance. Many people do not realize this, but upon being medically retired from the military, servicemembers are eligible for Social Security Disability Insurance, or SSDI. I'll never forget sitting in a classroom in Naval Medical Center San Diego, along with a dozen or so other Navy servicemembers being retired for medical reasons. We all listened as we took the required out-processing class so that we would be better informed about the process. For context, everyone in that room had two arms and two legs, and none had been wounded in combat except for me. For any number of reasons, the military can allow (or force) a person to be medically retired. It does not have to be combat related or even related to training. But I illustrate the nature of the medical ailments in that classroom for you because I want to make it clear that none of us in that room were *disabled*. I have a disability, sure, but I am not disabled. And there was no one in that room, even me with my half-blind state, who could argue that they were unable to work because of their disability or medical condition. The very fact that everyone was functioning just fine at that moment, and that they would all go back to their command and continue to function just fine, was proof that no one was truly disabled. And yet, the

Navy was encouraging us to apply for SSDI, a program that most Americans believe is set aside for people who have disabilities so severe that they cannot get a job.

This was mind-blowing. Due to the fact that all of us in that room would be retired, it was guaranteed that we would be getting VA disability payments and retirement payments. Additional government payments would just be an extra perk on an already generous package. If I were to ever be the "hero" that I describe in this chapter—resilient and self-sufficient—how could I possibly take that money? The SSDI program exists for a reason, and it isn't for people like me, or anyone else in that classroom for that matter. I went on to become a student in a master's program at Harvard immediately after being retired, so I easily could have been receiving up to $2,000 in monthly payments from SSDI until I started working full-time. There would have been nothing heroic about that, and so I never applied.

The problem with our current cultural trend is that we are far more likely to be cheered on if we embrace victimhood. The Navy actually encouraged me to take even more government handouts than I was already owed. It was a message literally embraced by the classroom curriculum. And that message—to reward a victimhood mentality—continues unabated. In fact it continued from the very place that I graduated from in 2017: Harvard.

The episode of Chelsea Manning and the Harvard Institute of Politics fellowship is instructive. You may recall that Bradley Manning, as he was known back when serving as a low-level United States Army intelligence analyst, chose to violate his oath and betray his country. He downloaded an astonishing quantity of classified information about the American efforts in Iraq and Afghanistan and sent it all to WikiLeaks.

Manning was tried, convicted, and imprisoned for nearly seven years. Deservedly so.

From a reputational standpoint, that probably should have been the end of it. But it was not: the prisoner Bradley Manning became Chelsea Manning, a transgender woman, and the societal forces that endorse and celebrate victimhood transformed a wartime traitor into a persecuted hero. When Chelsea Manning emerged from prison in May 2017, the perceptual transformation was complete.

This was the background to the announcement on September 13, 2017, when Chelsea Manning received a visiting fellowship at the Harvard Institute of Politics. A prestigious institution was taking on board a controversial progressive celebrity—despite the fact that Manning had no experience in the very thing that the Institute of Politics specialized in: politics. Manning didn't even know much about national security, considering her time in the Army was brief and low-level. There was no evidence whatsoever that Manning's qualifications met the standard for such a position. What exactly were students expected to learn from her? How to betray their country? But Chelsea Manning was a persecuted "whistleblower" turned LGBTQ activist—and so Chelsea Manning was receiving elite institutional approval. It was victimhood worship manifested into reality at one of our country's most preeminent institutions.

Luckily, the remnants of the American conscience that still believe betraying your country is actually *not* something to be celebrated, took action. Former CIA director Michael Morrell resigned his own Harvard fellowship. Then–CIA director Mike Pompeo canceled a public appearance at Harvard.

And two days after it was announced that Chelsea Manning was a Harvard visiting fellow, it was announced that Chelsea Manning was not. Student activists at Harvard tried to cry foul, claiming LGBTQ discrimination. But of course that had nothing to do with it. Manning had no business being elevated to the status of Harvard fellow in the first place, and everyone knew it.

That's how it should work: Victimhood should not be a cover story for crimes, excuse traitors to the country, open doors of opportunity, nor secure a Harvard visiting fellowship. For two days, Harvard was going to allow victimhood to do all those things—until people stood up to it, and the house of cards collapsed.

What worked for Harvard can work for America too, if we choose to collectively rebel against the victimhood narrative.

And what are the stakes if we don't? As we trend toward characteristics that do not value mental toughness, but actually elevate victimhood and outrage, our culture faces a truly existential threat. We must seriously question whether our modern-day population could confront the hardships of the not-too-distant past. There was once a time when we were occupied by a seemingly indomitable monarch, there was a time when the White House burned and the flames could be seen from the Potomac River. A time when we split ourselves in two over the great moral injustice of slavery, when a depression laid waste to our land, and when Nazi and Communist thugs were stopped from world domination only by the courage of our Greatest Generation. Now I wonder how a generation shaped by the comforts of victimhood culture, unaccustomed to adversity and allergic to sacrifice, with less and less desire to preserve our values and way of life, will react when we are faced with the next great war, or depression, or civil conflict. We can't even be sure of their reaction to offensive Halloween costumes, let alone invading armies.

This becomes a question of societal and cultural sustainability. As each new American is admitted into the postmodernist club of self-indulgence and self-pity, we eventually run out of tough and responsible individuals to carry us forward. With every newly admitted fragile mind comes the expectation that a more resilient person should take on additional responsibility. I think we observe this to be true at both the family level and the societal level. And instead of this counterproductive expectation being discouraged by cultural leaders, it is actually encouraged. Little by little, behaviors start to change. The prism through which we view life begins to morph from a competition between free people to a story of oppressors versus the oppressed.

As this trend manifests, it is no surprise that many people seek status in the ranks of the oppressed. Senator Elizabeth Warren, at the time of this writing, has now been caught claiming victimhood status not once, but twice. First, she claimed to be part Native American, even going as far as to put it on her résumé. Second, she falsely claimed she was denied a renewal of a teaching job for being pregnant early in her career. But further investigation of county records and Warren's own 2007 interview told a different story, wherein she chose not to return to her teaching position. Neither claim turned out to be true. But the surprising part is more that there was cultural incentive to make the claims in the first place. Why is it better to be thought of as oppressed? Why is that the more compelling story to tell? Why are hate crime hoaxes becoming more common? Why did Jussie Smollett, a successful actor, choose to go to great lengths to claim that two men wearing MAGA hats assaulted him in a hate crime? Why is this a status that some people are seeking out? Thomas Sowell, the preeminent economist and social theorist, put it in stark terms. "One of the sad signs of our times," he wrote, "is that we have demonized those who produce, subsidized those who refuse to produce, and canonized those who complain."

This cultural trend is driving outrage culture. True victimhood leads to outrage, which is human and understandable. If a *real* injustice has been committed against you, you are understandably enraged. But as our culture expands the definition of victimhood, even celebrating victimhood status as a heroic attribute, then the obvious psychological consequence is an angrier culture. And these new hero archetypes, manifested by the angriest and most passionate voices, start to be rewarded by public opinion. This phenomenon is clearly observed in mainstream and social media.

Consider the following comparison, for instance. After sixteen-year-old climate activist Greta Thunberg made her landmark UN speech in 2019, media attention soared. While her efforts and sense of initiative were undeniably impressive, especially for a teenager, the fact remains that her credentials on the subject were non-existent, and her scowling message offered no practical solutions whatsoever. Compare her accomplishments to another young environmentalist named Boyan Slat, who doesn't make passionate speeches or hurl angry slogans, but did design a revolutionary ocean cleanup system that captures debris ranging from one-ton ghost nets to tiny microplastics. At the time of this writing, a quick Google search shows 69 million search results for Greta, and just over 500,000 for Boyan. Greta was named "Person of the Year" by *Time* magazine. Boyan was not.

Passion successfully overrides reason and accomplishment. Who gets more attention? The public figure who calmly sees both sides of an argument or a perceived grievance and tries to mediate? Or the activist who angrily marches down the street proclaiming their righteousness? Who gets more traction on social media: a think tank spending millions of dollars on careful research, or a kid making memes on Instagram? You don't get likes on Twitter with nuanced disagreement, you get likes on Twitter by "owning" the other side. This phenomenon creates incentives for seemingly normal people to engage in hysterical behavior.

I've encountered them face to face. During the summer of 2019, I exited my office in the Cannon building to go vote on the House floor, as I normally do. A group of four young veterans was standing casually outside my office. They were wearing dark blue ball caps with VETERAN inscribed on the front in bold gold letters, which is unusual for younger veterans unless they are engaging in some sort of activism. They asked for a picture, which seemed normal. I obliged. But then it became clear the picture was just meant to slow me down so they could get their camera ready to record video. As I walked to the elevator on my way to vote, they proceeded to *lose it*. They were anti-Trump activists, surrounding me as I walked, and began asking loudly how I could "support a traitor." What about your duty! they screamed. Not getting the reaction they wanted, their emotions started to escalate dramatically. One man's voice cracked and he was visibly shaking. I began to worry that he might get physical with me, which was problematic considering he was on my right side (the blind side). It forced me to stop, turn to him, and sternly say, "You need to calm down." The emotion and hysteria coming from these grown men was and remains perplexing. (I wasn't the only one confused: The man's own father called our office to apologize.) But the motivations become clearer if you understand the rewards our society now gives to such actions. These activists did what they did because they knew their excessive passion would get more traction on social media than a reasonable conversation with me would.

Passion is contagious, and thus anger spreads quickly. That is exactly what these angry activists want. I am consistently amazed by the ability of one YouTube video—even one mired in falsehoods and lacking in context—to ignite a firestorm of enraged opinion across the interwebs. Our outrage culture is increasingly drawn to the voices perceived as authentic, which is usually just code for excessive emotion. Thoughtful argument is downgraded while fist-shaking activism is rewarded. There is an assumption that anger must be connected to righteousness. Passion replaces reason. Attitude—owning the libs or the cons—replaces sophisticated argument.

My problem with this trend is not the guy making snarky memes. Memes can be fun, and I share them myself from time to time. Activism can draw attention to important issues. My problem is with the imbalance of rewards—in the form of attention paid and respect bestowed—given to passionate clamoring versus thoughtful commentary. My problem is that the list of good attributes I listed earlier—take a joke, be even-tempered, take responsibility—are being pushed further down the list of character priorities in favor of the wrong hero attributes:

Don't take a joke—find offense where you can!
Don't settle for a tempered reaction—take to the streets!
Don't take responsibility—you have been wronged, and *they* owe you!

These attributes aren't just wrong on a moral level; they are wrong on a practical level. They do not benefit you, objectively speaking. These are the wrong heroes and wrong examples to follow, because *this sort of behavior doesn't work.* Not for your mental health and not for your relationships, let alone your success in a given career field. Assuming one's goals are more meaningful than Facebook likes or Instagram follows or other short-term attention seeking, what success could possibly be achieved from being outraged and victimized? What benefit to your mental well-being can arise from consistent hyperbolic and angry reactions to what is objectively the most progressive and least oppressive society in human history? If passionate outrage were really a virtue, wouldn't there be at least some measurable benefits? Does such behavior result in upward movement on a given hierarchy? Are relationships improving or deteriorating? Is one getting *more* promotions and opportunities? Is one happier? I highly doubt it.

But hey, they're probably getting more Twitter followers.

★ ★ ★

Heroes matter. For as long as civilization has existed we have aspired to be more like them, carefully extracting the right lessons to apply to our own personal growth, becoming better versions of ourselves. If we are going to be fortified against the tribulations we will inevitably face and be a tougher culture that endures for generations to come, then we should start by admiring tougher heroes—and ignoring the wrong ones. The American spirit, if we are to reclaim it, depends on getting it right.

CHAPTER 3

NO PLAN B

Quitting is a choice. And it is never Plan A.

Perseverance is also a choice. It isn't always easy—but it is simple. You tell yourself you won't quit, and then you don't quit. Do it in that order.

Failure becomes inevitable the moment it is embraced as a possibility. Once you have a Plan B, Plan A goes out the window.

You may be thinking, "Sure, easy for *you* to say, Dan." And you would be right. Everything is easy to *say*. Many things are hard to *do*. Perseverance in the face of hardship is a pretty simple concept, but what is simple isn't always easy. The simplest things—courage, focus, perseverance—can also be the hardest. And if you are to remain on the path toward a tougher and more resilient mind-set, free from outrage and impervious to microaggressions, then removing the words "I quit" from your lexicon is a good place to start.

Let's define "quitting" by stating what it isn't. Quitting isn't bowing to reality or unavoidable facts. My desire to spend like a billionaire crashes hard into the reality of my bank account: Curbing profligate spending doesn't make me a quitter. When Sancho Panza persuades Don Quixote that those are just windmills, and suggests that charging them may not be the most advisable action, he isn't making his friend a quitter. When a defeated candidate concedes on election night, the acknowledgment of more votes for the other candidate doesn't make that person a quitter.

Quitting isn't about succumbing to reality or failing to change what can't be changed. Quitting is not the same as failure. Quitting means giving up—in a context where there are other options. Options you know you have.

That context isn't always clear, to yourself or to others. It's possible, for example, that there's a young man or woman out there who very much wants a career as an artist. Maybe they pursue it for several years, and in the end choose to stop. There are many reasons they might make that choice. Perhaps they need to spend time working and supporting their family. Perhaps they acknowledge that they are utterly talentless. Perhaps something happens beyond their understanding that sends them down new paths. Changing trajectories isn't necessarily quitting. If a working couple has a new baby and one parent gives up their career to stay at home, they are reprioritizing, not choosing Plan B.

The story of Arthur Brooks is illustrative. The former president of the American Enterprise Institute in Washington, D.C., is one of the most compelling and learned scholars of freedom and human happiness. To say he is academically accomplished is to understate his credentials: His undergraduate and graduate work in economics was capped by a PhD and a master of philosophy in policy analysis from RAND. He's an expert in what he does. But he didn't start out that way.

He started out as a French horn player. He tells the tale in the July 2019 issue of the *Atlantic*:

As a child, I had just one goal: to be the world's greatest French-horn player. I worked at it slavishly, practicing hours a day, seeking out the best teachers, and playing in any ensemble I could find. I had pictures of famous horn players on my bedroom wall for inspiration. And for a while, I thought my dream might come true....

But then, in my early 20s, a strange thing happened: I started getting worse. To this day, I have no idea why. My technique began to suffer, and I had no explanation for it. Nothing helped. I visited great teachers and practiced more, but I couldn't get back to where I had been. Pieces that had been easy to play became hard; pieces that had been hard became impossible.

Brooks eventually understood that, for whatever reason, his singular goal of being the world's greatest French horn player was never to be achieved. That dream was over. His challenge was to move to excellence in something else—and he did. Arthur Brooks is not a quitter. What happened to his playing was beyond his control—and he shifted, rather than abandoned, his pursuit of excellence.

A quitter is someone who has the meaningful option not to quit, but does so anyway. The act of quitting is known only to the person who does it and is not always obvious to the onlooker. A lot of people quit and the world doesn't see it. A lot of people quit and the world excuses it. They excuse it because the polite assumption is that "they found a different path," as Arthur Brooks did.

But quitting is *always* obvious on the inside, to the person who does it. There is always the voice that acknowledges that you could do better. There is always the voice that whispers you could have kept on. There is always the voice that quietly informs you that you didn't do your best. I have spent nearly my entire life trying to silence that voice. That doesn't mean I haven't heard it. I have. I have succumbed to it at times. I remember it vividly the first time.

It was my eighth-grade year, and we were back in Houston after a year in Ecuador. Soccer was my sport, and before moving to Ecuador I played on a club team in Houston called the Hurricanes. I was pretty good—not overly skilled, but a valuable player. My value was in my intensity. My comparative lack of skill was more than compensated for by my work ethic. I ran harder than most and played harder than most. I never dragged. I never felt sorry for myself on field or off.

My internal motivation was strong. I had a sense of duty toward myself, an obligation to excellence for its own sake. I had a sense of duty toward my teammates. I wasn't going to let myself down, and I wasn't going to let them down.

My coaches noticed. They knew Crenshaw would play his heart out. I vindicated their trust.

But my motivation and character were not unblemished. There was a flip side to my drive and intensity. When I was young, I had a real problem with losing. In fact, if I lost on the soccer field, I would act like a crybaby. The problem went way past soccer. For example: I'll never forget losing my cool and surrendering to real anger and fury at the tender age of eight because my mother beat me in a croquet match. In that case, my rage was twofold—not only did I lose, *she should have let me win.*

(There are some things I'm glad got beaten out of me—by Mom, by Dad, and by life. She looked at me, perplexed by my outrage, and wondered aloud why on earth I should have been allowed to win. I didn't earn it. My croquet skills were not good enough to win. You don't get to win just because you *feel* entitled to it. Your status as an eight-year-old does not beget privileges that outweigh your merits. Croquet, sports, and *life* are meritocracies by which you shall be judged on your performance and the content of your character. Thank you, Mom and Dad.)

The fear of losing wasn't quite beaten out of me when I was thirteen, though. I still hated losing, but my mentality was evolving at least. Evolving into a healthier sense of competition and a desire to *win*. When I first moved to Ecuador, my parents enrolled me in a summer soccer camp at the local American school. During one scrimmage, my team lost. I was devasted and I let my emotions get the best of me. It was embarrassing. But at least I never felt *entitled* to the win. What I had failed to understand is what I understand now: The problem isn't failing; the problem is when you choose to fail, and rationalize that choice. Only you can know the difference.

When I started my seventh-grade year at Academia Cotopaxi, an American school in Quito, my father made me practice with my school's varsity soccer team, even though I was on the junior varsity team. I hated it at first. Junior varsity showcased my dominance. Varsity practice exposed my shortcomings. Then, though, I got better. By the time we returned to Texas only a year later, the varsity squad down in Ecuador had made me a pretty good soccer player.

Back in Houston, I returned to my old soccer team, the Hurricanes. The coach was psyched to see me. He thought I was going to be his secret weapon, because I had just spent a year in South America, in a real soccer culture. I, too, thought I would sail through practice, tryouts, and right back to the starting lineup. Back to winning state championships like we had only a couple years earlier.

But the first few practices went badly. Small mistakes led to small losses in confidence. Small losses in confidence became big losses in confidence. What I needed to do was refocus, reengage, explore the reasons for my paradoxical decrease in performance, and fix whatever was needed. I had just spent an entire year doing pretty well as a player in South America. I should have been blowing everyone away.

I didn't do any of that. Faced with my own diminished performance and unwilling to accept responsibility—not just for the problem, but for the solution, too—I adopted a teenage posture of apathy and decided not to care.

More accurately, I decided to *pretend* not to care.

I made a choice. I chose to quit. Quitting was my Plan B. With the existence of Plan B, my failure became inevitable.

At tryouts, I didn't make the cut. The coaches could see my fire in the gut was extinguished. Deep down, I knew I had poured water and sand directly onto that fire. I heard that little voice inside, whispering that I could have done better, that I could have kept on, that I did not do my best.

It was right.

Right after that, we moved again—this time to Bogotá, Colombia. It was for the best, because the change of scenery gave me a chance to reflect, revise, and reset. I had quit once, and I can keenly recall that teenage apathy was setting in. But that didn't mean I had to live as a quitter. In the more competitive soccer leagues of Colombia, I brought myself back. I excelled and finished my high school years as the starting forward on the varsity team.

You don't entertain the Plan B option because when you do, you're entertaining failure, and in entertaining failure, you will embrace it. Ultimately, the No Plan B mentality isn't about keeping you from doing something, rather it is about embracing a *positive* goal as your *only* choice. It is about enabling you *to* do something. It's about clearing the paths to your goals, to your achievements, to your tasks, to your responsibilities.

The importance of No Plan B as it relates to responsibility is worth spending a moment on. Living responsibly—cleaning your room, paying your taxes, treating people with respect, the basics—is a core element of personal success. Deeper than that, it is a core element of America's foundation in liberty. It has to be: After all, how can you trust a people with liberty if they choose to live within their Plan B, devoid of responsibility? You can't.

A generation back, in 1995, St. John Paul II reminded an audience of Americans at Camden Yards in Baltimore that the meeting of those tasks and responsibilities is the very essence of our national character:

> Every generation of Americans needs to know that freedom consists not in doing what we like, but in having the right to do what we ought.

The pope was getting at a foundational truth of American society: We are not founded on unbridled freedom that consists of "doing what we like"; we are founded on ordered liberty. This is an important difference. The Statue of Liberty is not a representation of pure freedom, but of liberty supported by the rule of law, both legislative and moral in nature. When French sculptor Frédéric Auguste Bartholdi designed Lady Liberty, he placed a *tabula ansata* in her left hand, evoking the concept of law. Inscribed on the tablet is the date of the Declaration of Independence, July 4, 1776. There is important symbolism here. First is the notion that our liberty is based on a legal and moral order. And second, the purpose of government as outlined by the Declaration of Independence: Our government exists to protect our inalienable God-given rights, among them life, liberty, and the pursuit of happiness. The purpose of government as per the Declaration of Independence is to protect the "right to do what we ought."

Pure freedom is chaos, anarchy, and moral decay. Freedom to do what you like—without any moral compass—can quickly result in the temptation to indulge in habits that may feel good momentarily but are wholly detrimental to yourself and others. Pure freedom detached from a higher sense of purpose results at best in overindulgence, lack of discipline, unfaithful relationships, and some minor drug use. At worst, it can result in the total deterioration of a society as moral relativism takes hold and humanity's darkest proclivities become justified in the name of "doing what we like."

Ordered liberty is at the heart of our founding, not pure freedom. Ordered liberty is the understanding that law exists to prevent individuals from infringing on the inalienable rights of others. As French philosopher Frédéric Bastiat observed in 1850, the law exists only to secure justice, and justice is defined as the protection of one's life, liberty, and property. And as our Founders argued, and St. John Paul II would have certainly agreed with, our laws must also be written in the context of a higher moral calling, derived from God and the teachings of the Bible. After all, our laws can be traced to the Ten Commandments, whether you believe in God or not. This is what St. John Paul II was saying when he mentioned "having the right to do what we ought." Our society's foundation came with an understanding that we would not only live free, but that we would live with good intent and moral purpose. As John Adams said, "Our Constitution was made only for a moral and religious people. It is wholly inadequate to the government of any other." The gift of liberty is accompanied by an expectation of living responsibly, both in the practical and moral sense. A person living their Plan B, effectively quitting on themselves and on those depending on them, cannot be said to be living responsibly.

By the time we set up house in Bogotá—where I spent my high school years—the question of "what we ought" to do was pretty well answered in my head. I was going to be a SEAL. My dad had given me Marcinko's *Rogue Warrior* and I was hooked. Around this time I also watched the 1990 movie *Navy SEALs*, starring Charlie Sheen, which I sheepishly admit only deepened my determination. Like most teenage boys I wasn't an avid consumer of high-concept art and literature. Sheen's movies are not known for that. But I did have an eye for the truth at the heart of books and movies, and both Marcinko and Sheen managed to communicate something vital about the SEALs: This was a community of men who worked hard, played hard, and didn't quit.

For young Dan Crenshaw, it was message received. I added "SEAL training" to the list of teenage to-dos in my already unique set of experiences growing up in Colombia. On weekends I was trying (unsuccessfully) to fit in by learning to dance merengue and cumbia. I was also reading up on SEALs in Vietnam. I didn't just train for the varsity soccer team—on which I was a starting forward—I also got into weight lifting and calisthenics to better prepare for a future at BUD/S. During my junior year, our class took a field trip to the beautiful Caribbean island of Providencia (it belongs to Colombia, much to the chagrin of the Panamanians). Freed from the burden of American-style liability laws, our school allowed us to embark upon an "Eco-Challenge." We were split into small groups, given a map, a compass, and a machete, and told to get from point A to point B in the wilderness of the island. It was one of the coolest experiences of my high school years. My classmates were thinking, "This is an experience I'll never forget," but I was thinking, "SEAL training." I had my Plan A.

When I got to BUD/S and met my peers there, I found that I wasn't alone. Nearly everyone present had harbored a singular goal of becoming a SEAL for most of their lives. This was no casual commitment. You didn't sign up for BUD/S on a whim. For the first time in my life, I was in a community of men who had dispensed with any thought of a Plan B.

Having no Plan B—I *knew* I would be a SEAL, and I pursued *only* that goal, with all other goals including my college education subordinated to it—meant that I gave my all to my efforts over a period of years. Every major decision was made in service of that pursuit. It made those decisions simple. It made life simple.

It did not, though, make life easy. And that's good. Things that are easy are often less rewarding. Hard work in pursuit of a dream?

Now that's a reward. My goal drove my action, and my action propelled me to my goal. The personal challenge associated with those actions was a reward in itself.

This is a point worth noting: A goal isn't necessarily the only end. Let's say I spent my youth pursuing the goal of becoming a SEAL, and for reasons outside my control—which is to say, for reasons other than quitting—I didn't make it. (In fact, I almost didn't, thanks to a fractured tibia bone during my first Hell Week. I had to start all over.) Would that mean all the effort was squandered and meaningless?

Not at all. For one thing, the preparation to become a SEAL—physical fitness, academic excellence, leadership positions, character development—is nothing more or less than *preparation for life*. We should hope every American seeks and embraces something similar for themselves in preparation for simple citizenship. The time and effort was never wasted. Even if I was never commissioned, to say nothing of becoming a SEAL, it would never have been wasted.

There's another and deeper reason it would have been time well spent: Purpose is meaning, and meaning is happiness. We don't think about happiness enough, and when we do, we do not necessarily think about it properly. Happiness is neither joy nor entertainment. It is an ontological condition, fundamental to our existence as humans. It's notable that when the Founders drafted the Declaration of Independence, they listed up front three things to which we are all entitled: life, liberty, and the pursuit of happiness. That's two things that we ought to have *as such*—and one thing that we deserve merely to *pursue*. The Founders didn't think government could or should guarantee happiness. They only knew it should clear the path for us to chase it.

The chase, you see, *is* the point. The pursuit *is* the purpose.

When I ran for Congress in early 2018, Marcus Luttrell was kind enough to have me on his podcast. You may know Marcus as the author of *Lone Survivor*. That story is one of the great battlefield epics of post-9/11 American history. Marcus, Danny Dietz, Michael Murphy, and Matt Axelson took on hundreds of Taliban fighters in the mountains of Afghanistan. Only Marcus lived to tell the tale.

It's no accident his podcast is entitled *Never Quit.*

Marcus asks every guest to tell their Never Quit Story. He asked me mine. When he asked, I requested that he stop recording. I needed to think. I wanted to get this right. This was the most important thing I could share with his audience. Not the war stories, not the tales of camaraderie and suffering in the field. This. How to never quit.

After a few seconds it came to me.

Here is what I said: You have purpose in this life. God has you here for a reason. You may not know it, but He does. Your job is to find it. No one else can. You need to understand that your purpose may be great in the eyes of the world, or it may be commonplace and seemingly small.

Your purpose might be your family, your children.
Your purpose might be tutoring a child and changing their life.
Your purpose might be the business you started.
Your purpose might be cleaning up your block.
Your purpose might be in the help you give others.
Your purpose might be in the example you set.

Only you and God know. Only you and God *need* to know. Search until you find it—and until then, *act as if you have it*, because you're wasting time otherwise. "You were designed to use your reason and your natural gifts—and to cultivate those assets toward fulfillment of a higher end," as my friend Ben Shapiro writes.

Your purpose allows for No Plan B.

Maybe this sounds religious. I'm not a man who wears his faith on his sleeve. Make no mistake, though, this *is* religious. The Bible tells us to embrace our purpose, and even suggests what it might be. St. John Paul II was probably riffing off Galatians 5:13: "For you were called to freedom, brothers. Only do not use your freedom as an opportunity for the flesh, but through love serve one another." I'm not here to persuade you that the Bible ought to be your moral touchstone from which you derive purpose and meaning—there is a higher and better-qualified authority who can work on that. My point is that this question of purpose touches upon themes fundamental to our existence on this earth.

Focusing on purpose centers your actions, even the small ones, around a cause. It's helpful in maintaining a sense of stability and direction when, say, a television comedian is leveraging your war injury for a joke. It's also helpful when you're at BUD/S, in the middle of Hell Week, and realizing that it is in fact...hellish.

BUD/S brings cold, fatigue, sleep deprivation, fear of drowning, hunger, and sand to bear in the world's toughest training environment. The sand—so beautiful to onlookers visiting the pristine beaches of Coronado—actually acts as the unspoken horror of BUD/S. It gets everywhere, and it thoroughly scours your entire body. During Hell Week, when we are soaking wet at all times, the sand combines with your fatigues to create the perfect hundred-grain fine sandpaper against your skin, making BUD/S students the most well-exfoliated people on the planet. Not surprisingly, the temptation is to quit. Hell, it goes beyond temptation. It is a burning impulse, mercilessly encouraged by instructors.

There are two things to understand about quitting BUD/S. The first is that the six-month experience, and Hell Week in particular, is designed to bring those quitting thoughts to the fore. If you think you've ever been miserable before, you'll find you were wrong when you encounter true misery at BUD/S. BUD/S makes up for the past century of comparative ease we have enjoyed in the post-industrial age. BUD/S practically invites you to quit—and you've got instructors yelling often and early at you about just how easy it would be.

Some men listen and they start to think about it. They start to think about what it would be like to take a hot shower. They imagine eating a nice dinner. They think about the feeling of a warm bed. They allow themselves to miss the embrace of a wife or a girlfriend. They do all this as they are shivering uncontrollably, as salt water is stinging small abrasions across their bodies, and while holding aloft a boat or a log well past the point of muscle failure.

They start to form their Plan B. "Maybe I really don't want to be a SEAL anyway. I would still be happy doing something else in the Navy, right?"

The second thing to understand about quitting BUD/S is it is a very public process. There's a brass bell—polished daily by dutiful BUD/S students—right outside the instructor's office where much of your suffering takes place. But to make the process of quitting even more convenient, the instructors bring the bell to each evolution—each boat race, log race, obstacle course run, two-mile ocean swim, all of it. The instructors want it to be *easy* to ring that bell. If you decide to quit and they start driving you back to the office, you may change your mind. They don't want that. They want it to be right in front of you at all times. They want to take advantage of that small moment of weakness you have. They make sure you know there are coffee, doughnuts, and warm blankets waiting for you. Over and over you are reminded that your suffering ends the moment you walk up to that bell— and ring it three times.

There is a calculus here and it is much more sophisticated and goes much deeper than just cruel hazing techniques. They make quitting easy and convenient because they *want to weed out the people who have the shortest mental path to Plan B.* In combat, we have no use for those people. They are dangerous, in fact. If quitting is an option when your life isn't on the line, there is no telling what you will do when lives *are* on the line.

Sometimes I've wondered if there were actually coffee and dough-nuts, as the instructors so frequently promised. I never found out. Ultimately it didn't matter to me. It also didn't matter to the fewer than one in five of my peers who made it to the end of BUD/S.

That was why we were left standing at the end.

More than that, we lived according to a purpose. The smallest of tasks, habits, and decisions were executed in service of the higher goal of earning the SEAL Trident. A No Plan B mind-set is useful for the big goals like BUD/S, recovering from my blast injuries, or running for a seat in the US House of Representatives. But it is the small choices that matter just as much. After all, your big goals are accomplished by an infinite number of smaller decisions. Resisting your temptation to accept Plan B is more than just *not quitting*. It is also refusing to engage in bad, unproductive, and immoral behavior, even when it seems unimportant.

It is the refusal to cut corners on that report for your boss, turn in an essay that meets only the bare minimum of standards, or lie to a friend or spouse. Will you decide to skip that workout (Plan B) because you're tired, or go to the gym (Plan A)? Will you decide to throw your trash on the ground when no one is looking (Plan B), or save it until you find a trash can (Plan A)? Will you decide to put that extra hour into your résumé before sending it in, or decide that it's good enough? You refuse to do these things because the proper standard of behavior is Plan A, a life lived with purposeful and good intent, and Plan B is the shortcut that chips away at your success.

When I ran for office in an against-all-odds Republican primary, I did so without a Plan B. This isn't to say I neglected to consider my career options after March 6 in case I lost. It would have been irresponsible not to set aside some savings and think pragmatically about the future. But the truth was that I didn't waste an ounce of effort or time dwelling on the possibility. Every small decision was purposeful and oriented toward winning. We relied on our personal savings in order to survive. We worked out of my parents' game room in Spring, Texas. We didn't waste a penny on any luxury. Every day was hyperfocused on connecting with new voters and spreading the message that I believed was right for America. The big goal was winning the election, and the smaller daily goals were the supporting efforts. Every day I faced a choice to sleep in or get up and start working. Every day we could fit in one more event on the calendar, or we could take a break. More often than not, as you might have guessed, we chose Plan A every day. Plan A led to victory, and I'll never know what Plan B even was.

This approach has a proud history in America. What works for individual Americans—perseverance toward a higher purpose— has also worked for America, not surprisingly. We are, after all, a country whose success relies upon responsible citizens who fulfill personal duty and purpose. From George Washington to Harriet Tubman to the men on the beaches of Normandy, American history has been deeply inspired by a No Plan B mind-set.

America has been successful because the backup plan was never an option. We are a nation, unique in world history, that is built upon *purpose* rather than geography or ethnicity. America exists because of a proposition about the nature of humankind—that our nature is not to be forcefully molded by government, but instead that government exists to protect our inalienable rights. In exchange, we expect our citizens to live dutifully, morally, and responsibly. That purpose has informed us and our national destiny at key moments throughout our existence.

At the close of 1776, the Continental Army was near dissolution. Summer and fall had seen defeat upon defeat, with the British driving General George Washington's forces from Long Island, from Manhattan, and from Westchester. Having lost the region of New York City, the humiliation of the Americans was crowned with a dispiriting retreat across a frozen and desolated New Jersey, until the armies came to rest facing one another across the icy Delaware River. Washington had remaining with him a tiny force, poorly supplied, and with the experience of defeat fresh on their spirits. The hopes of America were dimmed, and shortly to be extinguished.

Therefore, General Washington and the Continental Army— outnumbered, outgunned, and out of hope—attacked. They shocked the Hessian garrison at Trenton with a Christmas assault, and won. Days later, they fought again at Trenton, and held off the British main force. Then, deceiving their foes, they disengaged from Trenton and surprised the British garrison at Princeton, defeating it entirely. On Christmas Eve, 1776, the British assumed that America would be extinguished within weeks. Weeks later, they were evacuating nearly all of New Jersey because George Washington and the Continentals refused to stay beaten.

Washington's sheer will to triumph accepted nothing less than victory, and victory followed.

Just over one year later, with the British finally in possession of the American capital at Philadelphia, His Majesty King George III sent a peace commission to the rebellious Americans. Here is what that commission offered to the Continental Congress in June 1778:

Peace.
Trade.
American consent to any British forces in America.
British aid for American public debts.
Full American self-rule under the Crown.
American representation in Parliament.

The British, in short, offered the Americans a wish list of concessions beyond the wildest dreams of any revolutionary radical before July 4, 1776.

But this was *after* July 4, 1776. America wasn't fighting for a good deal within the British Empire now. America was fighting to be free. America had its purpose.

America had no Plan B.

So, eight days after receiving the peace commission's proposal, the Continental Congress sent back its reply: no. For America, it would be full independence or nothing. Against the world's mightiest empire, which also happened to be occupying the American capital at that moment, they said *no*. Our purpose was independence and freedom, and it wasn't negotiable. It isn't just purpose that saved us—it is purpose that *made* us. It was this purpose that authored the American story as we know it. In our lives now, I think we have an obligation to live up to that truth.

Never quit.

No Plan B.

★   ★   ★

Plan B is an alternate universe which only you can choose to engage in. It should be less satisfying in every single way because it represents a lesser version of yourself, the antihero. It represents the version that decided to give up and convince yourself that you never really wanted your dream in the first place. It is a habit that must be broken in order to develop the fortitude necessary to face life's challenges. Leaving Plan B behind means you believe that you will succeed, even if it kills you. It is a marker of the mentally tough, because to quit is to choose weakness. It is the decision to live with good moral intent and purpose, to live dutifully. It is the decision to take every small choice seriously, because it is the small habits that drive you toward your purpose, and ultimately your success. Your purpose is yours.

So is the choice of whether to fulfill it.

CHAPTER 4

BE STILL

The CH-47 Chinook helicopter—those giant two-rotor air beasts that can carry way more weight than seems physically possible for a helicopter—packed with thirty men and two dogs approaches the landing zone, or LZ, after a two-hour transit. The small clearing, tucked behind a small mountain (or large hill), is about ten kilometers away from the target, a cluster of mud buildings where we believe a Taliban shadow government meeting to be taking place. The LZ was chosen carefully so that the sound of the helicopter would not alert anyone nearby. Previous aerial ISR (intelligence, surveillance, and reconnaissance) revealed this area to be pretty desolate, making it ideal for an insertion location. We begin preparation for landing. The sound of magazines being inserted into the mag wells of our SCAR Heavy rifles and M4s reverberates throughout the fuselage. The bolts are slammed forward, each chambering a round. Infrared lasers, attached to the barrels of our guns, are turned on and quickly tested. Helmets are adjusted and night-vision goggles—"nods" for short—are turned on and focused. Rucks are tightened onto backs, adjusted so that all the first-line gear—gun, magazines, nods, and so on—is not interfered with during our ten-kilometer patrol to the target. When you walk off the ramp, you must be ready for all things that war may bring.

We exit and form into a preplanned security perimeter. We stop, look, listen, and smell. We call this simple action SLLS, pronounced "sills." After any activity, in this case a helicopter landing, there is a disturbance in the environment. Someone might have heard you or seen you. Maybe it was locals, maybe it was the enemy. It is standard operating procedure to take a minute, be silent, and observe the environment.

Silence. Nothing.

We begin moving. Two hours later we wake up an unsuspecting enemy and ruin their night.

SLLS—which also kind of sounds like "still," hence the name of this chapter—is simply a reminder to stop and observe your surroundings every once in a while. It is a patrolling tactic. But I attribute far more meaning to the term than simple tactical procedure. For our purposes, it is a mind-set to live by. It is a reminder to *literally* be still. Don't overreact, don't let your emotions drive your action, think before you act. In other words, stop and count to ten. Like your mom and dad taught you.

This is stillness in the Stoic sense. SEAL training never mentions the word "stoic," but it certainly teaches the principles. The best doctrines to live by—the ones that lead to the best outcomes and the happiest people—are generally the oldest ones, having stood the test of time across centuries of human history, trial and error, and diverse experiences. So, if people have been reading Marcus Aurelius for almost two thousand years, *then there might be something to that.* Marcus Aurelius was an accomplished Roman general and emperor, considered one of the last "good emperors" before the Pax Romana ended in the second century AD. He was an ardent follower of the Stoic philosophy—founded by Zeno of Citium in Athens in 301 BC—and the author of the great philosophical work *Meditations.*

Stoics had a few things to say about outrage and unbridled emotions, though they didn't call it outrage culture. They called it passion. In modern times we usually define "passion" as "intense enthusiasm or conviction." One can be passionate about their work, for instance. But it can also be defined as "strong and barely controllable emotion" or "an outbreak of anger," which is how the Stoics used the word. There's a big difference in those two definitions, so it's important to distinguish them for our purposes. Being passionate about your work and being in a state of "barely controllable emotion" are two very different things. Stoics were highly critical of the latter.

"The mind which is free from passions is a citadel, for man has nothing more secure to which he can fly for refuge and for the future be inexpugnable," wrote Marcus Aurelius. And "Let thy chief fort and place of defense be a mind free from passions. A stronger place and better fortified than this, hath no man." According to the Stoics, mental toughness and freedom from passion were directly related. A mind free from passion is a "citadel," and "fortified." I think this is a fairly intuitive concept. After all, what does an intense emotional outburst get us? Do you make better decisions when you're angry? Do raw displays of emotion improve anyone's opinion of us? Probably not. Aurelius addresses the utter futility of heightened passions and the need for perspective:

> Run down the list of those who felt intense anger at something: the most famous, the most unfortunate, the most hated, the most whatever: Where is all that now? Smoke, dust, legend...or not even a legend. Think of all the examples. And how trivial the things we want so passionately are.

An emotional response is a human response, I get it. I too have succumbed to emotion, more often than I care to admit. But it is also a futile response. It isn't an objectively beneficial response. This is central to Stoicism.

Stoic wisdom has guided men through experiences that make BUD/S look like a day at the beach. (Although, I suppose, technically a lot of BUD/S *was literally* a day at the beach—you get the picture.) Take, for example, the late American hero and Medal of Honor recipient Vice Admiral James Stockdale, USN, who endured years of hell in the Hanoi Hilton. Admiral Stockdale had spent years absorbing Stoic thought, in particular the teachings of philosopher Epictetus. In a 1995 lecture at Quantico, he spoke of the day thirty years prior when he was shot down over North Vietnam. It was the first day of seven years of brutal captivity.

Imprisoned, isolated, wounded, and often tortured, Stockdale had little but his faith and the perennial teachings of the great Stoics:

> What I had in hand was the understanding that the Stoic, particularly the disciple of Epictetus who developed this accounting, always keeps separate files in his mind for: (a) those things which are "up to him" and (b) those things which are "not up to him."...Among the relatively few things that are "up to me, within my power," within my will, are my opinions, my aims, my aversions, my own grief, my own joy, my moral purpose or will, my attitude toward what is going on, my own good, and my own evil.

Subjected to torture, deprivation, and humiliation for the following seven years, Stockdale was wholly reduced to "the relatively few things that are 'up to me, within my power.'" Yet it was enough. He survived. He survived specifically because of that Stoic mindset, which simultaneously gave him a sense of control *and* a sense of reality. More than thirty-five years later, the writer Jim Collins in *Good to Great* would call the juxtaposition "the Stockdale paradox." The aged vice admiral told him:

You must never confuse faith that you will prevail in the end—which you can never afford to lose—with the discipline to confront the most brutal facts of your current reality, whatever they might be.

It is a mind-set instantly familiar to any SEAL. And with apologies to Collins, it's no paradox. Stillness is not a denial of reality; it makes it possible *to deal with* reality. It is a source of power. The power to honestly assess what is in your control and what is not. It's the power to be wet and cold and miserable at BUD/S, and acknowledge that you are all those things—and still not ring the bell. It's the power of a single mom struggling to make ends meet, acknowledge that hardship, but persevere anyway. It's the power to eject from your doomed A-4 Skyhawk on September 9, 1965, and as you're descending beneath your parachute, think, "Five years down there at least. I'm leaving the world of technology and entering the world of Epictetus."

That inner dialogue, as he floated down into enemy territory, was his first act of survival. Acceptance for what you truly can't control, but responsibility for what you can control. The Stoic does not believe in categorizing so many things as "outside your control" that you simply become a victim of circumstance. Far more is within your control than you might think.

Responsibility for what you can control leads to the power to defeat outrage culture. As Stockdale said in another of his talks on Stoicism and Epictetus, "There can be no such thing as being the 'victim' of another. You can only be a 'victim' of yourself. It's all in how you discipline your mind."

No victimhood; no outrage. That's the promise and the value of stillness.

The alternative is unreasoned emotion. In many cases you can rationalize and justify your emotional response to a comment or headline or tough question, but we shouldn't pretend that the emotional response leads to a better outcome. Unless the goal is to manipulate other people's emotions—the goal of a political activist, for instance—then outrage is neither a moral nor a productive response. To be clear, I hope your goal is *not* to manipulate the emotions of others, and I also hope that in some small way I can encourage you to be more skeptical of those "passionate" talking heads that seek to manipulate yours.

Speaking of mass media talking heads who like to spin their viewers into a hysterical frenzy, here is another scenario, post military career. I'm starting out in politics and getting used to being on live TV and answering tough interview questions. Sometimes the questions are fair; sometimes they are designed to surprise you. Sometimes they are simply gotcha questions meant to elicit a controversial response. Putting aside for a second why journalists see any value in gotcha questions or what value they bring to public discourse, let's just agree that they are the norm these days. The producers told us there would be a certain set of topics, and we trusted the news anchor wouldn't veer from that. But of course they do. They ask a question midway through the interview that is less of a question and more of a moral judgment wrapped up in a question atop a false premise ("How can you support a tax bill that hurts America's workers?!"). Being surprised on live TV in front of millions of viewers isn't easy to deal with if you are prone to quick emotional reactions.

So, don't be. Be still.

When I went on *Saturday Night Live*, the producers were pretty nervous that I wouldn't be funny, which was a fair assumption considering the many unfunny politicians who had appeared previously. They were nervous that I was going to be too nervous. I explained to them that I was used to preparing for live interviews where anything could be asked of you. Reading rehearsed lines on cue cards would be a cakewalk.

Part of preparing for these difficult moments is simply anticipating them ahead of time. Imagining the scenarios you might be confronted with—called "war-gaming" in the military and just "preparation" in normal parlance—is an effective tool to blunt the emotional effect that events may have on you. Your nervous system will simply be more ready for it. The ancient Stoics called this *premeditatio malorum,* or the "premeditation of evils." Seneca, the first-century Roman Stoic philosopher, was famous for meticulously imagining all the potential pitfalls of a journey before departing. He wrote, "Nothing happens to the wise man against his expectation." In politics, we watch how an interviewer asks questions, and what talking points they use. We get a sense for how fair or unfair they might be, and what kind of topics they usually cover. Then we practice answering questions that are meant to confuse and distract. We get better at it.

Early on in my career, I was far less experienced with such gotcha questions. I remember one interview on CNN, discussing my campaign. At one point the host went off topic and asked me, "Are you comfortable with the fact that President Trump has not visited a military base in a combat zone since becoming president?" Let's unpack what this question was meant to do. On its face, it isn't a crazy question to ask of a former servicemember turned politician. On the other hand, one might question why such a topic would be newsworthy at all, unless the goal was to create a narrative that President Donald Trump was a bad guy who didn't care about the troops. The intent of the question was obvious: Imply a character flaw in the president and get me to reactively agree with that character flaw. That in turn would generate a round of news headlines: "Retired Navy SEAL turned GOP candidate questions President Trump's ability as Commander in Chief." Normal tactics for CNN, which like all cable news networks favors spectacle and drama over informing the public. But the bad-faith aspect of the question no longer mattered, because...*it was asked*. On live TV, where there was no escaping it. They could have acted in good faith and told me they wanted to discuss it, which is a common practice in the world of cable news producers, so I could have reviewed the facts surrounding the topic instead of relying on CNN's narrow (and likely biased) explanation. But they didn't. It was totally unexpected—I never war-gamed it—so I had to fall back on deeper training, back to being *still*.

On live TV, and especially on short news interviews, you don't get to roll your eyes (well, you can...it's just not a great idea) or hem and haw and scratch your head while you think about the question. You have to just answer. And your answer better not suck. Being still is about acting properly under pressure. And so I did that. I gave them an answer that would still push back against their premise (that the president was a bad guy) in a coherent way. I said something to the effect of "I was in the military for ten years. I never once saw a president visit a base, and I felt that I could do my job just fine. The president gives our generals and troops the ability to execute the mission we've given them. Troops feel like the president has their backs." Not perfect, but it didn't suck, either. Crisis averted.

The "calm inside the storm" quality takes practice. It's hard to know you even have that quality until you have been tested. Some people develop it through experience and adversity, others through training. The best and most emotionally resilient people develop it through both hardship *and* hard training. But the unfortunate reality is that fewer and fewer Americans are developing that quality because, well, life has become too comfortable. We no longer need to hunt for our food, defend ourselves from mountain lions, or figure out how to get water. The simple act of not having to find new and reliable sources of water should collectively blow our minds. The notion that nobody in this vast country worries about dying of dehydration would astound our ancestors. The miracle of modernity has done some amazing things, but it has also softened us a great deal. The likelihood of experiencing a truly harrowing situation, let alone many of them, is near zero and our resilience has suffered for it. This means you'll never know how you would react, and it means you have very few opportunities to practice for it when the time comes. It is one reason why even the smallest hardships elicit emotional breakdowns from many Americans, why so many are diagnosed with anxiety disorders, and why therapy and psychiatry are booming industries. Prior generations would be bewildered by the strange upward trend in both our fragility and our standard of living.

The way we millennials and Gen Z-ers have been raised also plays a role. Haidt and Lukianoff, in *The Coddling of the American Mind*, observe that independent activities—like walking by yourself to a friend's house—are occurring later and later in life. Younger generations report that the first time they leave their home by themselves—to walk more than six blocks away—usually occurs around fifth grade. Older generations report first grade. This change has occurred despite the fact that the crime rate has fallen dramatically.[1] Helicopter parenting, the incessant micromanagement of a child's activities, has created a generation of people who rarely experience conflict or traumatic situations, and as a result they are more prone to emotional overreactions.

The first way out of this mess is to simply choose not to be that person. Recall the importance of heroes? It's a valuable first step: Visualize what right looks like. If you want to *be* something, then you have to imagine being that first. Be someone who is cool under pressure. Value serenity instead of outrage. It seems that our

---

1   https://www.pewresearch.org/fact-tank/2019/10/17/facts-about-crime-in-the-u-s/

culture is moving in the wrong direction here. If you are blessed enough to not be on social media, you might be surprised to learn that the angriest, most passionate public figures are rewarded with the most clicks and biggest audiences. Our culture has begun to confuse passion with substance, reward the loudest and angriest voices, and thus incentivize behavior wholly at odds with Stoic wisdom. The number of decibels your voice hits as you scream about how right you are is not necessarily an indicator of how much sense you are making. As a society founded on reason and Western Enlightenment ideals, we must hold ourselves to a higher standard. We have to collectively stop allowing emotion and passion to pass for reason and factual debate.

In the SEAL teams, our first exercise in training the mind to be still is "drownproofing." And yes, it is as ridiculous as it sounds. As legend has it (and it may indeed just be legend), drownproofing originates from the story of an American POW in Vietnam. As the Viet Cong transported him along the Mekong River, they decided they'd had enough of him and threw him overboard. But this was not some magnanimous gesture of human civility. He was not being released for good behavior. They expected him to drown.

It was a reasonable expectation: His hands were tied behind his back and his feet were tied together. Visualize that for a second. This creates quite the predicament, especially when you are trying to *not* drown. He had to figure out how to swim to shore. And, as the story goes, he did just that. Ever since, a key element of SEAL training involves drownproofing us, making sure that we too can jump from a boat with our hands and feet tied.

There are two ways to not drown when tied up. The first is to methodically bounce yourself off the bottom. You let yourself sink to the bottom, slowly exhaling, and calmly springboard yourself back up after you hit the bottom. You must launch yourself off the bottom strongly enough so that the apex of your jump just reaches the surface, and you can grab a quick breath. Launch too hard, and you will not only waste energy but also throw off your apex. Launch too lightly, and you won't reach the surface and get that much-needed breath of air. If you panic, your rhythm will be broken and you will become out of breath. You will drown. If the water is shallow enough (ten to fifteen feet), you can do this indefinitely, and even move forward in a given direction. During BUD/S we do practice this indefinitely. It is one of the easier challenges we face in the water. Few fail.

Then there is the second part of drownproofing. After all, it's hard to claim you are "proofed" if you can only survive in shallow water. SEALs need to be able to *swim* with their hands and feet tied together. You know, *just in case* (even though real-life examples have proven elusive and the Vietnam story may be apocryphal). This is a little more challenging, and as you can imagine, it is much easier to panic. For starters, you may be surprised to learn that it is indeed possible to swim with your hands tied behind your back and your feet tied together. You do so by staying flat on your belly and methodically dolphin-kicking while also maneuvering your head to barely clear the water. You sink slightly after taking a breath, kick, and let your full lungs float your upper body back up to the surface. It requires flawless execution to work. It also requires that you not panic. (Imagine instructors screaming at the top of their lungs, "DON'T PANIC!!" as you calmly try and do this.) The slightest amount of panic will cause you to sink, and you aren't coming back up once you've sunk even a little bit. There's no method for swimming up once you have started to sink.

This exercise isn't about the tiny chance that you will be confronted with the aforementioned Vietnam scenario. That would be highly unlikely, and terribly unlucky. The point of this training is to teach SEALs to engage in a deep calm when they need to. Many training scenarios build upon this, usually using the discomfort that being underwater brings with it as a training tool. For instance, we do underwater knot tying—during which an instructor ever so slowly examines your knot while you wait fifteen feet below the surface on a breath hold. The knots are simple enough—square, bowline, and half hitch—but many people fail nonetheless, unable to be still.

The culmination of underwater discomfort occurs during Second Phase in BUD/S, also known as "Dive Phase." During Second Phase our big test is called "pool comp," short for "pool competency." This may be my least favorite test in BUD/S, simply because I hate it when I can't breathe (I know, how wimpy of me). It involves a lengthy test during which you must conduct underwater problem solving with your open-circuit scuba rig. Sounds simple enough, but it's not. First we are equipped with the more classic version of modern dive equipment. Two large tanks on our back, with a dual rubber hose regulator that feeds into both ends of the mouthpiece. The use of the traditional, older-style regulator for training is purposeful: It is easier for instructors to tie knots in your breathing hoses.

Oh, great. Every new scuba student's dream.

Pool comp begins with a "surf hit," where an instructor attempts to simulate a large wave disorienting you while you dive. He grabs your mask just as you exhale, rips your regulator out of your mouth (goodbye, sweet, sweet air supply), and begins spinning you around, all while adding a few jabs in the ribs for good measure. And of course, this particular "wave" also manages to tie your hoses in tight knots. What an amazingly complex wave.

Then the test begins. Your job is to collect yourself and get your air working again, using the proper procedures. This the key element of training: proper procedures. There are very specific steps required of you, in a specific order. You can't just rip off the rig; you have to feel the hoses behind you first. If you do remove the rig, you have to undo your straps in a specific order. Everything has to be done exactly to the prescribed method, or you fail. You cannot shoot to the surface, or you fail. You cannot do anything out of order, or you fail.

Remember, the goal is not actually to get good at fixing the dive rig. No one believes this particular scenario to be encountered in the real world, especially when we use these particular dive rigs only in training. Not a single SEAL remembers what these pool comp procedures actually were, when asked years later. The goal is to force you to remain calm and perform a task in the worst of conditions—when you can't breathe or see.

There were many moments when this training came in useful. In a gunfight, for instance. Yelling and screaming is a fairly natural reaction to bullets flying at your head, but it is also a useless reaction. Panic causes more panic, but calm breeds calm. So we are drilled day after day to be calm. Be still. One particular instance was my injury in 2012, in Afghanistan, when I was hit by the IED blast. An initial instinct is always to scream. It feels good, it feels natural. There may even be some evolutionary reason why we scream in pain (perhaps to signal for help from others). But it doesn't matter. It isn't useful in combat. Your buddies know you got hurt, they don't need to hear you complain about it too.

But there was actually another life-threatening experience where being still truly mattered for me. It happened about a year after I survived my encounter with fifteen pounds of explosives in Afghanistan. It happened on a beautiful, peaceful beach just outside Rio de Janeiro, Brazil. Tara and I were on our honeymoon, exploring local beaches. I found a boogie board and decided I would try my luck with the waves, like I had done hundreds of times before in my life. The waves were solid, but it was difficult to swim past them to the break point. Dragging the foam board through the surf was a difficult task, and I was putting in quite the effort to move past each set of waves. I was out of breath, and getting more out of breath with each large wave crashing over me. Not a big deal, I was fine. I could handle it. My heart rate was about at a quick jog. As long as nothing else disrupted that rhythm, I'd be fine.

Then an enormous wave broke right on me. The board was quickly detached from me, the cord breaking. The water was deep. Too deep for me to ever touch the bottom. The wave was violent, and kept me under for much longer than I expected. This was not the fake wave from pool comp; this was real. I struggled to get back to the surface, and when I finally did, I was completely exhausted, gasping for air. I was not a weak swimmer by any standard (Navy SEAL, remember?), but this was kicking my ass.

And then another wave hit. Same thing. So much turning in the water made it difficult to swim effectively, because bubbles prevent you from pulling through the water. All of a sudden, this situation was extremely dire. This particular set of waves was relentless. I was a good one hundred yards from shore, and there were no lifeguards. There was no one to see me go under.

That stillness training had never been more important. In that moment it was even more important than the day I was hit by an IED. In Afghanistan I had my teammates, on this secluded beach I had no one. I consciously prevented myself from panicking and began breathing in slower, more methodical breaths. I began to problem-solve. I quickly decided that despite the strong and reflexive urge to keep my gasping mouth above water, I would be better off if I dove into each incoming wave, just below it. In between waves, I slowly and calmly got on my back, in a sort of lazy backstroke, and moved toward shore. If I had attempted to stay afloat the normal way—treading water with bicycle kicks and circular arm motions—I believe I would have drowned. It's a crazy thing to say that a Navy SEAL with my amount of training could have been close to drowning, but I was. The situation was just that unexpected. And the only way to properly confront the unexpected is by facing it as calmly as possible. You never know when your life may be at stake.

I eventually made it back to shore. My wife, Tara, looked up from her book. She asked, "Why do you look so tired? And where is the boogie board?"

It's not fun for a Navy SEAL to tell their wife that they almost drowned.

I'll put aside the dramatic stories, as I admit they are extreme examples. Because the truth is, your life is usually not at stake. But your reputation is, your relationships are, and your mental well-being is. And that's where this Stoic ethos, this stillness that SEALs learn in the cold water, is instrumental to daily life: the disagreements with your spouse that get unnecessarily intense, frustration with a coworker, or political disagreements on social media.

First of all I want to say—maybe "admit" is a better word—that I am not some Zen master in my personal life. I have proven myself to be capable of maintaining my cool during political disagreements, near-drowning experiences, or debates, but I won't claim I am the best at doing the same during private conversations. I didn't write this book because I am perfect. Far from it. I just think I have a pretty good idea of what I should aspire to be. Romans 3:23 says that we have all sinned and fallen short of God's glory. But wisdom is immune to our humanity and tendency to fall short.

Let's dissect the reason why I fail at this sometimes, and in doing so I think I will reveal some lessons in how to toughen up. It comes down to emotion. In public, you will have a hard time getting me to react emotionally, especially with politics. But there are people who do have an ability to get me agitated, and those are usually the people I am close with, or the ones who are "on my team." Why is that? Maybe it is because there is a sense that they know you best, and their observation or criticism is painfully accurate. Or maybe it's the opposite: Their critique or observation is terribly inaccurate, and you feel *they should know better*. It depends on the situation, I think. The point is that it is worth thinking about. I have had to analyze why I overreacted, in a deep and honest way, and then apply it to my future war gaming. It can help you be still during the next round of emotional agitation you are sure to encounter. Frankly, I should do it more often.

War-gaming doesn't just apply to, well, war. It applies to life. As I stated earlier, war-gaming is just the simple mental act of imagining a scenario. It is the practice of mentally walking through various scenarios and then imagining your ideal reactions to those scenarios. In training and in combat, we are war-gaming constantly. If this happens, how should I react? What if, during our patrol, we begin taking fire from our left flank? What call would I make? What cover should we maneuver to? So when it does happen, you've already thought through the action and it comes with ease. You are better prepared. Your mind is freed to embrace new, unexpected challenges. And in a firefight with the enemy, those new and unexpected challenges will come up fast. Better to consciously prepare for that which can be anticipated and be mentally prepared to deal with that which cannot.

I war-game constantly, mostly with respect to political debate. It happens to be my job and my passion, so it comes naturally. My wife will catch me talking to myself in the living room and then ask, "Hey, babe, who are you debating?" She has become accustomed to this strange habit of mine.

Anyone who has ever practiced for anything—sports, debate, a biology test—is familiar with that particular idiosyncrasy. I am simply encouraging you to do it more often, as it relates to confrontational and uncomfortable situations. Imagine how you would want to be seen reacting to a difficult situation, and simply think about reacting that way. You will be amazed at the effects.

Soldiers certainly know the benefits. In training, it is sometimes lost on us why we train using the drills that we do. They may seem redundant, boring, or unrealistic—or any number of descriptions. But then the real thing happens. In the real world. The bomb goes off, the bullets start flying, the truck rolls over, the radio breaks. You're stressed and mostly unable to calmly rationalize or problem-solve. And yet you solve the problem. Why? Because you've thought about it before. War-gaming simply means you have bothered to think about it before. You have played the what-if game…and you have won.

Now let's apply this to the most emotionally taxing and divisive category in our lives today: politics.

In our political disagreements today, our emotional attachment to certain positions has taken on new extremes. Whether or not this is something new is anyone's guess, but it certainly seems more intense than ever before because of the loudspeaker that social media provides to everyone's opinion. In his book *The Smallest Minority*, Kevin Williamson writes, "This exudate of outrage and dread has arrived together with the rise to prominence of social media and other instruments of communication that not only are better-suited for emotional outbursts than for reasoned discussion, but which, as a consequence of their basic social architecture, reward rage, extremism, and hostility while they suffocate intelligence, charity, and gentleness."

The likelihood of anyone saying, "Oh, I hadn't thought of it that way thank you for clarifying your position" during a debate in the depths of Facebook comments is laughably small. It is even more unlikely in the 280-character-limit depths of Twitter. But the real reason it is unlikely isn't because of social media, it is because it is human nature to dig in and double down. Your gut tells you to never back down from a position that you are emotionally invested in. Politics has become a team sport, and that makes it extremely difficult to swallow your pride and admit error.

I speak at a lot of high schools. One question that I am inevitably asked is, "How should we get more involved in politics?" My answer is always the same: Take it slow. Don't choose a side. Just keep learning and take pride in having an open mind. Your opinions on complex matters should come to you slowly, over time, within the context of new facts and experiences. Most adults simply haven't had access to all of the information yet, let alone most teenagers. Your experiences are few, and your knowledge of any given subject incomplete. *And that's OK.* There is nothing wrong with not knowing, but there is something deeply wrong about having a strong opinion based on very little fact or reason. A cautious approach to opinion formation is also better for your mental health. Discovering you were wrong about a subject is psychologically taxing, especially after investing serious emotional energy into that opinion. The first reaction is often to dig in, stay wrong, and get angry. By emotionally attaching yourself to an opinion so early in life, you've set yourself up to be the person you never wanted to be: outraged.

I view this tendency toward extreme emotional attachment to an argument as both a societal problem and an indication of mental weakness. A mentally tough, confident person does not have a problem admitting they are wrong or unknowledgeable on a subject. A weaker person, captive to emotions and unsure of themselves, does. This is the hard truth. And the next hard truth: Many of us are in the latter category. And if we aren't fully in the latter category, we have certainly dabbled in it.

This is partly because our hero-archetype architecture is miscalibrated. As I've said earlier, we elevate the public figures that exude the most passion instead of the most sense. Passion becomes synonymous with "authenticity," and gives the loud-mouthed activist or politician an undue amount of credibility on an issue, even when completely wrong. As people admire these fist-shaking "leaders," they themselves are more likely to behave in the exact same way. When confronted with a disagreement, their likeliest reaction is to raise their voice and hurl insults. We see this all the time in our political discourse, and it's ripping the country apart. We have chosen the wrong heroes, and the wrong character attributes to elevate and value. We need a sharp recalibration in what we view as *good*.

So how do we fix it? How we do dabble more often in the first category of cool, calm, and collected? What do war-gaming, mental preparedness, stillness, and Stoicism have to do with the goal of political detoxification?

We can apply these lessons—tried and tested from the battlefield—to the way we absorb the news, interpret a friend's comment on Twitter, or hear a provocative speaker on a college campus. War-gaming—in this context—is applied as *imagining a scenario in which you don't freak out on someone else.*

What a concept.

Maintaining your stillness is about stopping for a second and asking a question. Preferably a good, constructive question that will elicit some form of truth. This is quite easy to practice, and I would certainly encourage you to do so. The news headlines are a great place to start. In the twenty-first-century news cycle where shocking headlines get more clicks, the incentive to write provocative headlines at the expense of truth and context is terribly strong. Words like "bombshell, "corrupt," "traitor," and "treason" elicit an immediate sense that the story is deadly serious, begging you to read more into it. As author Matt Taibbi notes in his book *Hate Inc.*: "Content is designed not just to be lurid and sensational, but immediately disquieting from a psychological standpoint." The media's goal is to literally challenge your ability to be still.

A tough American, intent on improving upon their current self, is not tricked into an emotional reaction by these headlines. You do not write an angry tweet, you do not hurl an insult. You are cool and measured, and *skeptical*. You are curious what the agenda of the journalist might be and what facts or context they might be leaving out. You seek out a different story on the same topic from an opposing view, and you find out that many of the claims made in the original story were convincingly debunked. And just like that, you are a Zen master of stillness and Stoicism.

A part of curing our political debate is having the courage to stand up for what you know and admit what you don't know. And when you do stand up for what you know, you better damn well know *why* you believe it. And just because you *believe* it doesn't therefore mean you should express your belief in the most emotional of ways. If you do, it may indicate that you are filling in your knowledge gaps with raw passion, and hoping that no one will realize it. Unfortunately, these days, too many people are overcoming their knowledge deficits with passion, and too many more people are mistaking "passion" and "authenticity" for righteousness and sophistication. It is an unhealthy trend.

I find this dearth of curiosity to be especially bad with many policy debates. Take regulations, for instance. When you hear "President Trump repeals twelve more Obama-era environmental regulations," what goes through your head? If you're being honest, probably images of fat-cat businessmen celebrating as they dump sludge into a pristine river, or some kind of ooze seeping into a green field, or dark black smoke suddenly emanating from a factory as birds fall out of the sky choking. Why not ask a few questions first? Why were the regulations put in only during the previous administration? Was there really a need for them in the first place? What was the cost-benefit analysis done? Or start with a more basic question: What *kind* of regulations were these?

Let's take one recent example. In August of 2019, the *Hill* ran a story on the Trump administration EPA's proposed rule changes to the New Source Review regulations under the Clean Air Act. The headline read "EPA Proposes Easing Air Pollution Permitting Process."[2] This headline clearly implies a particular message: More air pollution is coming from power plants.

But is it?

In this particular case, and in many cases like it, the story itself is actually somewhat balanced. The author notes what the EPA's argument is (current regulations actually discourage more efficient technology being installed, and this new reform will actually remove obstacles to the construction of cleaner and more efficient facilities), as well as the environmentalists' arguments (they believe net pollution will increase). But most people don't dig through the content of the story, and instead simply read the headline. And in this case, like so many others, the heavily editorialized headline gives the wrong impression.

The reality of this particular policy issue goes much deeper, which is what all fair-minded and mentally tough Americans should do: dig a little deeper. New Source Review (NSR) is a permitting process that is required by the Clean Air Act and impacts virtually every major manufacturing facility and power plant in the United States.[3] Put simply: If you are a new power plant or factory, you have to get a permit from the EPA to make sure your new plant is not going to adversely affect the surrounding air quality. Seems fair enough, since we all have an interest in cleaner air. But as most regulations do, this one has gotten out of control. The NSR process oftentimes costs companies millions of dollars, years of delays, and

---

2   https://thehill.com/policy/energy-environment/455854-epa-proposes-easing-air
    -pollution-permitting-process
3   https://media.rff.org/documents/472010026.pdf

uncertainty, as companies don't always know what will trigger an NSR by the EPA.

It begs the question: Is this regulation really keeping our air cleaner?

As currently written, this regulation has prevented the very thing it's advocating for: cleaner air. Because NSR also kicks in for major modifications—like adding a carbon capture facility to a power plant—it impedes companies from investing in even cleaner air quality.[4]

Take Petra Nova, a carbon capture pilot program in the greater Houston area. Petra Nova and its parent company, NRG Energy, have had incredible success with their carbon capture project. By capturing five thousand tons of carbon dioxide per day, they've taken the equivalent of 350,000 cars off the road, generated power for thousands of homes in Houston, and recycled the carbon that would have been otherwise released into the atmosphere.

But when they were building their plant, they had a decision to make: Would they trigger the costly NSR by modifying their existing power plants? Or spend $100 million to create a completely new system and thus bypass NSR? They chose to spend the $100 million—an incredibly costly way to avoid the even costlier expense of triggering NSR to *decrease* their carbon dioxide emissions.[5] The EPA's new rules would change this incentive for the better, by changing the criteria that trigger NSR to encourage carbon capture investment by both the manufacturing and energy industries. If your project decreases the overall amount of pollutants, rather than

4   https://www.epa.gov/sites/production/files/2018-05/documents/hhrg-115-if18 -wstate-wehrumw-20180516.pdf

5   https://www.epw.senate.gov/public/_cache/files/c/c/cc38b124-4842-4794-b883 -21e1cd08f2c2/AA4D18981D364A7D686D95523F8EB5FD.greeson-testimony-09.13 .2017.pdf

increases, the project will not be subject to NSR.[6] It's an elimination of a regulation for the sake of *better* regulation—and one that actually helps achieve the goal of cleaner air.

The *Hill*'s headline missed all of that context, and their story barely scratched the surface of the issue. If you are predisposed to think that Trump and Republicans are anti-environment, then that headline was all you needed to confirm that bias. But more context changes the story substantially.

These days, there is so little space to wonder *why*—in good faith—someone might be making the decision they are making. Just because we all agree on having oil and gas regulations does not therefore mean that any and all of the regulations make sense. Imagine if that were the case. All a regulatory agency would have to do is simply say, "Well, it makes the air cleaner," and we must line up blindly behind them or be bullied into submission. That's absurd, of course. Many regulations have been feel-good measures that have a marginal positive impact on the environment but enormous costs. It also ignores the important question of what other preventive measures might be taken aside from top-down, one-size-fits-all regulations. No one disagrees with smart regulations, especially on the environment. But to pretend that all regulations are good or even necessary is an analytical leap that is based on emotional reasoning and not careful analysis.

It is also indicative of a society that is losing the ability to assume good intentions about people on the opposite political team, and has a lazy tendency to judge without evidence. The media's grotesque behavior only worsens this trend. Remember the angry veterans that confronted me outside my office? Shortly after that incident, they colluded with *Newsweek*—the former news magazine

6   https://www.epa.gov/sites/production/files/2018-03/documents/nsr_memo_03-13-2018.pdf

turned left-wing tabloid—to write a blatantly misleading headline: "Crenshaw Tries to Hide in Elevator while Confronted by Combat Veterans."[7] The false headline is easily debunked by simply watching the video embedded in the article. I wasn't hiding at all. I was on my way to vote, and the elevator is simply part of that journey. The crazed young men entered the elevator with me. The writers knew this, of course, but wanted to write a salacious headline at the expense of factual reporting.

A *still* person has the ability to stop, look at a news story or another person's arguments, and ask objective questions without emotional overreaction or assumptions of ill intent. One is centered, rational, and respected; the other is frantic, unhappy, and intellectually stagnant. Don't be the latter.

Because of this reality, I have gotten into the habit of explaining controversial votes or issues with videos on social media. I call them #Heresthetruth videos because, well, I feel there has usually been some dishonest narrative put forth about what the legislation in question was really about. One particularly egregious example was H.R. 986, the Protecting Americans with Pre-existing Conditions Act.[8] I voted against it. Why? Because I don't want to protect people with preexisting conditions? Of course not. I voted against it because that particular bill had *nothing to do with protecting people with preexisting conditions.* At the height of political dishonesty, Democrats crafted a bill that would have removed the recently expanded ability of states to use different methods to insure people. Some states, for instance, have seen huge success by using reinsurance programs to protect people with preexisting conditions, while also not forcing those additional costs on the healthy population's

7   https://www.newsweek.com/gop-rep-dan-crenshaw-tries-hide-elevator-while-confronted-combat-veterans-over-his-support-1460313

8   https://www.congress.gov/bill/116th-congress/house-bill/986/text?q=%7B%22search%22%3A%5B%22Protecting+people+with+preexisting%22%5D%7D&r=2&s=1

insurance premium costs. They do this by using a 1332 waiver within the Affordable Care Act ("Obamacare"). The bill in question would have actually made these waivers *less* flexible, and therefore made it more difficult to experiment with different options. So not only did this bill *not* protect people with preexisting conditions, it actually limited our options *to protect* people with preexisting conditions. Knowing that Republicans would vote against it, the Democrats slyly named the bill "Protecting Americans with Pre-existing Conditions" so that they could use it as a campaign commercial in 2020.

Why would they do this? Because they know they can take advantage of a population that jumps to conclusions and doesn't engage in a be still mentality. And they aren't the only ones. We see this daily on the left and the right, where a single social media post will send users into a confirmation bias–driven frenzy. Fake news stories (literally fake news, not the intentionally biased mainstream media headlines I noted earlier) that sensationalize preconceived notions of a given issue are a surefire way for the purveyors of such stories to get more clicks. They have it down to a science,[9] and they take advantage of the fact that our society is becoming less still, less skeptical, and more inclined to overreact in the most emotional of ways. I am consistently amazed that social media users will exercise cautious skepticism toward their politicians (and rightfully so!), but accept as fact the ramblings of an anonymous Instagram commentator deep in the comment section of a post. I've watched it happen in real time, and it is utterly bewildering.

---

9   I don't mean this figuratively. Experts studying this phenomenon noted that the groups generating this content are not interested in politics, but in clicks. Filippo Menczer, a professor of informatics and computer science at Indiana University who runs the fake news tracking site Hoaxy, noted "sometimes they generate similar messages for the right and the left" (https://www.bbc.com/news/blogs-trending-39592010).

In November of 2019, a single social media post got people to *physically* show up to protest Putnam County, New York, police officers as they confronted an Army veteran during a seven-hour standoff. Why? Because this particular young man went on Instagram, drinking whiskey, and told everyone the police were coming to arrest him because a fellow vet told the cops he owned thirty-round-capacity rifle magazines (illegal in New York). Social media activists quickly rallied to his cause, spreading a story that he was being unconstitutionally targeted for his firearms. His Instagram following jumped to 150,000 followers overnight, more than $10,000 was raised for a "legal fund," and his newfound supporters succeeded in causing chaos within the 911 dispatch system with hundreds of calls. It is hard to imagine a more emotional and *real* reaction to a situation in which the only evidence came from an intoxicated Instagram user. And the kicker? It was all a farce. The police were arresting him because he had multiple warrants—burglary, aggravated harassment, and larceny, to name a few—and deputies reported hearing what sounded like a gunshot from the man's home. *It had nothing to do with firearms or thirty-round magazines.* But that didn't stop literally thousands of people from engaging in full-on emotional reasoning without an ounce of self-doubt.

Less extreme examples can be found on social media daily. The point is this: Be still; delay your reaction. Be skeptical and consider alternate possibilities. Hold multiple potential scenarios in your head at the same time. If an argument is wildly passionate, it may indicate that the person is compensating for a lack of substance. Envision yourself as that thoughtful skeptic (be your own hero) and you will *be* that person.

This applies to personal interactions as well, and the increasing tendency for people to immediately assume hostility, discrimination, or otherwise ill intent from others. We appear to be losing the ability to consider alternate explanations for someone's behavior toward us. For instance, is it right to assume that someone's treatment of you is motivated by some form of discrimination? Or is it possible they treat everyone that way? Maybe they are having a bad day? How many other possibilities are there, and shouldn't we consider those possibilities before assuming they mean us harm?

Haidt and Lukianoff discuss this type of problematic "us versus them" thinking, and how the theory of intersectionality[10] has been corrupted and interpreted to mean a power struggle between the privileged and the oppressed. In any power struggle, there is a perceived "good" and "bad" side, thus pitting us against each other before the conversation has even begun. This form of identity politics combined with microaggression training "creates an environment highly conducive to the development of a 'call-out culture,' in which students gain prestige for identifying small offenses committed by members of their community, and then publicly 'calling out' the offenders." The authors write, "They have learned to interpret mere words and social behaviors as acts of aggression. They have learned to associate aggression, domination, and oppression with privileged groups. They have learned to focus only on perceived impact and to ignore intent." This learned behavior of assuming the worst of intentions has had a chilling effect on freedom of speech and a supremely caustic effect on political discourse.

This leads to situations where even innocent gestures are

---

10 The theory of intersectionality, originally advanced by UCLA law professor Kimberlé Williams Crenshaw (no relation!), was intended to illuminate the fact that some individuals may face discrimination along multiple "intersecting" lines, to include race, class, sex, age, etc. As an analytical tool, this may be useful. The problem is the way it has been used to advance tribalism and moral arguments against the most "privileged."

labeled as insidious aggressions by an overreactive media. Take, for example, the Army-Navy football game in December 2019. During this great American tradition, a number of cadets and midshipman were seen making a peculiar hand gesture behind a sports newscaster, forming a circle with their thumb and index finger. It looked like an upside-down OK symbol. For anyone familiar with military culture, this is known as the "circle game." If you are unlucky enough to glance down at the circle, you earn yourself a swift punch to the shoulder. It's a harmless, if some-what immature, game. But that wasn't the media's take. Within hours, major news organizations pounced, decrying the gesture as a white power symbol[11] and encouraging mass hysteria from social justice warriors across the internet. It led to an actual investigation, from actual military personnel, into the "scandal" of the hand gestures. I noted sarcastically on Twitter soon after: "Glad we needed to waste our military's time investigating the hysterical cries of the outrage mob."

Why on earth would our first reaction be to imply that a group of future military officers were not-so-secretly taking part in a racist ideology on national television? What happened to grace and charity, where we interpret the statements of others in the most reasonable possible form?

It turns out there is bipartisan agreement on this point. In his 2016 exit interview with NPR, President Barack Obama said he gives his own daughters this advice: "Don't go around looking for insults," he tells them. And on the excesses of political correct-ness, he said, "If you're narrowly defining political correctness as a hypersensitivity that ends up resulting in people not being able to

---

11   They claim that the OK sign has been appropriated by white supremacists to
      mean "white power," because a W is formed by three fingers, and the P is
      formed with the index finger and thumb.

express their opinions at all without somebody suggesting they're a victim...our social discourse and our political discourse becomes like walking on eggshells."

A mentally weak person reacts to the most offensive potentiality; a still person has the power to simply...not know. Which person do you think is happier? Which one do you think has less stress? The person who finds ill intent with every interaction, or the person who chooses to give the benefit of the doubt?

★   ★   ★

To be still is to be much, much happier. Not only that, but you'll be better prepared. Spend some time imagining those bad scenarios—whether it is a bad day on a boogie board or a mean tweet—and then imagine overcoming it. Don't kick yourself later when you finally think of a better response to angry Twitter trolls. Instead, war-game the scenario ahead of time so you have the carefully crafted—and far less emotional—reaction ready to go.

And what if life hits you unexpectedly, in a way you could never anticipate or war-game? When that unfortunate moment comes (it will), promise yourself that you will encounter it with tenacity, thoughtfulness, self-awareness, and self-control. You will be ready. You will be ready to listen before you react. You will be ready to admit you don't know the answer and seek it out before becoming emotionally attached to a particular argument. You will be unmoved by the haters and trolls because you anticipated them. Hell, you feel sorry for them. Their anger is both foolish and unproductive. Reactive emotional states are useless. You know this now, because you live with stillness.

CHAPTER 5

SWEAT THE SMALL STUFF

T his is the chapter where I give you permission to complain. Permission to moan and groan about the nitty-gritty, small-but-annoying, ankle-biting inconveniences we face in our everyday lives. Permission to gripe about even your smallest troubles, grumble about long lines at the drive-thru, and whine about the imperfect weather. I am actually going to encourage it.

You're welcome.

OK, don't thank me yet. There are certain ground rules:

1. Sweating the small stuff is OK, *but* exercise your complaints lightheartedly. Seek out humor in your whining. Be humble. Be self-aware.
2. If you allow yourself to sweat the small stuff—and I think you should—then you also must force yourself to be detail oriented.
3. If you allow yourself to sweat the small stuff, then you must try your hardest not to sweat the big stuff.

That's the deal we are making in this chapter. I will declare that it is acceptable to complain every once in a while, and you will agree to do it only with the small stuff and not the big stuff. I am giving this advice because *venting* is extremely healthy. And it is also good practice for self-awareness. Venting about the little things provides you with perspective on how silly and unproductive complaining really is. At the same time, we should recognize that pent-up frustration can have real consequences and be detrimental to our mental health. I firmly believe that allowing yourself the space to complain every once in a while about the little things frees up mental bandwidth to deal with more consequential life events. It is a frustration-release valve.

We have all witnessed someone snap. It ain't pretty. It happens suddenly when that one thing just sends them off the edge. Maybe a white shirt got turned pink because it was mixed with a red shirt in the laundry. All hell breaks loose—detergent is splashed against a wall, the pets go running for cover. Maybe a snide comment by a coworker causes a meltdown in the office. Things are said. Tears are shed. Rumors are spread.

It's never about the one comment made or the shirt ruined. It is usually a whole slew of built-up frustrations that just piled on day after day. Your subconscious is a holding tank filling with stress and frustration from the little stuff we deal with. (Like when traffic lights in a city grid are not properly synchronized, and you just keep going from one red light to another, and you wonder *why* city planners can't synchronize the damn green lights to improve traffic flow. *Why?*) Eventually that tank hits capacity, and that frustration makes its debut in the conscious mind...manifesting in a human firework display of flipping the fuck out.

You do *not* want to be that person who is known to flip out. That should not be included on your hero-attributes list.

Most advice you get on this subject is just the opposite of what I am telling you. "Don't sweat the small stuff," they say. Just be bigger than that jerk on the highway who cut you off before the exit you needed, smile when the power goes out, don't cry over spilled milk, and so on.

I disagree.

Let it loose, my friend. Because let's be honest, that little stuff probably still genuinely pisses you off. You can't actually change your emotional reaction to it. So in reality, saying, "Don't sweat the small stuff" is actually a suggestion to pen it up (or in the words of my last chapter, be *still*). There's some good reason for this. It is generally socially unacceptable to be seen as the person getting bent out of shape because their steak arrived slightly overcooked. It seems petty, because it is.

You're probably thinking: "OK, Dan, you just got done telling me that I should be *still*—stop, think, listen, question—when confronted with the bullshit occurrences in life. Aren't you now telling me the opposite?"

Not exactly. Remember we have a deal: You can complain about the small stuff, but it should be lighthearted, quippy, and avoid personal attacks. Being still is about having the ability to delay an emotional reaction and replace it with a preplanned response. The response is intentional and deliberate, not reactionary, and based on the qualities and attributes that you have already aspired to as part of your hero archetypes. You are choosing to sweat the small stuff, but you are choosing to do so with some grace, humor, and self-awareness.

This isn't easy. It can go wrong. It may take practice and keen observation of how people react to you. But don't overthink it—just remember a few key principles.

1. Incorporate humor and sarcasm when possible. Sarcasm is a uniquely American and British attribute, and I think we should embrace it.
2. Smile.
3. Don't overdo it. Just sweat the small stuff enough to make sure the frustration valve is released a little bit.

This is *how* we sweat the small stuff. It's an art, really. I am personally not sure I have mastered it. My wife thinks I complain too much, but I feel right at home among my fellow SEALs. You'd be amazed how much we complain about the small stuff.

Overall, I think our culture has healthily embraced sarcastic, dry humor as a coping mechanism. Our comedy culture largely relies on it. Tony Stark, taking a break with fellow Avengers in between battling mortal enemies, abruptly complains, "Who put coffee grounds in the sink? Who does that?" Comic relief, a lighthearted quip that relieves the tension during a tense situation, is more than just a film technique. It's a life lesson. Remember, your whole life is a tense situation. Scriptwriters are intuitively picking up on this very human need to relieve stress with humor. Sweating the small stuff is about doing just that.

Stand-up-comedy routines are often a litany of complaints about life and society that are framed in a way that is both relatable and funny. Every parent, for example, can relate to Jim Gaffigan's riff on what it's like with multiple kids: "Imagine you're drowning—then someone hands you a baby."

I fear we are in danger of losing this ability to laugh off the small stuff, and we are even closer to losing the ability to laugh at the big stuff. Comedians like Jerry Seinfeld and Chris Rock no longer perform on college campuses. Why? The PC culture has driven comedians away. In a 2015 interview, Seinfeld observed: "They just want to use these words: 'That's racist. That's sexist. That's prejudice,'" he said. "They don't know what the hell they're talking about." Comedians are worried that they'll offend an overly sensitive generation of students looking for any reason to be offended. This is deeply unfortunate, and not just for the sake of comedy.

It is unfortunate because it robs us of our most fundamental pressure-release valve: humor. The basic truth is that we—humans—like to laugh, and oftentimes eliciting that laughter requires some sort of shock factor, inappropriate comment, or politically incorrect observation. For the same reason that I am telling you to sweat the small stuff, I am also telling you that we can't lose our sense of humor. The alternative is a stuffy, emotionally bottled-up society walking on proverbial eggshells. Sounds a little bit like hell.

So be funny. Watch some shocking comedians. Screw it. Take some risk. See if it offends you. And if it does, start this book over.

When working in teams—whether in the office or the military or sports—I find this comedy useful, as it pertains to criticizing our coworkers or teammates. As a general leadership rule, you want to punish in private and praise in public. Good leaders build their subordinates up, but also correct them when they're wrong. Corrections are best done in private because good leaders don't seek to humiliate or embarrass their people. There is a small caveat to this law. Sometimes it is OK, and even called for, to punish in public. But in moderation and with a specific intent in mind. There can be value in it, and you do it by sweating the small stuff.

In my experience (being in thick-skinned Navy SEAL platoons), we call guys out for both the small and the big stuff. Public shaming is useful for us. That doesn't mean it is useful for all organizations or groups. Not everyone is desensitized to public critique, and I am not sure we can expect people to be. However, I do believe that there is a certain degree of bonding that occurs when good-natured call-out culture thrives. Again, it's a pressure-release valve.

I went from the SEAL teams to graduate school to the United States Congress. Graduate school was useful in the sense that I was able to observe academia's gentle nature of civilian human interactions, after having come from the far more direct, rough-and-tumble nature of the military. It was eye-opening (no pun intended). Joking in tense or awkward situations is a necessity on the SEAL teams. In the university system, it can land you in an administrative review or worse. On the teams, we would rip each other for failing to secure some gear properly, or forgetting a key piece of kit, often in the full presence of the platoon. In academia, discipline is eschewed and feelings reign supreme. I soon learned that my sense of humor might not work with these people. I evolved.

In running my congressional office, I have to take those lessons to heart. In the SEAL teams it was perfectly normal to open a discussion with the phrase "You are fucked up right now, and you need to unfuck yourself." Turns out I don't hear that phrase very often anymore. And that's OK. It wouldn't be appropriate anyway. There are other ways to get the point across. And I don't need my congressional staff to have skin thick enough to survive combat deployments.

But I do want to create an atmosphere that is at once accountable, detail oriented, *and* fun. The way we do this in the SEAL teams is by sweating the small stuff, and I carry these lessons over to my congressional office. We pick on each other. I use sarcasm and a smile to point out a minor flaw ("Oh, I guess we didn't need to be on time to my event today?"). I don't pick out truly important aspects of people's work to poke fun at, just the little things. I also encourage my staff to pick on me relentlessly. And they do so, with a bit more enthusiasm than I anticipated.

This requires careful judgment. For instance, I wouldn't recommend saying, "Oh, I guess you thought this briefing on the next Homeland Security hearing was actually well done?" That is less funny and more just being a jerk.

This entire philosophy flies in the face of everything you have been taught, I get it. For too long we have accepted the notion that being relaxed and "chill" about everything is the right way to be. Don't be a narc, don't sweat the petty things, don't enforce certain standards because that would make you petty and uncool. But it isn't self-evident that being relaxed about the small stuff is a virtue. While there is some societal romanticizing of the cool, surfer-dude,

Big Lebowski–type character, especially for teenagers, it isn't at all clear that this is a good thing. The cool kid in high school who doesn't care about anything may also be the most accepting of bad grades, and consequently he may have a mediocre future. The Dude in *The Big Lebowski* was far from a productive member of society, and even though his "don't sweat the small stuff" lifestyle was entertaining, it was also an utter mess.

Ignoring many of the small problems in life can build up in two ways: It can make you crazy, or it can make your life crazy. Both are bad. We went over how it makes you crazy, because pretending that the little things don't bother you and bottling up your frustrations risks setting off an emotional time bomb. But what if these little things truly don't bother you? What if you really are among the coolest of characters that just "chillax" and hang loose? Again, it isn't self-evident that this is a virtue. It *might* be, for some people. Some people can ignore all the small things in life but still be productive members of society. But I think the more likely outcome is that the chillax attitude toward the small things carries over to the bigger, more important aspects of life also. And this can be a problem. For instance, it may be a perfectly good thing to keep your cool over a flat tire or lost dry-cleaning, but that devil-may-care attitude is less endearing when you are running your business or trying to complete a project on time. When it comes to *performing*, you must be engaged and detail oriented. And being too apathetic with certain behavioral habits can chip away at that necessary intensity and focus. It becomes more and more difficult to switch it on when you need it.

Details matter. Ignoring them can be the difference between success and failure. We had a deal, remember: If you're going to sweat the small stuff, then you must also seek balance. You must agree to engage in productive, detail-oriented behavior to offset your newfound love of complaining about the small details of everyday life. You have no right to complain about your coffee order being screwed up if you can't even clean your own room.

"Attention to detail" is a mantra in the SEAL teams that is repeated over and over. For good reason: Details matter in life-and-death situations.

If your parachute cord was misfolded, or wrapped slightly incorrectly around a riser, well then, your parachute malfunctions. You die.

If you make one misstep in your procedure when diving, you become hypoxic. You die.

If you don't program your radio correctly, you can't communicate when it really matters. You die.

In combat, attention to detail is the barrier between life and death. We generally don't like death, so we pay attention to details. We also don't like failure. We don't like failing in our mission and we don't like failing the people who are relying on us. Ignoring the small stuff leads to both of those unenviable failures.

You may be thinking, "This life-and-death talk is a little extreme. I don't have to go into combat." True, but you take more risks than you are giving yourself credit for. You drive, for instance. You get into a vehicle and fly down the highway way too fast and barely look in the side-view mirror before you change lanes. Pretty risky. But hey, party on, you rebel.

Even in that somewhat irresponsible moment, you are paying attention to details. Especially if you just started driving. So is everyone else around you (thank God, because you're a jerk driver). The fact that everyone has an unspoken agreement to pay attention to the details of driving is what allows all to travel exceedingly fast down the highway in an organized pile of sharp metal and glass and rubber.

This mutual understanding is important, and it is representative of a broader truth—that we must pull our own weight in order to live together peacefully and properly. Once somebody starts to think that cutting the line is OK, society unravels. It is just that simple. The rule of law and societal norms matter. And paying attention to details—even selfishly for your own success—is part of that social contract.

You ever wonder why we are always doing inspections in the military? Why do we obsess over perfect creases, shiny shoes, and crisply made beds? It's simple: If you can't get the small stuff right, you won't get the big stuff right. If you ignore the relatively unimportant details, then you are more likely to ignore the very important details, the stuff that actually counts. This is true of running a town, a city, or a country, but also for running your own life.

We start our two-mile ocean swims in BUD/S with all of our gear perfectly prepared. Our underwater demolition teams (UDT) lifesaving vests have their valves scraped of all rust, and they are evenly oiled with CLP, a special lubricant used to protect weapons and key pieces of kit. Your name is stenciled clearly with white paint marker, exactly where it should be on each piece of gear. Your dive knife is especially well cared for, being the most thoroughly inspected item. It is not only clean, without a hint of rust, but also sharp enough to shave the hair off your arm. Only then are you approved to enter Davy Jones's locker and start your two-mile battle against time and sea.

All in all, the two-mile ocean swim, conducted once a week during BUD/S, is a fairly low-demand evolution with respect to details (high demand with respect to effort, however). Your detail-oriented requirements essentially amount to a very obsessive-compulsive gear inspection. If the paint stencil isn't bright enough, you fail. Drop down and do pushups until we feel like telling you to stop (not ideal when you have to swim a fast two miles immediately after). If the chest strap on your UDT vest isn't tucked correctly, fail. Even the inflation valve lever has to be in a certain position for inspection, or you fail.

The truth is that none of this matters, at least not in the way you think. If your knife has a bit of rust, it will still work. If your stencil is faded, it won't affect your ability to swim two miles. But the point is not that these details matter for this particular swim, the point is that these details matter *because they are details*. These small, relatively insignificant details that we start with in the early days of BUD/S are merely the foundation. They are the first and most important lesson in our obsessive "attention to detail" mantra. If you can't get the small details right, there is no reason to think you can be trained to get the more important details right. SEALs like to find out early on if you have what it takes.

Because here's the thing: That simple two-mile swim gets a lot less simple later on in training, and unbelievably complex in a real-world operation. The next stage of training is Dive Phase, where we add navigation tools (a compass and a stopwatch, nothing fancy), weights, and a closed-circuit, bubbleless Dräger dive rig with a whole variety of additional complexities. The next stage is diving with weapons and other pieces of gear. How do you keep them dry? What mix of water and gun oil do you need to bring to keep the weapon functioning? How do you keep it neutral underwater? Next comes a radio, with waterproof headsets. After all, the whole point of being able to swim for two miles is so that we can use the water as an infiltration route onto land or a ship (unless we are conducting underwater demolitions, the water is always just an infil-exfil route, never the final destination). This means we need *all* our equipment with us when we start that swim or dive. The details start to get a lot more complex than just a knife and a UDT vest.

And that isn't even close to the end of it. Now imagine a real-world scenario. The planning considerations become immense. You must think of contingencies, medical evacuation plans for both the water infiltration and when you reach your land-based objective. What kind of assets will you have to communicate with—drones, C-130s, a submarine?—and what kind of radios do you need to bring to do that? What about backups? If you're taking over a ship in the middle of the ocean, who is going to drive it once we detain the crew and captain?

All that is barely scratching the surface.

I don't think this is unrelatable. Anyone who has run a small business, done payroll, or led a complex project can relate to this. Details matter. They are foundations for success, and cutting corners early on in the learning process builds bad habits that are hard to break, making success all that much more elusive. In the SEAL teams, we are brutally unforgiving about attention to details during our training so that we forge that mentality into our men's psyches. It is life or death, so we must. The civilian world isn't quite life or death, but it is certainly about your *life*. And if you choose to make the best of the one life you have, getting in the habit of paying attention to details is a good place to start.

There is also a real psychological benefit to a detail-oriented mind-set. In addition to maintenance of an even temperament, there is evidence that deliberate attention to detail yields long-term benefits in pattern recognition and informational synthesis. In short, you may not be smarter—but you'll look it, because you'll be faster when new information and systems present themselves in your life.[1]

But this book is about mental toughness and battling outrage culture, so how does being detail oriented really fit in? Well, first of all, if something makes you better at life, I will also suggest that it

---

1   "The Perks of Being Detail Oriented," *Association for Psychological Science*, November 10, 2014, https://www.psychologicalscience.org/publications/observer/editors/the-perks-of-being-detail-oriented.html.

makes you more mentally resilient. But more than that: If your goal is to be less triggered, less outraged, and less prone to emotional overreaction, then a detail-oriented approach is beneficial.

This is because you are more likely to ask questions, be curious, and be measured. A person who is concerned with detail is more likely to ask about context and intent and make counterarguments when confronted with a potentially inflammatory idea or comment. A detail-oriented person is a deeper person, concerned with that next layer of meaning on any given subject. They seek perspective and historical context. They want... details.

Bogging yourself down in the details on any given subject, especially policy or politically related, is guaranteed to make you less outraged and less extreme. It is the inevitable consequence of adding more context. And it's a good thing. Let me give you some examples.

The minimum wage has long been debated. The argument in favor of raising it is deceivingly simple: We want workers to have more money, so we enact laws that force businesses to pay their employees more. So simple. Not only that, but it's a policy that affords lawmakers a sense of moral justice—we are fighting for the little guy and doing the right thing.

But the reality is far from simple. There are consequences, second- and third-order effects, to every action that exist beneath the warm, fuzzy, feel-good layer of being helpful to low-income earners. A mentally tough individual is someone who pushes back on the simplistic instinct to do what feels good, feels morally righteous, and instead questions the details. Passion and knowledge can have an inverse relationship. Details are a natural moderator of strong opinions.

The details surrounding the minimum wage debate get quite tricky. First, the economics become problematic. According to a 2019 Congressional Budget Office study, a federal minimum wage increase to $15 an hour could cost up to 3.7 million jobs.[2] Why? Well, for starters, just because we change the minimum wage doesn't change the overall budget a business has for its salaried workforce. The first workers they will cut will be the least skilled. At best, they will cut their hours. And this is exactly what we see in cities that have gone to a $15 minimum wage, like New York City, San Francisco, and Seattle.[3] It also isn't true that people earning minimum wage are the main breadwinners of their family. Half are under twenty-five.[4] About 40 percent of low-wage workers come from a household that earns three times the poverty rate, meaning these are usually young workers getting their first job and adding income to their household.[5] These are the people being priced out of the job market. The result is that the minimum wage hurts the people we are trying to help the most—because it pushes companies like McDonald's toward automation and prices entry-level workers out of their first jobs. When a hardware store owner is forced to increase her payroll expense by 15–20 percent, the owner has a choice. She can cut jobs or increase prices. Both are bad for the low-income earner. We also are pricing people out who are simply trying to work part-time to add money to their household's overall income. Even worse, overall product prices go up in businesses that use a lot of minimum-wage workers—like grocery stores and fast-food chains.[6] Whom does this harm the most? The poor.

If that weren't bad enough, there is a second problem with the minimum wage: It should never be federal policy. Why? Because different states and different cities have totally different costs of

---

2   https://www.cbo.gov/system/files/2019-07/CBO-55410-MinimumWage2019.pdf
3   https://www.nber.org/papers/w25182.pdf, page 38.
4   https://www.bls.gov/opub/reports/minimum-wage/2018/pdf/home.pdf
5   https://www.cbo.gov/system/files/2019-07/CBO-55410-MinimumWage2019.pdf
6   https://reason.com/2019/08/06/minimum-wage-hikes-in-nyc-are-forcing-businesses-to-cut-jobs-and-raise-prices

living. You can't pretend that the minimum wage in San Francisco, where rent is on average $3,600 per month, should be the same as in Lubbock, Texas, where the average rent is $693 a month.

My point isn't to make the argument against the federal minimum wage (though I do make a good one), but to hopefully stop and make you think less extremely about the debate surrounding a minimum wage. When faced with strong arguments, I would hope that you would be less inclined to become radically opinionated about this particular issue. By way of illustration, I think it is safe to assume that anyone angrily waving a $15 MINIMUM WAGE! sign has never seriously studied these details and internalized them. They willfully embrace the outrage that stems from a shallow and simplistic reading of the problem. A shallow reading of a problem begets outrage; a detailed approach to a problem encourages moderation.

That's a common policy example (and I assure you that most policy deep dives will moderate your thinking or maybe even change your mind). Here is another example, where an initially shocking announcement turns out to be rather mild in nature, upon learning the details and context. Imagine a hypothetical local-government announcement about an elementary school. You hear from the city council that they are canceling plans to refurbish the cafeteria and older west wing. That's the headline. Seems absolutely senseless at first. You're pissed. You post a strongly worded Facebook message. But then, more details emerge. The plans weren't finalized in time to make it into the final budget. The city just voted last year to raise $500 million in bonds for local schools and infrastructure, and this project wasn't included by that time. Probably because the repairs needed were mild compared to the other projects the city needed to prioritize. City officials debated it for weeks. Experts were brought in. Careful consideration took place. Yet you believed you had the answer when you posted on Facebook! You were so *sure* of yourself…because you read the headline. Has this ever happened to you? I'd be lying if I said I have never reacted that way. We all have.

I encounter people with this kind of emotionally driven, self-assured opinion *all* the time. Forming an opinion without the relevant facts is a phenomenon that I believe is getting worse— probably because of social media and the echo chamber of disinformation it can create. Our tendency to react wildly to headlines, which are already largely crafted to elicit emotional responses rather than inform the public, is asphyxiating the deliberative system of government designed by our Founders. It has created a troubling new reality where even new or more complete sets of facts cannot sway opinions. I am not saying you *have* to change your opinion, but you should at least have a serious, honest, and coherent reason for why not. Reactive dismissal of new information is indicative of mental weakness. Absorbing new information honestly, even if you don't ultimately change your mind, is a sign of fortitude.

The last part of this lesson is the most important: Sweat the small stuff so you can deal with the big stuff. This is the heart of the message, and the most relevant "sweat the small stuff" lesson as it pertains to the theme of the book, which is mental toughness. Sweating the small stuff is your pressure-release valve. It's like that built-in drain at the top of your sink or tub that lets water out before it overflows. That drain is your conscious self, bitching and moaning about the dumb stuff so that your unconscious emotions don't overflow. This shouldn't be news to anyone. It is, after all, why most people see a therapist. They just need to get some issues off their chest. It's why you go to happy hour after work, to blow off some steam and complain about your boss and coworkers. This is healthy behavior and it should be encouraged.

SEALs are not trained Stoics. We are human. We complain about the same things that you complain about. We complain about getting wet and cold. We complain about our boss and our command atmosphere, and we complain that our equipment isn't the latest and greatest like it should be.

A good leader allows this to happen, to an extent. A good leader understands that part of cultivating a healthy social environment is allowing some complaining. Allowing your team to blow off steam over the small stuff is natural and healthy. Trying to stifle it will not make it go away, just hide it, only to see it boil over later on when you least want it to. A good leader even partakes in some of the complaints, but they are careful how they go about it. It is one thing to complain about the bitter coffee and stale food, but quite another to make substantive complaints about the chain of command in front of your team. Big difference, in fact. One complaint is "sweating the small stuff," and the other is fostering true discontent with the institution itself.

A favorite memory of many veterans is their time sitting around grumbling incessantly about their circumstances with their teammates. I have to admit that we do this *way* more than the average group of people. It's like a continuous group-therapy project. When the guys stop complaining, leadership starts to worry. What's wrong with them? Are they depressed? Something wrong at home? The reality is that in these high-performing environments, where everyone is a perfectionist and an overachiever, people like to point out deficiencies in the most over-the-top fashion, usually with a side of sarcastic and cutting humor. The good news is that they also aspire to fix those problems.

Or maybe we are just a bunch of divas. I don't know. Maybe it's both.

The point is that it seems to work. The SEALs are regarded as perhaps the finest fighting force on the planet. The ethos on the teams works both as a mechanism to be aware of smaller deficiencies and blow off some steam. Both of these things are important.

The SEAL's terror of wet socks—yes, I said wet socks—illustrates how menial and hilarious the complaints can become. SEALs go through some extreme punishment, both physical and mental, in training and in combat. Many people therefore believe—wrongly—that this sense of perspective gives us the superhuman ability to *never* sweat the small stuff. This could not be more wrong.

Wet socks are like our kryptonite. They are like a nightmare wrapped around your feet. Soggy. Squishy. Incapable of drying. Sapping your feet of their energy as they cause your skin to prune. Wet socks were created by the devil to punish men for their sins, crafted by the wicked as an antidote to order and all things good. We emphatically and unambiguously hate wet socks.

And it's not just wet socks, SEALs hate a lot of things that involve cold and wet circumstances, probably because we were born in them, molded by them, forged by them. BUD/S is basically a six-month experience of cold, wet, soggy pain infused with extreme physical exertion. That about sums it up. So as a result, we don't like being wet. And we feel perfectly entitled to complain about it when we do get wet.

The difference—well, one of the differences—between a SEAL platoon and a Special Forces team is this: When we come upon a river, let's say knee-high water depth, and we have another fifteen kilometers to go, the SF guys will just walk across it. Not SEALs. Not if we don't absolutely have to. We will walk another kilometer to find a better crossing. We will build a bridge if we have to. Anything to keep the feet dry.

OK. So the wet-socks thing is a bit maniacal, born mostly of our somewhat traumatic experiences on the beaches of beautiful Coronado, California, where the BUD/S training center is located.

And truthfully, I am half-joking about the wet socks (but only half). Any SEAL reading this is nodding in agreement. I am illustrating a point: We sweat the small stuff so that the big problems don't bother us as much. We let in a little weakness, blow off a little steam, so that we are well rested for life's true challenges. Because on the other side of that river might be a hundred bad guys armed with PKMs and AK-47s, and surrounded by buried pressure-plate IEDs that we can't see or detect. That's the big stuff.

Fundamentally, this is an exercise in control. We can control wet socks. We can't control what is on the other side of that river. As I noted previously of the Stoic philosophy, it is useful to focus on what you can control and accept what you cannot. Sweating the small stuff is, in essence, about regaining control over the smaller problems we face. When I said that I complained, almost irrationally, about the little problems I faced while hospitalized—bad food, uncomfortable clothing, the inability of those around me to say exactly the right thing—and less so about the big problems, like permanent blindness, I was *focusing on what I could control*. I accepted what I could not. Perhaps it wasn't that irrational after all.

How you complain is important. *What* you complain about is important. Again, think about *who* you want to be. Negativity is unpopular, and so are negative people. "Dan is generally pretty pessimistic" is *not* how I would want to be described by my peers. It isn't who I want to be. A good rule of thumb is this: If you aren't making someone laugh with your complaints, then you might be doing it wrong. Lighthearted humor wrapped up in your menial grumbling should be the goal. During my hospitalization, I certainly could have made improvements in how I complained, even if I may have justified the act itself.

We allow ourselves to sweat the small stuff because we strive to be detail oriented. Details matter. Paying attention to detail is an absolute must for performing successfully in life, whether in the life-and-death situations of combat or doing payroll for your business. Small mistakes pile up and make everything harder in the long run.

This accomplishes a few things, and I'm speaking mostly to how the average American interacts with politics here. For one, you won't be so outraged. Anytime you are paying attention to the detail and nuance of a controversy or topic, you will be decidedly less extreme about it. Using your deductive reasoning to dive into a topic will moderate your emotions on the subject. You will also be happier. Outrage is antipathetic to happiness, after all. You will blow off steam in a healthy way so that when bigger problems arise, you are more emotionally capable of dealing with them. And most important, you will be a better citizen. You will be more understanding of your political opponent and their ideas. You will also be better equipped to debate those ideas, and, *gasp!* more likely to find a reasonable compromise agreeable to both sides. Be self-aware, be happy, make people laugh. Not just for your sake, but for the sake of everyone around you.

CHAPTER 6

THE RIGHT SENSE OF SHAME

In America today, we too often look at personal failings as things to overcome, move past, or forget. Sometimes we should do one or all of those things, but we should also do something else: Learn our lesson.

The list of public figures who run headlong into self-inflicted failure—personal, political, or otherwise—and then reemerge shameless without having appeared to learn a thing, is long. Don't get me wrong, I'm no opponent of redemption. Far from it. I certainly believe there should be space for reemergence from public scorn. I believe redemption is a trademark of an enlightened society. One of the more detestable social trends now is the mocking of redemption, and the dismissing of the idea that it is possible or even desirable. In place of a system of repentance, justice, and mercy we have a culture of mindless fury—an outrage culture. Outrage culture has contorted our ability to seek redemption and recover from failure, which in turn has contorted our sense of shame. Not only do we feel no shame for being outraged, but that same outrage incentivizes a lack of shame for just about anything—lies, dubious news reporting, scandals, even simple cases of clumsy commentary.

Redemption is harder and harder to come by. Take my experience with *Saturday Night Live*. It would have been easy to call for Pete Davidson to be fired after his infamous joke about my appearance in November of 2018, only a few days before my election. I remember finding out about the previous night's skit. I woke up Sunday morning unaware of what had happened. I started my day as I usually do, checking the calendar on my phone. My first election to public office was days away and my Sunday was packed. After church, we would meet up with volunteers doing door-to-door canvassing for the campaign, and then head to Huffman, Texas, for a campaign event at the local bar, which meant I would need to change into jeans and boots after church. This was my routine.

Then I checked my text messages.

"Dude, *SNL*! You made it!"

"Those expletives, expletives, expletives at *SNL*."

"Hitman in a porno. Brahahahaha."

That was the general nature of the reactions. Keep in mind, my friends in the SEAL teams are cut from a certain cloth. The lengths to which we go to make fun of each other are often extreme, and as a result we grow pretty thick skin. That being said, we keep it in the family. My friends will often say, "I get to make fun of your injury, but they sure as hell don't." Lucky me, I guess.

So I looked up the clip on my phone as I made coffee. My Apple news feed already had a couple stories about it. "Wow," I remember thinking, "how bad could it be?" I started the video. The skit in question was from *SNL*'s longest recurring sketch, Weekend Update. The sketch is a faux news segment where comedians poke fun at the biggest stories of the week. The hosts, dating back to 1975, have been a veritable Who's Who of comedy: Chevy Chase, Dennis Miller, Jimmy Fallon, Tina Fey, Seth Meyers, to name a few. The skit typically runs after the musical guest plays their first set. That week, the producers had comedian Pete Davidson jump on Weekend Update as a special guest. Davidson's segment poked fun at some of the politicians running that year. It's fair game, there's no shortage of characters in the United States Congress. Sometimes we make ourselves easy targets.

Pete flashed through photos of candidates and had a joke or two for each. He's a gifted comedian, with a sharp wit and an amusing, contagious habit of laughing at the camera when he delivers his jokes. Davidson knocked through a few senior politicians: Senator Rick Scott of Florida (Republican) and New York Congressman Pete King (Republican) before he came to me (also Republican, in case you didn't know).

"This guy is kind of cool," Davidson cracked, "Dan Crenshaw." As the producers flashed my photo to go along with the commentary, Weekend Update host Michael Che sensed the danger and gave an "Oh, c'mon, man" as a warning shot to Davidson. I carry my worst war wound on my face, and the only way to mask it is with a patch or prosthetic. It's visible and impossible to hide (not that I want to), and that night it was the target of Davidson's crack. "You might be surprised to hear that he's a congressional candidate from Texas and not a hitman in a porno."

As the audience howled, Davidson jumped in with a quick aside. "I'm sorry, I know he lost his eye in war ... or whatever."

The first thing I noticed about Pete Davidson's monologue was that he referred to the list of candidates running for office as "gross people." So it was pretty clear that this was not going to be a favorable analysis of my venture into the public sphere. Not surprising, really—it is *SNL*, after all, and the whole point is to make fun of people. But here's the thing: Calling someone "gross" isn't really funny, at least not in the way it was portrayed in the skit. It was just a statement of fact, and it set a clear tone for the real objective of the skit: discrediting the character of those they were about to roast. It was the first shot across the bow of this cultural micro-battle. Definitely not enough to offend me, but it certainly set the tone for the true intention of the joke.

Then I got to the part of the skit that I have to admit was pretty funny. The "hitman in a porno" line made me chuckle a little bit. Maybe because it brought to mind so many questions about precisely how that particular film would play out. For the sake of this narrative, those are questions best left unanswered. Suffice to say this part of Davidson's joke was not what offended people.

The line that riled everyone up was, "I know he lost his eye in war...or whatever." It felt like an ad lib, perhaps prompted by Michael Che's warning to Davidson seconds beforehand. It was dismissive and clearly an indication that the reason behind my "gross look" didn't really matter. What really mattered was my political affiliation and therefore all bets were off, all decency eschewed, because this was really about winning a battle in the culture war.

I don't think I am rushing to judgment on this point, either. Why am I so sure that this was meant to be a dig at conservatives in particular? Well, it's simple, because right after Pete got done roasting me, he went on to take jabs at the one Democrat on the list of "gross people," and before leading into a pretty mild joke set, he said, "Here's a Democrat so I look fair." Right. Enough said.

One of the reasons I didn't demand an apology was that everyone deserves some space to seek redemption and forgiveness. Now, it was pretty clear that the intention of Pete Davidson and *SNL* was to berate and demean Republicans running for office, at least in this particular skit. *SNL* pokes fun at Democrats plenty, but the bias in this skit—right before an election—seemed obvious. But I wasn't sure that his motivations went any deeper. I doubted he was out to belittle and mock my war injuries. It sure sounded like that, but maybe, just maybe, that wasn't the intention. Maybe, just maybe, I didn't have to act offended (I wasn't) and demand that he atone for his transgressions.

Redemption prevailed, and I had the opportunity to forgive Pete on next week's episode of *SNL*. More on that shortly.

But nine months later, the *SNL* showrunners had another cast member come under fire. Shane Gillis, a young comedian, had just realized his dream of joining America's greatest and longest-running sketch comedy show. After he was hired, reporters and bloggers pored over his past routines and found instances of him using a racial slur against Chinese people and a slur against gay people on a podcast. The slurs are not good and I am not defending them. But we should also ask: Was the intent of his comments based in prejudice? Aren't comedians supposed to push boundaries and make mistakes in the process? And while his comments would be utterly unacceptable in regular conversation, it was clear that Gillis was using them in a form of shock comedy rather than a reflection of deep-rooted biases against those communities. Intent matters.

SNL could have granted Gillis the same redemptive opportunity they gave Pete Davidson, a chance to apologize in a way that was funny and unifying, and that acknowledged the deep-felt pain those slurs might cause others. He could have been allowed to explain that he meant no offense and was just doing as comedians do. They could have explained that context matters, mistakes can be made, and sometimes they go too far. They didn't. They caved to the outrage mob and fired Gillis before he could shoot his first episode.

This is how shame is used as a weapon in the modern era. Gillis isn't a one-off event, either. Kevin Hart had to step down from hosting the Oscars for similar reasons. Even outspoken progressive Sarah Silverman was fired from a movie after unacceptable past comedic content came to light. That we even have journalists whose job it is to act as inquisitors, combing through a comedian's past (of all things) in search of wrongthink or blasphemy, is absurd.

But it demonstrates how hungry mass media is to find a public figure to humiliate and thus toss to the wolves of an outrage mob. These were once tactics reserved for politicians aspiring to run our government—which is understandable given their role as representatives. Now it infects every element of our culture, this need to shame and see people shamed. Pete Davidson survived. Shane Gillis didn't.

But most important, it shows how shame has been overused and mishandled. Public shame once had a purpose. It was a politician resigning for carrying on an extramarital affair and thus not acting worthy of his office. It was a CEO caught using slurs in a *literal* way that reflected true bias against a race, gender, or creed. A sense of shame is what regulated bad behavior and purged it from office. But today, shame has lost its meaning and its direction.

Every day it's a new outrage, especially on social media. Every day the mob roots out someone who tweeted an off-color remark or misspoke on the news, and cries, *"Justice!"* as they seek their ruin. The notion of shame is losing meaning, and if it were a stock it'd be plummeting. The mob is crying wolf, not revealing legitimate wrongdoing. We have simultaneously deprived it of its value and meaning while still wielding it as a club with which to swiftly ruin careers and reputations.

This loss of meaning has warped the incentives public figures face when engaging in a sense of shame. In short, they have stopped feeling shame altogether. What does this new world look like, where traditional remorse and redemption are things of the past?

It looks like former South Carolina governor and congressman Mark Sanford, who disappeared for four days while serving as governor. Confronted by the press after his story of "hiking the Appalachian Trail" fell apart, Sanford admitted he had been in Argentina pursuing an extramarital affair with a mistress. He should have resigned from office. He didn't, and instead successfully ran for Congress in 2012.

It looks a lot like former congresswoman Katie Hill, who resigned from the House of Representatives in 2019 after being caught in an unethical personal relationship with a member of her staff. Her resignation statement gave no admission of wrong-doing, even though a relationship with a staffer is a serious ethics violation. Not only that, but she was given a hero's welcome at a rally soon after her fall from grace, proof yet again that our culture has elevated the wrong heroes and the wrong attributes to aspire to.

It looks a lot like United States Senator Richard Blumenthal of Connecticut, who served in the military stateside for much of the 1970s, but later claimed to have served in Vietnam. When the misleading implication of service was exposed, he apologized for having failed to be "clear or precise"—rather than taking personal responsibility for his actions.

It looks a lot like Andrew Rosenthal of the *New York Times*. In 1992 he fabricated an incident in which then-President George H. W. Bush was "amazed" at seeing a supermarket scanner. Rosenthal wasn't even present for the incident—the truth was that the president was perfectly familiar with ordinary grocery stores—but the deliberate falsehood soon became a popular by-word for an out-of-touch narrative against the president. For his efforts, Rosenthal eventually rose to become editorial-page editor of the *Times*.[1]

It looks a lot like the governor of Virginia, Ralph Northam. His page on his 1984 medical school yearbook contains a picture of two men: one wearing blackface makeup and the other wearing

---

1   https://www.snopes.com/fact-check/bush-scanner-demonstration/.

a KKK mask. If that picture was ever considered humorous, it shouldn't have been, and it certainly isn't now. Questions were rightfully raised. But Governor Northam didn't apologize. After acknowledging his place in the photo, he changed his story and actually denied that the photo was him at all, and gave no plausible explanation for why it was on his yearbook page in the first place. He refused to resign, and his only attempt at redemption was to spend the coming months pushing for the most progressive agenda possible, earning him praise and forgiveness from left-wing journalists. A December 2019 *Washington Post* op-ed titled "How Ralph Northam Came Back from the Political Dead" outlined in glowing terms the reasons why his shameless lack of explanation should be forgiven and forgotten. It is impossible to imagine the *Post* giving the same generous treatment to a Republican governor and impossible to ignore the fact that Northam *never even admitted wrongdoing*. Shouldn't forgiveness be a two-way street? Shouldn't there be some admission of guilt prior to redemption?

It looks a lot like G. Gordon Liddy, who committed real crimes—burglary, conspiracy, illegal wiretapping—in the course of his service to President Richard Nixon yet remains unrepentant for them. His career since, especially as a media figure, has flourished.

It looks a lot like the entire cabal of left-leaning mainstream journalists and news anchors who wrongfully indicted the Covington Catholic kids in the court of public opinion after their relatively uneventful confrontation with a Native American activist. Because Nick Sandmann, one of the students, wore a Make America Great Again red hat as he silently faced the activist, news anchors were quick to describe the group of kids as an angry racist mob. Even when more videos of the incident came out, and it was made clear that the kids acted rather appropriately in the face of chaos, the media never backed down. Nick Sandmann sued the various news agencies for hundreds of millions of dollars after their refusal to admit wrongdoing.

If you're well connected, or you can claim that you're a victim, or you can hide behind a façade of noble journalism, failure doesn't touch you.

Americans know all this instinctively, even if they don't know the details. They know that failure, for *them*, has real consequences. They know that failure to pay their debts means they lose their house. They know that criminal acts mean they go to jail. They know that public notoriety stemming from an ill-thought-out social media post means it will be impossible to find a job. They know failure is *real*.

They know that failure is not real to the wealthy and the powerful. Not like it is to them.

What *should* a story of failure look like?

Failure—and its companion, redemption—should look like a young United States Navy ensign assigned to a destroyer in the Philippines in 1907. One day, entering a familiar harbor, he decides to get by with an estimate of his ship's position instead of taking proper bearings. He runs it aground, and the ship must be pulled free of the mud bank into which its keel has settled. It is a grave error and tremendous offense for a naval officer. He reports his error. The young officer is rightly court-martialed and found guilty.

Our naval officer's career future is uncertain, and he is denied the opportunity to serve on the Navy's crown jewels, the battleships. Instead he is shunted over to a relatively new and unglamorous branch of the naval service, the submarines. But he doesn't quit in the face of adversity. The young officer becomes an expert on their use and theory—and the experience places him in good stead when, as arguably the greatest admiral in American history, Chester Nimitz leads America to victory in the Pacific.

That is how to handle failure. Nimitz exhibited a willingness to internalize rather than externalize. He assumed responsibility. He learned. He changed. He grew.

Outrage culture doesn't have room for a Nimitz. And that's the problem.

★ ★ ★

A little shame is good. It keeps you accountable, and on course. It is a necessary element of personal responsibility, which is a necessary bedrock for a successful life. Shame leads to humility (the good kind), which leads to thoughtfulness, a desire to improve, and ultimately mental fortitude.

Outrage culture has had an unfortunate effect on our society's sense of shame. We rarely get it right these days. One of the reasons my moment on *Saturday Night Live* was so unique and so surprising was because it was *just the right amount of shame*. The public interactions between myself and *SNL* during the seven days between Pete Davidson's famous insult and my appearance were characterized by temperance instead of outrage. After it happened, I was careful not to demand an apology, careful not to call for the online mob to scream, "Shame!" I was careful not to play the part of the aggrieved victim. When crafting a response, the words that stuck with me came from a brief presentation I heard during student orientation at the Harvard Kennedy School, where I did my master's program after retiring from the military. A wise professor advised us, "While you're here, try hard not to offend, and try harder not to be offended." It was both simple and profound, and it always stuck with me. It certainly wasn't a lesson I needed, but I was well aware of the hypersensitivity on college campuses that had formed in recent years, and this professor was addressing that issue in a pretty thoughtful way. He was implying that we should consider the intentions of someone's words before defaulting to feeling "offended." And so that was my statement.

This allowed the producers at *SNL* the space to react in a way that exhibited the right amount of shame. They wanted to apologize, but they wanted to do it their way. They wanted to do it the right way. By the next weekend, producer Lorne Michaels had convinced me to fly to New York and make an appearance on the show. I said no at first. I had other events planned, it being Veterans Day weekend and all. Couldn't we do it another weekend? I asked. No, he replied, precisely *because* it was Veterans Day weekend, and we had the opportunity to give America's veterans a heartfelt message. I could say whatever I wanted, he told me. So I agreed.

The experience was surreal. We got to work as soon as we arrived in New York on Friday evening, going over the initial drafts of the jokes. My wife and I made some edits, and offered some additional ideas—such as suggesting Pete looked eerily similar to a Troll doll. We got our own dressing room, right next to Robert De Niro's. The hallways were small and the set crowded, which I guess isn't that surprising considering the location in Manhattan, where space is hard to come by. I got to meet Kate McKinnon, who is just as funny and cool as you would expect. My wife, Tara, a longtime fan of Kenan Thompson in *All That,* was able to show her gratitude to Kenan for publicly showing support for me after the initial skit with Davidson, when he stated that such a joke was "never somewhere I would go." I found out that Pete wasn't a terrible guy, just a comedian who had made a mistake. He apologized privately and asked if I wanted some pot. I laughed and said no. The hallways were already plenty smoke-filled from Lil Wayne and his crew.

The next night we rehearsed the skit in front of a live audience. *SNL* does this to test the jokes and make last-minute changes before the show goes live. The entire staff of writers and producers gather in Lorne's office to trade notes and rework the scripts. It is an intense and purposeful process, and frankly a lot of fun to be a part of. As the scripts get changed, the staff gets to work rewriting the cue cards, which are all done by hand and shuffled through manually during the skits. There are no teleprompters. It is truly an old-school sketch comedy environment.

My time onstage came about halfway through the show. The stagehands prepared me to be rolled into the scene on a roller chair from offstage. There was no turning back now. "Better not screw this up," I thought. The crowd cheered and we started the skit. After Pete's apology, he offered to let me "get him back" a little bit. And so I did. In keeping with the tradition of poking fun at appearances, I let loose a series of jokes that likened Pete to a Troll doll with a tapeworm and Martin Short's character from *The Santa Clause 3*. At one point my phone started ringing, and it just so happened that the ringtone was a song by Ariana Grande— Pete's ex-girlfriend. The audience particularly liked that one.[2] We wrapped up the skit with my monologue about Veterans Day, and my "Never Forget" message to America. We succeeded in turning an offensive jab at wounded veterans into a heartfelt message to the same. Americans seemed to feel pretty good about it.

Now imagine a different scenario. Imagine I had done what is normally done in these situations: demanded that my allies focus the entirety of their rage on *SNL*, shame them into submission, and not give them even the slightest benefit of the doubt. This scenario easily could have happened. I was new to this outrage game. I might have quickly tweeted out something snarky and hard-hitting, given I hadn't quite realized the gravity of the situation when it first happened. Truth is, I initially struggled with the right message. I

---

2   The full clip is easy to find on YouTube.

didn't feel offended, but I also had to take into account that I wasn't just responding for myself; I was responding on behalf of many veterans who felt *SNL* had gone too far, diminishing their sacrifices for the country. I couldn't just dismiss that. I needed to acknowledge that righteous feeling of anger felt by many, while also avoiding fanning the flames unnecessarily. This, of course, goes against the very nature of our current politics. The laws of modern politics dictate that you never throw water on the flames of a good controversy if you can use it to your advantage. You're supposed to play the part of aggrieved victim to the greatest extent possible and use that moral superiority to club your opponents into submission.

If I had done that, *SNL* would have been put in an awkward position and become more entrenched. It's highly unlikely that they would have reached out and invited me on the show. It's far more likely that they would have done one of two things: refuse to apologize and weather the storm, or apologize profusely to appease the mob. Neither would have been inspiring nor satisfying. The battle would have continued to rage either way.

The second scenario is the one that normally plays out. The troubling part about my *SNL* story was that it was actually *surprising*. America breathed a collective sigh of relief because I didn't freak out, and Americans smiled when Pete and I joked about it a week later. The reaction was so positive precisely because it was so unexpected.

And this fact should trouble us. Shouldn't we pause and ask: Should it really be all that surprising? Isn't it indicative of a decaying culture that we can no longer just expect people to assume the best of intentions of one another? That we can no longer expect some degree of forgiveness, or at least an uninterested shrug when someone "offends" us?

Unfortunately, the outrage mob's usual reaction is to demand an extreme level of shame from their target. The degree of the impropriety doesn't appear to change the intensity of the demands, either. The mob's goal is to beat its opponent into total submission until they are literally begging for forgiveness, or destroy their reputation should they refuse to apologize. I could have easily unleashed that outrage mob, and it would have been fully in keeping with the expectations of most Americans.

This normalization of outrage has consequences. The result is an equally extreme—and unhealthy—*reaction* to the outrage mob. Imagine the reactions to the outrage mob as a bell curve, with the most nuanced responses in the middle ("I'm sorry you took my comments that way, but here is how I meant it"), the most subservient responses on the right side ("I apologize deeply for my insensitive comments"), and the most unapologetic responses on the left ("I'm not resigning!"). Note: The left and right distinction is not meant to indicate any political affiliation. It's just a bell curve.

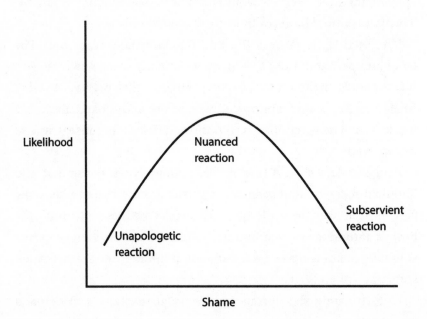

Now imagine that bell curve totally inverted:

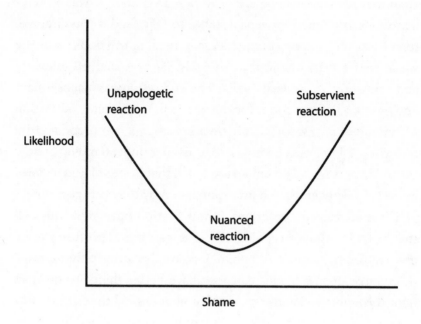

Which one seems more accurate in today's society? If you said the second bell curve, then I agree. The truth is that proportional responses to the outrage mob seem fewer and further between, whereas the extreme responses are increasingly the only option. The extreme nature of the outrage mob, willing to pounce at even the slightest offense, devoid of any benefit of the doubt, has forced the shame response into extreme categories. Everyone has two options now: show deep shame, or show no shame. The middle option of showing a little amount of shame in proportion to the actual offense is hardly an option at all. There is simply no reward for it. No grace is given, no outrage will subside.

I grew up as a fan of *Saved by the Bell* (don't judge me), so I am going to use Mario Lopez as an example. In the summer of 2019 during an interview, Mario was quoted as saying that he did not believe a three-year-old was old enough to choose their own gender. He said he believed it was the parent's job to explain to the child that its biological gender is in fact its gender. It was a pretty commonsense, uncontroversial stance to take (and if you disagree, then I am very happy you are actually reading my book). But the social justice warriors pounced quickly. He was shamed intensely and consistently on social media. The end result was a subservient apology that left no room for nuance, only a complete admission of wrongdoing. He called his own comments "ignorant and insensitive," adding that he now had a "deeper understanding of how hurtful they were." The self-assured man that Lopez played in *Saved by the Bell* had been beaten into submission by the outrage mob.

These are extreme reactions. I think Mario Lopez knew full well that he had nothing to apologize for, at least not as profusely as he did. He did so because of public pressure, because of the outrage mob. Most people in this category have better things to do than fight through the Twitter storm that condemned them. Attempts to engage in discussion or nuance would be lost on their audience, and they know it. So they choose the most subservient mea culpa response they can, exhibit an extreme level of shame for their actions, and hope that it will be enough to move the mob on to the next victim. Tim Keller's quote comes to mind: "Fear-based repentance makes us hate ourselves. Joy-based repentance makes us hate the sin."

This has two unfortunate effects: It empowers the outrage mob and it normalizes improper shame responses. We should ask ourselves: Do we really want to live in a culture where reactive apologies are the norm, even when clearly not required? When we think back to our heroes, do we look up to someone who engages in strong discourse and pushes back against unjust accusation? Or do we value someone who gives in to unjust accusations immediately just to get the accusers off their back? Again, I am not judging the victims of the outrage mob I mentioned above. Like I said, they have their own priorities and lives to live. But I worry greatly, and we all should, about the trend taking place and the notion that extreme shame should be normalized. I argue that we must fight back.

But there is a right way to correct course and there is a wrong way. The other side of the bell curve is the other extreme: the no-shame extreme.

The other side of that inverted bell curve is Queen Cersei, whom you may recall from HBO's *Game of Thrones*. Walking naked down the streets of King's Landing, she smirks at the angry peasants as she is forced on the Walk of Atonement. She is being shamed but she feels no such emotion herself. The contempt they feel for her is immediately transferred back at them. She walks naked and embarrassed but is ultimately shameless. There is no introspection, no calls for greater understanding, no well-meaning dialogue between her and the mob. Just mutual contempt. She will never apologize to the angry mob because there is no reward for doing so. Their anger will not subside.

This is the other extreme of our culture's reaction to the outrage mob, and it is just as unhealthy. It is especially true in politics, where politicians descended upon by the outrage mob no longer have an incentive to give in at all. This is true even when the accusations leveled against said politicians are *actually legitimate*.

The governor of Virginia has never taken any kind of responsibility for an obviously racist costume from his past. Hillary Clinton has never admitted that putting highly classified information on a personal server deserved any kind of punishment, as any of us in the military would have swiftly faced for the same violation. Congressman Steve King never really apologized for racist comments but instead tried to rationalize them.

I want to be clear that I am not giving any of these politicians an excuse for their lack of shame. There really isn't any excuse. I am saying that this lack of shame didn't just appear out of nowhere. It is a conditioned response that originates from previous experiences, where the outrage mob never forgives and never forgets. There is no space given for benefit of the doubt, and therefore no space for any apology whatsoever.

That is the large-scale cultural problem with shame, in a nutshell. So how do we fix this? What is the right amount of shame? First of all, we must begin with inverting the curve back to normal. We have to normalize proportional shame responses again. We have to engage in nuance again. We have to be bold enough to defend ourselves and humble enough to admit some wrongdoing. And just as important, we as a culture must reward that proportional response instead of punishing it.

In short, we have to be more like Ellen DeGeneres, and *reward* people like her. In October 2019 she was confronted with the Twitter outrage mob when she dared to appear at a Cowboys game with her friend, former president George W. Bush. The outrage was pronounced enough that she felt the need to address it on a later show. Did she apologize? No. Did she dismiss her attackers as mere outraged fools to be ignored? No. She simply explained herself. And in doing so she made a beautiful contribution to the eventual death of outrage culture.

She started off by noting the Twitter outrage that had occurred, summed up by "Why is a gay Hollywood liberal sitting next to a conservative Republican president?" She then went on to explain her side. "The fact is that I am friends with a lot of people who don't share the same beliefs that I have. We are all different and I think we've forgotten that that's OK that we are all different.... But just because I don't agree with someone on everything doesn't mean that I am not going to be friends with them. When I say be kind to one another I don't mean only the people that think the same way you do. I mean be kind to everyone."

Boom. Outrage mob completely deflated.

The controversy surrounding J. K. Rowling, author of the Harry Potter series, was also emblematic of the right response to the outrage mob. After learning that Maya Forstater was fired from a think tank for criticizing the notion that biological men can become women, and that private citizens should not be forced to acknowledge another's desired identity, Rowling jumped to her defense. Bear in mind, Rowling is no social conservative. Far from it. But she also believes that no one should be punished for stating their beliefs, especially when that belief is rooted in basic biological truth. On Twitter, Rowling stated:

> Dress however you please.
> Call yourself whatever you like.
> Sleep with any consenting adult who'll have you.
> Live your best life in peace and security.
> But force women out of their jobs for stating that sex is real? #IStandWithMaya #ThisIsNotADrill

It was obvious from Rowling's tweet that she has no problem with the transgender community. Again, she is no social traditionalist. But she understands a fundamental truth about the nature of rights that the British employment judge who ruled against Forstater does not. The judge ruled that Forstater's comments "were not worthy of respect in a Democratic society." But in fact, a truly democratic society is one that protects its citizens' rights to be who they want, while also not forcing others to believe the same. Much like the right to free speech, the freedom to be a transgender person is a protected "negative" right, meaning that no one has the right to stop you from doing so. But to make it a "positive" right, meaning others now have a legal obligation to participate in your beliefs, is utterly unthinkable. That is what J. K. Rowling was saying in her tweet. And she was raked over the hot digital coals of social media for it. According to the outrage mob, disagreement about the nature of sex was an unpalatable offense.

Rowling did not back down. Good for her.

This is all deeply related to our end goal: Fortitude. It is related because our individual sense of shame—and the way we engage in it—contributes to the toxic cultural transition to the extremes that we have seen. For us to fix the bigger problems, we have to fix ourselves first. We have to be mentally tough enough to both disengage from outrage and also develop a proper individual sense of shame in our daily lives.

Feeling shame is actually good. It is synonymous with feeling accountable for our actions, and consciously admitting that our actions might not have been the right ones. And I am not necessarily talking about the deep-moral-regret narrative of a Dostoevsky novel, where the murderer Raskolnikov agonizes over his crimes in an excruciating manner. I am talking about starting with the smallest of life's missteps and the substandard ways in which we live our daily lives. In other words, sweating the small stuff.

We should feel a sense of shame for not training hard enough, for sleeping in too late, for eating that extra ice cream scoop. We should feel regret after walking past a piece of trash next to a storm drain, knowing full well it is going straight into the ocean. We should feel bad for not tipping that hardworking waiter. We should be embarrassed when we owe a friend money and they have to constantly remind us to pay them back. We should feel lazy for leaving our food tray on the table in a fast-food restaurant even though trash cans are right there. We should feel ashamed after honking at the car in front of us when the light turns green, even though its driver may very well have been a single mom checking on her kid, momentarily distracted. We should feel shame for insulting the character and intent of someone on Twitter just because they disagree with us, knowing full well we would never have the guts to speak to them that way in person. We should feel discredited when we become emotionally attached to political positions and pretend not to hear facts or context that debunks what we previously thought.

I use these examples because we have all done it. We are all guilty on at least one account...probably more. And the truth is that all of us will probably continue to make these mistakes, and continue being the imperfect human beings that we are. But my goal is not to make us perfect—I certainly am not. It is to make us more aware. My goal is to encourage a healthy sense of shame so that, at the very least, we are *aspiring to a higher ideal, a higher sense of self.*

Having no sense of shame, for all of those transgressions I listed above, is a *de facto* justification for bad behavior and boorishness. And justifying inadequate behavior isn't very different from promoting it, practically speaking. "I didn't work out today because I was tired, and dang it, I have a good excuse for being tired!" Sure, maybe. Maybe not. Only you know the answer to that. But if you truly feel no shame for skipping leg day at the gym, what on earth will motivate you to go the next day? And the day after that? If you really feel no shame for leaving your trash behind (it's a city street, it's already dirty, and we have street cleaners!), then who's to say you won't keep doing it and contribute to the littered mess that you surely disapprove of? Feeling shame for the small stuff takes practice, and it takes mental dedication. It requires one to let go of their ego and admit imperfection. It may be unrealistic to demand that everyone act perfectly virtuous at all times, but it should be less idealistic to hope that we are at least aware of our imperfections and seek to mend them.

In short, be accountable for everything you do. It was why Commander Jocko Willink, one of my mentors in the teams, wrote an entire book about the subject called *Extreme Ownership.* The premise of the book is quite simple: Everything is your fault.

Be accountable. Take ownership. Take responsibility. From this responsibility you will find freedom.

Feeling accountable is the only thing that is going to make you better. Hell, it is the only thing that keeps you *alive*. When we debrief operations in the SEAL teams—whether in training or in real-world combat—we are relentless with criticism. There is no coddling, only truth. The mistakes must be well known to everyone because that is the only way to ensure that everyone actually learns from them. There isn't time to make that mistake a second time, because it could very well be fatal.

On one debrief after a mission in Iraq, our chief gathered us around. He was exactly the spitting image of a SEAL chief you might imagine: quiet, professional, ruthlessly aggressive, careful and direct with his words, and built like an NFL running back. He didn't like to lift heavy weights because his stature was already too damn muscular. He was naturally stronger than everyone in the platoon. When he spoke, we listened. Like the SEAL chief played by Dennis Haysbert in the movie *Navy SEALs*, he was a well-respected leader. Being an officer and the acting platoon commander, I was technically his boss. But I always listened when he had something to say.

"Gents," he began. "You're all fucked up."

We weren't sure exactly why at first. Nothing major had gone wrong on this op. We were on time, and we hit the right target. We'd left Camp Ramadi at 0200 hours and drove straight into one of the worst neighborhoods in Iraq. We weren't perfectly clandestine (we were driving giant armored vehicles, after all), but we were still good enough to wake the bad guys up from their beds. They never saw us coming. No one got hurt. We coordinated well with our Iraqi partners and they took custody of the al-Qaeda operative we had captured. Our intel team had been tracking this guy for months, and when we confirmed his location, it was game on.

But it wasn't *perfect*. And Chief was going to tell us why. He pointed to our guys in charge of getting the vehicles ready. "The seating assignments were screwed up, we looked like idiots trying to figure out who was supposed to be in which vehicle before leaving the base. Unfuck yourselves."

"Roger." That is the only acceptable response.

"And you guys," he said, pointing to our comms team, "why the hell didn't we have SATCOM when we were on target? I thought you said you fixed the antenna. Didn't you test that?"

"We did, but the angle—"

"Shut up. Fix it."

"Yep. Will do."

"And sir," he said, looking at me. But it wasn't a real "sir." It was an "I have to call you sir because that's good military bearing and I am a professional but we both know I have a decade of experience that you don't."

He was right.

"Tell your boys at NIIA"—the National Iraqi Intelligence Agency, with whom I was the primary liaison—"that they better start bringing actual guns on these ops and not that dumbass sniper rifle that guy carries around." He was referring to the NIIA commander who always carried this Russian Dragunov rifle with a nonworking scope into close quarters. It was definitely not the optimal weapon, and it should have been my job to say something about it. We ignored it because he was always out in the back of the assault anyway.

"Roger that, Chief, we will fix it."

No one can quite make you feel as small as a SEAL chief can. But here is the thing: He can't *make you feel shame*. No one can. A sense of shame only really comes from within. I think we know this intuitively, and in the SEAL teams it is deeply embedded in our culture. As a SEAL, you simply cannot fathom committing less than 110 percent effort at all times. Every SEAL does his duty, even the smallest job, simply for the sake of the duty itself. The mantra "If you are going to do it, you might as well be the best at it" is repeated constantly. We live by it.

And this high expectation works only if it comes from within. It is impossible for leaders to make you feel something and then enforce it. A teacher or boss or parent can certainly correct our behavior or misdeeds. And we may nod in agreement about our transgression, but only we can actually *feel bad* for having done it. You either internalize it, or you don't. I would argue that the more immune you are to a healthy sense of shame, the more susceptible you are to contributing to big cultural problems: the outrage mob and the extreme response of shamelessness.

Outrage mobs are born of many things, but one of them is the total unwillingness to learn and discover. Remember the advice I gave to high school students earlier in the book: Wait before becoming emotionally attached to an opinion. There is nothing wrong with saying, "I don't know." Ignorance on its own is not cause to feel ashamed. There are plenty of things that I am not an expert on and never will be. But ignorance coupled with strong opinions *is* a reason to feel ashamed, and it is one of the hardest things to get people to actually feel ashamed *about*.

This shameless ignorance is difficult to reverse once it takes hold. And I believe it is a primary cause of outrage-based call-out culture. As a politician, I am always in the center of a debate, either publicly or privately with constituents. I am often disagreeing with someone on the left or the right. I have noticed that both sides of the political spectrum hate nothing more than for you to tell them that you disagree with their long-held beliefs. The reaction is swift, severe, and highly emotional. Take for example the slogans "No more endless wars!" and "Bring the troops home!" repeated excitedly by both conservatives and liberals. I have spent a good deal of time explaining via social media and op-eds in the *Wall Street Journal* and the *Washington Post* why these slogans are hollow, wrongheaded, and severely lacking in the nuance necessary to understand our nation's overseas involvements. The reaction on social media, upon learning of my contrarian viewpoint, takes on the form of the emotional reasoning that I discussed previously. I am called a war-monger, a RINO, a neocon, responded to with everything *except* a reasonable policy debate.

People hate being told they are wrong, and seem to hate it even more when it comes from someone they thought was on their side. It is easy to understand why. I think we can all admit that once we have publicly defended an argument, it is a huge blow to our ego when we are presented with facts and arguments that clearly debunk it. It is damn near impossible to admit we were wrong, especially to some slimy politician who "sold out" as soon as he got to Washington, D.C. (I am still trying to figure out what the hell that even means.) Even though my beliefs are firmly conservative, I run into this sentiment often, and it comes from both the left and the right. People do not trust politicians, even when those elected officials work to be truthful and grounded in fact. This mistrust is a growing feature, not a bug, in our democratic system.

That distrust is perhaps justified, and maybe even emblematic of healthy skepticism. The problem is that most people are never skeptical of their *own* beliefs. Haidt and Lukianoff discuss this as one of the "great untruths" in *The Coddling of the American Mind*, in which they strongly condemn the notion that we "should always trust our feelings." Dr. Haidt uses a metaphor to explain why. He writes about the human mind as a rider on an elephant, where the rider is our conscious mind steering the unconscious mind represented by the elephant. The elephant is obviously larger and can easily overpower the rider, which is indicative of the emotional power of the unconscious mind. The role of the rider is to question that emotional reasoning, and use conscious reasoning to investigate what is actually true and based on facts and reality. "Emotional reasoning is the cognitive distortion that occurs whenever the rider interprets what is happening in ways that are consistent with the elephant's reactive emotional state, without investigating what is true," writes Haidt. This applies to a variety of psychological issues, whether they be depression, victimhood, trauma, or anxiety. Cognitive behavior therapy can be used to correct this unhealthy thinking by encouraging the patient to consciously question those preconceived notions.

If we are to engage in truth seeking and avoid outrage, we must aggressively challenge the beliefs and opinions that led us to that outrage in the first place. We have to start assuming that maybe, just maybe, there might be more to the story than our emotional elephant is telling us.

We must train the unconscious elephant to feel some shame for emotional reasoning. If we don't, the shameless outrage becomes normalized and the behavior continues to worsen. The rationalization that the rider engages in begins to rewire our brains. At first, there was a small voice screaming, "You screwed up, own it!" But eventually, after losing the battle so many times to a rider rationalizing your misstep, that voice stops talking. The elephant has been fully trained in the worst of ways, and the result is outrage behavior. The result is shamelessness. Your elephant is your unconscious mess of feelings and automatic behaviors. The rider of that elephant can question the elephant's instincts and drive it toward better behavior, but only the elephant can actually *feel* the shame that is necessary to hold you accountable. That feeling of shame should be encouraged, not rationalized away.

One thing I hear a lot is, "Well, that's just what I believe, and it's my opinion, so you can't really argue with that." Well, I can, actually. An opinion is valuable only insofar as it can be backed up by some element of reason and facts. The common story being told by many people, especially in the outrage mob Twitter-sphere, is that their opinion is true simply because it is *their* truth. There is no sense of shame whatsoever in their inability to explain *why* they hold that opinion. I have watched in dismay as this happens from both the left and right. When challenged, they default to talking points that don't even address the question, and attack a straw man argument (an imagined argument that is easily defeated, but ultimately not the argument being made by their opponent).

For instance, when debating the merits of building additional walls along the length of the border, left-wing activists often accuse Republicans of racism and xenophobia instead of addressing the actual question: Shouldn't we secure our southern border? Once past that, they attack a straw man argument, claiming Republicans want an expensive two-thousand-mile concrete wall. The actual proposal during the budget standoff in early 2019 was regarding 234 miles of steel bollard fencing where Border Patrol needed reinforcement, not a two-thousand-mile Great Wall of the Southern Border, as was often claimed by media and my colleagues in the Democrat party.

Or take the 9/11 truthers, the conspiracy movement that believes the September 11 attacks were perpetuated not by al-Qaeda but by the Bush administration. On every anniversary of 9/11 their pronouncements get thousands of likes on social media. It is rather concerning. *Popular Mechanics* did a great public service by painstakingly going through each silly tenet of trutherism, "A bomb took down Building 5," "Fire doesn't melt steel beams," and so on. When confronted with certain scientific realities, such as "Fire may not melt steel beams, but it sure as hell can weaken them to the point where they can no longer bear their load," truthers have a choice: They can admit that they have been suckered, or they can double down. A common truther refrain is to ignore *Popular Mechanics'* findings and instead accuse their writers and editors of being paid handsome sums by the government to help cover up the conspiracy. Though truthers are a tiny conspiratorial fringe, they represent a wider trend of Americans growing so embroiled in their own political beliefs that they will beclown themselves rather than simply admit that a fair point was made and move on.

This phenomenon has bewildered me. I get told how wrong I am all the time. Literally every day on social media and elsewhere. And it's fine. It's obviously part of the job. Sometimes it is simple disagreement on a policy approach. But sometimes it is disagreement on the basic facts. Sometimes I have been proven wrong and forced to reckon with it. During a Twitter-based policy dispute early in my term with Representative Joe Kennedy of Massachusetts, I made the mistake of misrepresenting a bill in one of my tweets. I screwed up, and Kennedy corrected me. Publicly. It sucked. But it didn't make me angry. It made me better. I reached out to him privately afterward to hash it out, and we have since developed a friendship that I value greatly.

Honest debate makes us better at thinking more deeply about why we believe what we believe. If you find yourself calling someone a communist, traitor, or RINO because they disagree with you, it is a good indication that your arguments are shallow and your emotions are driving your thinking. And shouldn't we feel a little shame about that? Dropping weapons-grade accusations, like that of racism, Nazism, sexism, homophobia, without cause or evidence is a sign of weakness, not strength. It is reflective of a mind that refuses to engage itself critically, and instead reaches for insult and ad hominem attacks to shroud ignorance and policy illiteracy.

I encountered this firsthand at a campus event at Arizona State University in the spring of 2019. During the question-and-answer session with students, a young man took to the microphone to tell me I was a Nazi and that I should be ashamed for my service in Afghanistan, not proud. There was no intellectual argument made, no debate to be had on the merits of America's involvement in Afghanistan, just ad hominem attacks fueled by too much time on the internet following equally angry activists. What are the chances his little outburst actually earned him respect or changed any minds? Certainly not mine.

Again, I'm OK with ignorance about complex subjects. Ignorance is fine. I have no problem with it. We all can't be experts on everything, even if Wikipedia makes us feel that way. But ignorance incorporated with overly strong opinions? Yes, that's a problem.

One of the greatest aspects of religion is that it imbues a deep sense of shame in us. I want to be clear, shame itself is not an inherent virtue. But shame, in particular shame in the ecclesiastical sense, has a way of forcing contrition. And contrition, along with the redemptive qualities that accompany it, is a fundamental good in our society. It correlates virtue with a higher power, and that we will be judged according to that higher power. This is exceptionally important. Without a transcendent moral authority, what motivation would we have to live virtuously? Wouldn't we be able to justify just about any action taken? I'm not here to evangelize. I know that many people do not look to the Bible for their moral guidance or feel that famous sense of Catholic guilt. But consider the value in having an hour or two every Sunday to reflect on your wrongs. It is the same as training with a rifle or a compass or practicing with a basketball or seven iron. It drills your conscience with a sense of shame, which becomes remorse, which becomes redemption and ultimately self-improvement. To have no shame is to wrongly believe you are fine as you are, with no room to grow. It is a self-imposed restriction on further development. To fill a country like the United States with the shameless, rather than the virtuous, is to allow vice and iniquity to define us as a people and stunt much-needed progress.

Shame is accountability. You may still decide to be a jerk and leave that trash on the sidewalk, but at least you felt a little bad about it. At least you felt some semblance of personal responsibility for failing to hit the gym three days in a row. You felt some regret for failing to check in on a friend you know is struggling. And it is this notion of personal responsibility that we are ultimately getting at. It's one of the most important concepts that make up the bedrock of a well-functioning society. Personal responsibility leads to empowerment, control, and ultimately success. A person who isn't personally responsible—and feels no shame for it—is by definition waiting for someone else to be responsible for them. This isn't empowering. This is disempowering. Someone else has responsibility for you and therefore control over your destiny. This frame of mind, where you accept that others must be responsible in your stead, is a prison. It is the abdication of agency and control in your life. It is the height of helplessness, and I wish it on no one.

A dose of shame is required for personal responsibility to manifest. After all, the fundamental desire to be responsible for your actions and destiny requires an intrinsic sense of right and wrong, good and bad, and therefore a sense of shame to help understand that choice. That sense of personal responsibility gives us control and leads us to other virtues that ultimately make us better and more productive people. It will give you a moral toughness that hardens your resilience to external and internal stress.

Don't be shameless. Train your unconscious mind to feel bad. Work hard to define what is good and what is bad. Think deeply about your hero attributes. What are they? Why are those heroes successful? Why do we look up to them? And are you feeling a sense of shame every time you engage in a behavior that doesn't live up to that hero? A healthy sense of shame means you are less likely to be outraged, and therefore less likely to be anxious, depressed, and neurotic. The road to mental toughness is paved with the knowledge that we don't always do what is right, but we are willing to take responsibility for it, humbly correct it, and be stronger as a result. A mind that cannot bend to admit wrongdoing is easily broken. Don't be breakable. Live with fortitude.

CHAPTER 7

A SENSE OF DUTY

G rowing up in Katy, Texas, I was in the last generation before overprotective, helicopter parenting came onto the scene. I think the demographers put me in the "elder millennial" category—a timeframe where we grew up with analog but became adults in the digital age. I had to call my friends on landlines to make plans. We navigated without Google's help. We looked up movie times in the newspaper, not the Fandango app. The internet hadn't yet scared parents into protecting their child's every move.

My parents didn't hover or monitor me excessively. I was allowed to explore the neighborhood, take risks, skin my knee or fall on my face. That's not a figure of speech: I came home with a black eye and busted lip more than a few times.

The 1980s and 1990s were a crime-ridden era compared to today. Gang violence was rampant in the Houston area. In 1981, Houston was proclaimed the "murder capital of the United States," with 701 homicides.[1] Today, despite a much larger population, that number fluctuates between three hundred and four hundred. It's still too high—but it is also a reflection of a vast improvement in policing

---

1 https://www.chron.com/news/hurricanes/article/Houston-homicide-rate-may-be-worst-in-a-decade-1911228.php

and society from then to now. A high murder rate was just the tip of the iceberg. Kids' faces showed up on milk cartons constantly. And yet even in those empirically more dangerous times, parents let their kids walk to school, ride their bikes to their friends' homes, and play unsupervised. All without a cell phone tethered to the child. Unbelievable. Mom, Dad, forget Afghanistan. How did I ever survive childhood?

But with that freedom came a scourge. The bullies.

Walking home from school every day in the third grade, my friends and I began having issues with another group of older kids. Each day was a challenge as these tyrannical little jerks chased us down. They specifically targeted a friend of mine whom they knew they could take on without fear of serious retribution. They would yank on his backpack and toss him around, sometimes throwing him to the ground.

One day I had enough. I don't know what came over me. I was not a big kid. I never have been. I just had enough. As the bullies were doing as bullies do, I decided to charge. I extended my arms and drove them straight into the back of one of our tormentors, slamming him to the ground. I then sprinted away like I had just won the Olympics. The third-grade admixture of selfless sacrifice and pragmatic self-preservation was perfectly expressed in both my attack and my flight.

Thus ended the scourge of bullying.

None of this was particularly dramatic or much different than any other childhood story. I share this story because elementary school was the first time in living memory that I felt one of the most important things a person can feel: a sense of duty.

It was, in retrospect, exhilarating. I felt a duty to protect my friend from harm, and to stand up against an obvious wrong.

I was also a good student. Why? Because I liked school and learning? Sort of, but not really. I was a good student because I felt a strong sense of duty to get good grades. Why? Because I felt shame if I got a bad grade. Why? Probably because it was imbued in me by my parents. Growing up, they simply highlighted the importance of academics, putting forth your best effort on the soccer field, and standing up for your friends. And not because of any transactional benefit to these "good" actions. Rewards or punishments were not necessary, only the satisfaction of accomplishment and, in the case of the bullies, righting a wrong.

These actions were good *because they were good*. And my parents imbued in me a sense of duty to do that which has inherent value.

This is duty at the most fundamental level. It is a sense that there are virtues and values in this life that should be pursued for the sake of virtue itself. We know deep down what those virtues are. We know we have a duty to clean our room, be patient, be polite, follow the law, get good grades, respect our parents, and so on. We know that. We don't always adhere to them, but we *know* them. And hopefully we feel a degree of shame when we don't adhere to them. Shame and duty are closely linked. You must feel shame so that you act on your sense of duty. Duty is a positive result from the negative emotion of shame.

A healthy sense of duty toward self-improvement, virtue, and responsibility for your loved ones must be pursued consciously. We have to remind ourselves of it constantly. If we don't, it is far too easy to rationalize selfish and irresponsible behavior, eventually shutting down any feelings of shame whatsoever for that bad behavior. When the shame is gone, it is pretty unlikely that a sense of duty toward higher and nobler purposes will ever materialize. This tradeoff manifests in the small stuff too: If you don't feel bad about littering, then you certainly won't feel a sense of duty to pick up the plastic bottles near the storm drain before they wash away into the ocean.

Duty is ingrained in the human condition. Our great religions are essentially based on a sense of duty to love God and live well. We have a duty to not only survive in this world but to pursue a higher purpose. We are here for a reason, and living for that purpose is our choice to make. It is the path to happiness. Many political institutions throughout history have also centered around duty, albeit in very different and interesting ways. The ancient Greeks believed in living for the sake of the polis.[2] It was your duty to live for the city, for the community. Sometimes, as in the case of a hoplite or Socrates, it was your duty to die for it. In Rome, it was deeply ingrained in the citizens to live according to law and tradition—which was one reason the early Christians, who refused to revere the civic gods and rites, were persecuted. Communists believe in an even more extreme version of duty toward the state. In America, our duty, as our Founders envisioned it, was to live virtuously so that the government could back off and simply protect our freedoms. The American sense of duty is the most enlightened version thus far, with the best results.

Our American sense of duty is based on Judeo-Christian history and teachings. In the United States Capitol, on the upper walls of the House floor, where the House of Representatives votes and debates, are the Relief Portraits of Lawgivers. The historical figures depicted are noted for their work in establishing the under-lying principles of American law. The lawgivers are historically diverse, including Jefferson, Hammurabi, Gaius, and Sir William Blackstone, to name a few. There are twenty-three lawgivers in total. Here is the interesting part: All the renowned figures' reliefs are in side profile, except one. At the center of the northern wall, only one portrait relief faces forward, looking directly down at the Speaker of the House.

---

2   A city-state in ancient Greece, especially as considered in its ideal form for philosophical purposes.

That portrait is of Moses.

It is easy to understand why. Moses received the Ten Commandments from God on Mount Sinai, providing humankind with the most basic rules governing our sense of duty to ourselves, to each other, and to God.

1. You shall have no other gods before Me.
2. You shall make no idols.
3. You shall not take the name of the Lord your God in vain.
4. Keep the Sabbath day holy.
5. Honor your father and your mother.
6. You shall not murder.
7. You shall not commit adultery.
8. You shall not steal.
9. You shall not bear false witness against your neighbor.
10. You shall not covet.

Even if you don't believe in God, these divine laws chiseled on stone tablets have an importance beyond theology. Divine law has long superseded human law. Indeed, human law draws most of its moral character from those ten simple rules. And, assuming you didn't shoplift this book, these commandments are also quite obvious to you. If you are reading these for the first time, your first reaction may be one of incredulity: "Why do I need these? I already know these things. I know right from wrong. I don't need the Bible to tell me that I should respect my parents and not murder people. I don't need Moses to explain to me that coveting my neighbors' belongings is bad."

I am sympathetic to that sentiment, but we do have to consider an important question: *Why do we know these things?* Who taught us? Our parents? Our culture? And who taught them? Where did these "truths" come from? There has to be a history of teachings and traditions that led to this modern moment, where all of us just happen to "know" that lying about your neighbor or cheating on your spouse is a bad thing. It isn't *necessarily* the case that humans naturally follow these laws if left to their own devices. In fact, it is quite obvious that we don't follow these commandments very well at all.

Human history is a story about the struggle to follow these fundamental truths, the struggle to live with virtue in the face of our own dark side. People of all types, including those of religious faith, have struggled to live according to this sense of duty. After all, the word "Israel" literally means "struggle with God."

Moses receiving the Ten Commandments was a defining moment in the beginning of Western civilization, where our sense of duty to live virtuously began. Whether you believe in the first four commandments, which instruct deference before the Almighty, or not, the truth remains that commandments five through ten have had a profound influence on what we consider to be virtuous rules to live by. So much so that we consider the Ten Commandments to be a basis from which we derive our modern laws, and place the relief portrait of Moses front and center in the House of Representatives, where we create our laws. Our Founders designed our republic with the understanding that citizens would strive to live under these divinely inspired rules. They understood that freedom could be protected only so long as citizens had a duty to live responsibly. Recall St. John Paul II: "We have liberty not to do as we wish, but to do as we ought." Government can enforce the law after it is broken, but citizens must still choose to first follow that law if we are to live free from chaos. A prosperous nation is one where citizens choose to follow laws for reasons other than threat of punishment. The law must be respectable if we are to respect it. And respectable law is based on timeless virtues such as the ones written in the Ten Commandments.

Our religious history doesn't just provide us with our basis for law, it also establishes the foundations for how we should live beyond the reach of law. It is not illegal to covet, but it is well established as a negative quality. It isn't illegal to commit adultery (although it is under military law), but courts still punish you for it during divorce hearings. But more than behavioral guidance, religion has provided us with a deeper sense of purpose. This is the benefit of believing in a transcendent power greater than ourselves. The Ten Commandments are not debatable, as man-made laws are. They are simply *true*. That sense of truth allows us to pursue virtuous living and act on our duties in this life.

This, in turn, provides a path out of despair. Most studies show that suicide rates among religious people are lower than among the nonreligious.[3] The reasons for this are likely complex, but I believe one reason is a sense of meaning that is greater than ourselves. That higher meaning produces a sense of purpose. Without it, nihilism can infect the head and the heart. And with it a sense of empti-ness, a sense of being lost. If we are truly just walking skeletons stuffed with meat and tissue, following the commands of our firing neurons, then what is the point of it all?

Living with purpose and virtue is not easy. Far from it. The default human condition is to *avoid* duty and honor and shame. Religion can be a real buzzkill here, as it instructs a soul that seeks comfort and pleasure to *stop seeking comfort and pleasure*, and instead pursue purpose. More and more people are leaving the church. Everyone may provide different reasons for abandoning God, but I am going to assert that freedom to pursue pleasure without guilt or accountability is a critical element of this disconcerting trend.

I understand that if you are agnostic or not particularly religious,

---

3   https://ajp.psychiatryonline.org/doi/full/10.1176/appi.ajp.161.12.2303

the Bible may not be a powerful or compelling source of authority. You may not believe in it, but you cannot escape its foundational impact on our government, our society, and our institutions.

I believe our modern-day outrage culture is partly due to a misunderstanding of what our duties and virtues are, where they came from, and why they are good. For the outraged, there are serious questions about whether or not many basic truths actually exist at all. The postmodernists driving this revolutionary thought question everything simply for the sake of questioning it. This isn't a surprising trend among young people, since the language of revolution is always romantic and idealized, and the youth are most susceptible to it. On small scales, this might be fine. It is part of every child's learning process to ask, "Why?" But mix this childlike curiosity with extreme political passion and social media–fueled outrage culture, and you've got a pretty dangerous mix. You have a cultural trend that seeks to tear down anything traditional simply because it is old.

Think of the parable about the fence in the forest. As you walk through the forest you come upon a fence. It extends out in both directions, beyond what you can see. Its purpose is not obvious. Why is this fence here? I didn't see any property on either side. What is it fencing in, or keeping out? The postmodern revolutionary simply says, "Tear it down. Its purpose is not immediately obvious, so tear it down." A more careful thinker says, "Let us investigate this further. Just because we can't immediately explain something's purpose does not mean it is not important. We should learn the history of the fence before tearing it down." Tearing down the fence results in a world where we throw the baby out with the bathwater.

I'm not saying all traditions are good or immune from criticism. Remember, we used to think women shouldn't vote. That was a bad, long-held tradition. We changed it, and thank God we have a political institution capable of making such a change. But the truth is that women's suffrage was always something that aligned with our most basic values. The problem wasn't our values, the problem was that we weren't living up to our foundational values or the Judeo-Christian history they were based on (nowhere in the Bible does it say that women can't vote).

Today, the results of questioning *all* of our traditional values are: fewer marriages, contracting birthrates, the erosion of interpersonal relationships, and declining church attendance. Instead of believing in our duty to overcome adversity, the outraged postmodernists want you to embrace victimhood. In this new world, it is of higher virtue to be oppressed than it is to be self-reliant. The modern outrage culturalists want you to speak truth to power with an angry fist, instead of seeking out truth for the sake of truth itself. This results in a lot of incoherent yelling and screaming, but not very much thinking. The outrage world is one where bad behavior has become justified simply because you feel angry and passionate about something. Anger and passion are becoming substitutes for righteousness. Attitude and arrogance are becoming substitutes for sophistication.

At a very basic level, this is a shirking of fundamental human duty and responsibility. A responsibility to what exactly? Politeness, open-mindedness, and grace, for starters. These are our duties to our fellow Americans. Just the basics. If we lose those fundamental virtues, we lose our sense of unity. Without a sense of unity under an umbrella of common values, this whole great American experiment unravels. This republic is rooted in the notion that a diverse people (perhaps more diverse than any nation in history) can only live together in liberty and prosperity if we share some common understanding of respect and decency. Again, the law can be enforced only after the fact. It can serve as a deterrent. Only we can choose not to break the law in the first place, and if we don't begin to see that living with virtue is more than just an aspiration but also a duty, then we fall victim to anger, outrage, and discord.

Duty is not just about others. It also begets a sense of self-worth and purpose. The story I told about moving the rocks on the ranch is an important lesson precisely because no one would have noticed if I hadn't done it. The ranch owner, unable to watch me continuously throughout the day, never would have been the wiser if my rock-moving efforts were subpar. It was summertime in central Texas, after all, and it would have been understandable for a thirteen-year-old to slow down a bit. I could have gotten away with moving considerably fewer rocks across that fence line. But I didn't. Because my parents taught me that a strong work ethic is not just a means to an end; it is an end in and of itself. Living with duty is the pursuit of virtue because it is good, not because there is a reward at the end.

That being said, the good news is this: *There is most likely a reward at the end.* But if your focus is only on the end reward, it is likely that your actions to get to that goal will be insufficient. This is where the connection to our main theme, mental toughness, comes into play. Let me explain it this way. If my attitude during BUD/S was simply "I am doing this only because I want to be a SEAL," then I don't think I would have made it. Even though that statement is objectively true (why else would you suffer so much?), it doesn't capture the mentality of the men who do make it through the gauntlet that is BUD/S. The mentality that is beaten, with controlled violence, into a student during BUD/S is that high performance is expected for the sake of high performance. It has intrinsic virtue independent of its utility toward an end goal.

Instructors often point this fact out. They can't possibly observe everything we do. They remind us constantly that we could easily "skate by" and do the bare minimum throughout BUD/S. We could put just enough effort into that four-mile run to get barely under the time limit. We could glide through the two-mile ocean swims instead of striving to beat our previous time. We could spend one less hour cleaning our room before an inspection and just accept the punishment for failing. Even with all that, there is a chance we'll still make it to the end of training and go on to become a SEAL.

But such a path to "success" is no path at all, in the world of the SEAL teams. It is deeply discouraged. The known half-ass, the man who skates by, the man who treats the minimum standard as his maximum effort, is not a man we want beside us in a firefight. We want the guy who puts every ounce of effort into everything he does. Anything less is failure, even if technically the job still gets done. For instance, when assigning something as simple as organizing a training day on the shooting range, there is a difference between getting the job done and a SEAL getting the job done. One could easily fulfill the bosses' orders by doing the minimum: ordering some ammunition and booking a time slot at the range. Let everything fall into place after that. But a SEAL who values a sense of duty doesn't stop there. He prepares the ammo so we don't waste time pulling it out of boxes. He writes out a series of shooting drills. He prepares paper and steel targets for variety. He brings in some outside experts to critique our shooting. He has a plan for cleanup at the end and makes sure everyone knows what it is.

A sense of duty is indispensable in combat, because the ultimate test will be on the battlefield, where your greatest fears come true and death surrounds you, begging you to join him. Walking across the fields of IEDs in the countryside of Afghanistan could occur only with the deepest sense of duty to mission, country, and teammates. We do it because our country asked us to. We do it because the mission is just and necessary. We do it because our teammates, our brothers in arms, will be there, and we can't let them down.

The first friend I lost to the war was Lieutenant Brendan Looney, killed in Afghanistan in 2010. A star lacrosse player at the Naval Academy, an exemplary husband, and an inspirational leader, Brendan embodied everything SEALs think about when we examine a sense of duty. His favorite value statement was "Be strong. Be accountable. Never complain." Sound familiar? He had a roommate at the Naval Academy whom I never met, First Lieutenant Travis Manion. They are buried next to each other in Arlington National Cemetery. Travis was killed in action as well, three years before Brendan. Their somber but undeniably American story is one of duty, expressed beautifully by Travis's words, "If not me, then who?"

When describing the importance of duty, that is one of my favorite phrases: "If not me, then who?" It isn't just applicable to joining the military; it applies to everyday life. If you won't help that homeless person get a meal, who will? Why is it someone else's job? If you care, if you really care, then why not take action? What is better, demanding that some kind of government "action" be taken to solve a problem, or getting a group organized and getting it done yourself? You might say, "Both." And if you are that person doing both of those things, then good on you. If you are just doing the first thing, then you are just asking others to do what you won't do yourself.

If not me, then who?

Is someone else going to discover that next medical breakthrough, or are you? Is someone else going to clean up your mess at the food court in the mall, or should you do it yourself? Is someone else going to stay late at the office and put the finishing touches on that big quarterly presentation, or are you? Big things and small things alike are driven forward by a sense of duty. We have to consciously apply it to every aspect of our lives. It is the path to self-reliance, responsibility, virtue, and striving to be part of the solution instead of the problem. It is hypocrisy to bemoan outrage Twitter mobs and then be one of the comments deriding the character and intent of the person you disagree with. "Delete your account!" "Nazi!" "Idiot!" are not exactly examples of thoughtful discourse, no matter how much you *feel* your comments are justified and true.

We have a sense of duty to be better, more polite, and smarter with our public disagreements. I'm not alone in thinking this. Recall President Obama's 2016 exit interview: "I think that I can have a polite dialogue with somebody who differs from me....And so, on the one hand, my advice to progressives like myself, and this is advice I give my own daughters who are about to head off to college, is don't go around just looking for insults. You're tough. If somebody says something you don't agree with, just engage them on their ideas."

We have a duty to be tougher; tough enough to engage in ideas. We have a duty to our entire society to be not just resilient, but antifragile, as defined by Nassim Nicholas Taleb in his book *Antifragile*. To be antifragile is to be the embodiment of the timeless truth: "What doesn't kill us makes us stronger." A resilient person can suffer through some punishment, but an antifragile person is made stronger by it. *Duty* is the pathway to self-improvement. It is applied to every aspect of your life. Your kids, your spouse, your job, your own self-improvement. You have a duty to those relying on you and you have a duty to be the hero that you imagined yourself to be in chapter 2. You have a duty because you are alive and you're alive for a reason.

I've been asked before what message I have for my fellow veterans who are struggling. Many veterans get out of the military—a place where duty and purpose are part of everyday life—and they are shocked by the lack of meaning they now experience. They are wandering, aimless, their sense of mission vanished. They feel empty. They had a duty to their teammates, their country, and the mission. Now what is their duty? I would say that it isn't any different. Your duty is the same. You still have a duty to your teammates, but those teammates are your family, friends, and community. It is to your fellow Americans. As an American you have a duty to contribute, even if it is a small thing. Make no mistake: There is no job that is undignified. Every small job is a contribution to your country. I'm not being facetious, and I say that with utmost sincerity. You are employed. Productive. Contributing. Making money and spending money, thus contributing to the tax base and to a healthy economy. It may not be glorious, but it is a duty done. Don't want to be at the bottom forever? Then there is opportunity to master a small task, to show up on time, to be a good employee, to be noticed, and to be promoted. Many of our grandparents and great-grandparents started off in small, seemingly meaningless jobs.

Every mission matters, even the small ones. And you have a duty to put the same amount of effort into the small things that you do into the big things. Because the small missions, done well, make up the big missions. Its your duty to recognize that. Every mission we did as SEALs was really a result of a multitude of smaller missions, accomplished by individuals who did their duty. In every smaller cog in the machine, it would have been easy to dismiss the small mission as unimportant to the larger cause. Easy to say, "I don't really need to put in the extra effort to this contingency plan, because it's so unlikely we will have to use it." Yeah, sure, until you *do* have to use it and everyone's life is on the line. A mission to capture a terrorist cell leader seems simple from the outside. Get to a location and capture the guy. Simple enough. In reality, it's possible only because of many separate missions executed extremely well. And that is only possible because each of those individuals feels an inherent sense of duty to make sure that if there is a screwup, it won't be because they were the weak link.

On one of our more complex missions in Iraq in 2010, the

duty of each team member could not be overstated. We had intelligence from our Iraqi partners that insurgents were using the rural region in central Iraq to hide out and plan attacks in the city centers. We wanted to investigate these remote locations along with them.

Side note: Even in 2010, our Iraqi partners were very reluctant to do any mission without us. Even though the threat was relatively low compared to the civil war of 2006–2007, the al-Qaeda insurgency still scared the hell out of the Iraqis. They could see the writing on the wall. Without an American presence, the insurgents hiding out in Syria would blitz through Iraq again. And this was exactly what happened after we left in 2011.

While the notion of patrolling to different locations on a map seems relatively simple, I assure you it is not. Once you start asking some basic logistical questions, the operation becomes pretty complex. How will we get there? How will you move around once you're there, on foot? Do we need to bring vehicles? What kind of air support will we have? Where will we hole up to spend the night?

Our plan was to drive our LTATVs (light tactical all-terrain vehicles—not much different from your commercial side-by-side ATV) throughout the rugged terrain, talk to the locals, and cautiously check out some of the locations described to us by Iraqi intelligence. To get the LTATVs there, we had to fit them in four CH-47 Chinook helicopters. In the movies, special ops teams just show up, get briefed on the target, and get on the mission. Hollywood doesn't show you how each one of those team members is in charge of an extremely important part of the mission. Ninety-five percent of warfare is logistics. Someone is in charge of making sure each LTATV is fueled, maintained, and equipped for a three-day journey. Someone is in charge of scheduling the airlift and making sure we have an appropriate landing zone. Someone else is in charge of making sure we have primary, secondary, and tertiary communications customized for the LTATVs. They can't just throw a radio in the back. It has to be secured and accessible. The antenna has to be customized and attached in a good place where it won't break, won't be in the way, and will still get a good signal. They could just throw the radio in the back storage bin and perform their other duties in the most minimum of ways. In theory, that fits the definition of doing your job. In reality, that half-assed approach could cost lives.

Not two hours into that particular mission, we ran into trouble. We touched down at about 0200 hours and began navigating toward our first checkpoint. Our first problem started almost right away, as one of the LTATV engines began to overheat. Great. And also typical. These things can usually go hard for days in the summer heat, and in the middle of the night this happens? We cooled it off and kept going at a slower pace to keep it from breaking down entirely.

Then things got really interesting. While moving forward in our unarmored LTATVs, we started taking machine-gun fire from a secluded compound that had previously seemed harmless. There was nowhere to take cover—we were in a pretty flat desert area—so the only option was to return fire and maneuver. We hit back with more firepower than they were probably expecting, including forty-millimeter grenade rounds. They were outgunned and quite surprised to see us on their home turf, so they split. As this chaotic situation unfolded, one thing stuck out to me. We were prepared for it. Why? Because everyone did their job. They did their duty. The communications lead made sure that the radio was ready at all times so we could communicate with air assets, in this case a Predator drone, instead of just tossing it in the back in case we might need it. And in the middle of a firefight, it is imperative you have comms ready to go at all times.

In that moment, everyone had a duty to slow their heart rates and listen for orders. They did that. No problem. Every single team member did their duty to ensure they would not be the weakest link. Even the smallest thing, like failing to check the batteries in your infrared laser, would mean that you would not be able to aim your gun at night, and would therefore be totally useless. The smallest things matter in huge ways. That single 1.5-volt battery is everything. And there is no one to blame but yourself if you don't carry an extra one with you.

So maybe you don't have imminent plans to go into battle. That's understandable. But this lesson carries over to your daily life, despite the absence of life-or-death consequences.

Because so what if it's not life or death? Pretend it is.

Otherwise it's easy to fall into the trap of mediocrity. You may *survive* the gauntlet that we call life, but you aren't really *living*. And this gets to another common misconception—one that really irks me—about what our duty here on earth really is. About what *living* really is. It is the misconception of what it means to live your life "to the fullest." In our modern world, full of fun and luxury and comfort, it seems that living life to the fullest increasingly means taking advantage of the modern world's luxuries: weirdly customized lattes, staying out late drinking with friends, exotic travel, and so on. I don't think there is anything inherently wrong with these things. I like all of the creature comforts of the modern world, too. But I don't pretend this means "living my life to the fullest." Far from it.

This is a trend that worries me. Teenagers are far less likely to get a job now. Millennials are less likely to work overtime and more likely to value leisure instead of work. Being a millennial myself, I have plenty of experience with this generation and its proclivity for some carefree indulgence. Again, a healthy dose of fun on weekends isn't *bad*. But it is folly to think that it has anything to do with the purposeful living that we have been talking about. This all ties back to a sense of duty. Do you feel you have any duty to contribute more to this world than you are taking from it? In a world where travel, mixed drinks, and soy lattes are always within reach, does it bother us that our actions don't contribute even a little bit to these modern comforts? Someone dedicated their life to invention, entrepreneurship, and world peace so that you could board an airplane to Europe while sipping a double espresso mocha. What an amazing world we live in. What will we do to earn that luxury? How will we contribute? Answering these questions is an exercise in defining our purpose.

When I left the military, I immediately started my master's program at the Harvard Kennedy School of Government. One of the oft-repeated mottos of that school is a quote from, you guessed it, John F. Kennedy. "Ask not what your country can do for you—ask what you can do for your country." It's one of the great lines in American politics, and I swear by it. Stop wondering who is going to create the next best thing to make your life better. Create it yourself. Help your community. I think most of my classmates in that master's program were intent on filling that goal, in their own way. That's the good news.

But I noticed something else as I transitioned from military to college life, especially with younger students. These kids had great goals and a dizzying array of personal accomplishments to speak of (it is Harvard, after all). But does that mean a sense of duty was really prevalent? Not in the small ways. And as I have argued, the small things matter. I was amazed by how few people actually showed up on time to class, for instance. I was amazed how many people typed away on their laptops—sending iMessages, not taking notes—while the professor tried to lecture. It struck me because it was so normalized in college culture. This lack of politeness and lack of basic manners was the norm, not the exception. Don't get me wrong—

the students were not disruptive. But they were, at times, rude. I couldn't help but think, "You are going straight into the job market after this. Who on earth will hire you if you can't show up on time?"

Maybe I'm just acting like an old grouch, I don't know. But this isn't just my experience. I talk to employers a lot, and I am often told of management challenges with the younger generation. I'm generalizing here, but there is a growing sentiment that supervisors can't get them to show up on time, and staying late to put the finishing touches on that presentation seems out of the question for them. They think they deserve more responsibility but aren't willing to start at the bottom in order to earn it. They move between jobs rapidly, thereby making investments in job training a real challenge. There is no sense of loyalty to an organization, no sense of duty to be part of that organization's success. It seems as if they believe the organization has a duty to them, but not the other way around. I accept that this is a perception about a group, and that such judgments are often incomplete. The staffers who work for me certainly don't fall into this category of mediocrity, for instance.

The good news is this: If you are young and ready to take on the world, engaging in the smallest sense of duty will set you apart. People will notice that you are humble, polite, and believe in the team's success before your own. People will notice that you aren't looking for reasons to be offended. Not looking for reasons to be outraged. You will be rewarded for it.

In summary, let me end with some lessons in duty, to be followed daily:

You have a duty to accomplish something every day.
You have a duty to live up to your best self, the person you want to be, the hero archetype that you admire.
You have a duty to embrace shame and learn from it.

You have a duty to be polite, thoughtful, patient.

You have a duty to overcome your hardships and not wallow in self-pity.

You have a duty to contribute, even if your contribution is small.

You have a duty to be on time.

You have a duty to do your job, even if your job sucks.

You have a duty to stay healthy, both for yourself and so that you do not become a burden on others.

You have a duty to be part of the solution, not the problem. In other words, don't join the Twitter mob.

You have a duty to try hard not to offend others, and try harder not to be offended.

We may all survive this great, big experience we call humanity if we can abide by some of these little rules. And while I think our country's continued prosperity and even its existence depends on a citizenry that understands and values duty, there is a selfish reason to live a life of purpose and responsibility: It will make you tougher and more successful. We aren't perfect and we won't always adhere to these basic duties. But I hope we can start to agree on what they are, feel some shame when we fall short, and begin living our lives with purpose. This is the time-tested formula for a stronger people and, more than that, a stronger America.

CHAPTER 8

DO SOMETHING HARD

In BUD/S, it's all about the next ten minutes. Sometimes it's about the next thirty seconds. If you are thinking about BUD/S in its entirety—six brutal months—then the thought is simply too much. The men who quit are the men who look up at the day before them and see all the days to come. They are the men who are miserable, and wet, and cold, and thinking about the hot coffee and girlfriend they miss—and suddenly, because they imagine the months-long suffering they will inevitably face, they break. They are already using every ounce of endurance and fortitude to survive what's happening *right now*. Expanding their horizons to an infinite number of miserable right-nows does them in.

So you focus on the next ten minutes, and remind yourself that the instructors can't kill you—even if they're claiming otherwise. Thousands have made it before you. You can too.

What's on the other side when those months and months of ten-minute blocks are over?

Liberation. Transformation. *Meaning.*

I won't suggest everyone go through BUD/S, but I will suggest that a life unchallenged by hardship is a missed opportunity, and you should therefore seek to do something hard. Something really difficult. Something that takes you from a place where you're not the kind of person who could rise to the challenge—to a place where you're the kind of person who *did*.

The achievement itself isn't necessarily the point. The point is the challenge. The journey is the destination. That's a cliché, but there's a reason it is. It's entirely true. In difficulty, in adversity, in *meaningful* suffering—there is transformation. That transformation is one of confidence and mental fortitude, derived from the challenge and hardships we seek out. These challenges are forgotten tools, some of life's finest instructors, wiped away by a society that increasingly values comfort and pleasure over accomplishment and triumph.

The source of that transformation doesn't have to be BUD/S. But for me, it was.

I started with Class 261 in August 2006. The first few weeks of BUD/S—First Phase—are a pure gut check. SEAL instructors want to see if you can push yourself past limits you didn't even know you had. They want you to find inner strength whose existence was hidden before being unveiled by extreme hardship. They want to make sure you will carry your weight in a boat crew, keep up with and lead your class on long runs, endure thousands of repetitions of the same exercise, and do so on sleepless days stacked upon sleepless days. They want to know you will never quit. BUD/S is the most effective screening process in the United States Armed Forces, unique in that it doesn't just test physical strength, but also stamina, focus, and raw willpower. It ensures that every single SEAL has the mental fortitude to survive in the worst of environments and still take care of himself and his team.

First Phase is primarily log PT and IBS training.

Log PT, short for "physical training," is simple. It means you and your boat crew—about six guys grouped together based on height—carry a log. Kind of like a shortened telephone pole. A heavy one. And carry it a *lot*. There are a variety of exercises that the instructors offer up that are generally terrible—endless lunges while cradling the log; "up log," which just means holding it above your head until your arms give out—but mostly "log PT" means racing other boat crews up sand berms for hours. Losers keep racing, and winners get to sit out a round. It always pays to be a winner. I still have scars on my inner forearms from cradling the three-hundred-plus-pound log while wet and sandy.

IBS stands for "inflatable boat—small," a cumbersome Navy term for what is in essence a military river-rafting boat. It also weighs two hundred to three hundred pounds, depending on how much water they have in them. As with the logs, there are a variety of painful games we play for hours on end. We race for miles and miles carrying the boat on our heads. It is estimated that during Hell Week we run two hundred miles with that sandy rubber atrocity bouncing atop our skulls and pile-driving our spinal cords mercilessly. We take it everywhere with us, never leaving it.

That was hard enough.

It got harder when my leg—my left tibia, to be exact—fractured. This is not a unique injury, of course. Tendinitis and its ensuing limping results in stress on your bone. Stress on your bones eventually breaks them. I spent most of First Phase limping around, especially in the early morning when I hadn't warmed up yet. Every day was like that.

Hell Week is the fourth week. You have been beaten down for three consecutive weeks and then you have to stay up for six days and go through, well, hell. Hell Week is every SEAL's first real awakening, when you realize the limits you thought you had don't really exist. This awakening gives you the confidence you need to always say, no matter the circumstance, "I've been through tougher things before, so why not this, too?" There is a lesson here. We force hardship upon ourselves because it gives us *confidence* in ourselves. "If I can do this one hard thing, maybe I can also do the next hard thing." Hell Week is an extreme example, but you better believe it builds extreme confidence (sometimes a little cockiness, too, which is less of a virtue). Your self-imposed suffering doesn't have to be extreme, but it must be habitual, so that you are in the habit of building up your confidence one challenge at a time.

Hell Week is rife with moments of choice, and the choice is always the same: Keep enduring the pain or seek comfort. The comfort, the coffee and doughnuts, are always there. Waiting. The instructors never let you forget how easy it is to quit. Hell Week starts on a Sunday and ends Friday. For the first couple of days, you watch as dozens of your friends—some of them in far better physical shape than you—simply give up. They made the choice. They allowed Plan B to become their reality. They probably thought it was a choice all along, and that was the problem.

The reason Hell Week is so trying on the human psyche is because it really doesn't ever seem to end. It is the most brutal workout you've ever done, over and over and over again. You reach total muscle failure dozens of times throughout the day. Just when you think the instructors will end an exercise that has broken everybody down, they call for another round. For men who have never experienced failure before, especially star athletes, this can be exceptionally demoralizing.

Many think to themselves, "I thought I was ready for this. I thought I had trained and prepared." As it turns out, the only real preparation was mental. The preparation happened years before, when you decided a long time ago that this dream wasn't something you could fail at. They would have to kill you or break you.

They can't kill you. But they can certainly break you. This was exactly what happened to me.

My left leg was getting worse each day. I was moving slower and slower but still able to pull my weight under the boat we carried everywhere. I had pushed through the pain on one of the worst runs, a seemingly endless seven-mile footrace with the boats on our heads from Coronado to the Imperial Beach "elephant cages."[1] We did this on Sunday night. It felt like we were running forever. It seemed endless. We stopped occasionally to leave our boats and sprint into the frigid Pacific water. After all, the instructors could not possibly tolerate our dry fatigues. Wet and sandy was the standard. By the time dawn arrived we were greeted by a desolate patch of land covered in sand and ice plants—with plenty of room to continue the boat races. We fueled up with salty MREs (meals ready to eat) for breakfast, with the just-add-water chemical heating pouches taken out so that we could enjoy the packaged and preserved "omelets" cold.

It was only Monday morning. The air was cold and biting and the smell of the ocean was already revolting to our senses. The new day reminded us that this demoralizing moment would come four more times throughout the week. It was unbearable to some and they rang the bell as soon as the sun rose.

Tuesday came, and we were racing the other boat crews to lunch on a mile-long stretch through the base. At one point, we had to cross Orange Avenue to get from one side of the base to the other. I find it amusing to think of the everyday commuters waiting at the red light, and how they must react to the brutal scene playing out in front of them, watching these beaten and exhausted young men sprint across the intersections with sandy rubber boats on their heads.

You have to earn your meals during Hell Week, and you earn them by winning the boat races. It pays to give it your all and push your boat crew to victory. Better to put in the effort initially instead of being forced to do another race. The drop in morale that occurs

---

1 "Elephant cages" was a nickname for this base, itself a remnant of WWII. An enormous radio antenna apparatus still existed there as of a few years ago, and looked like a giant circular zoo cage.

from losing a race is devastating to a boat crew, and continues building until the boat crew is exhausted to the point of breaking, unable to perform. The initial pain and effort are worth it.

I remember the exact moment when my left tibia snapped.

Soon after crossing Orange Avenue, I could feel it as I rounded a corner on our way to the galley (in civilian-speak, this is a cafeteria). I kept going. I was not going to fall out of ranks and draw attention to myself. The adrenaline was strong enough to keep me upright.

I got my food and sat down. One nice thing about BUD/S is that they don't try and starve you. Quite the opposite: They give you as much food as you need so that you have the calories to keep going. They want you to be healthy and energized because they are pushing your physical limits. They also want you to be healthy and energized because if you quit, they don't want it to be for any other reason than the fact that you chose to quit.

I tried to get up from my seat, and collapsed back down. The adrenaline had worn off. Something was wrong. I tried again. No luck. Shit.

An instructor noticed and said in the most typically unsympathetic voice he could muster, "What the fuck is wrong with you, Crenshaw?"

I told him. He responded with the question I knew was coming: "Are you hurt or are you injured?"

There is a big difference between hurt and injured. *Everyone* is hurt. *Everyone* in that room had something wrong with them. We all had deep and painful chafing from the combination of sand and seawater on our not-so-soft camouflage fatigues, creating the effect of basically wearing sandpaper. Men were swollen and bruised. Many were battling infections and the onset of pneumonia. *Everyone* was hurt. If you stop because you're *hurt*, that isn't much different than quitting. I was pretty sure I was injured. I felt my shin *snap*. Still, the stakes were high. I knew that if they did an X-ray on my leg and it turned out not to be broken, then my entire dream of becoming a SEAL would be shattered.

I told the instructor that I was certainly injured. I couldn't put any weight on my left leg at all.

As it turned out, I was definitely injured, as the X-ray showed a large crack in my upper left tibia. My time at BUD/S was done for now, and it was, in the moment, psychologically devastating. Exiting Hell Week involuntarily was never in my plan. A lifelong goal was at risk of slipping away forever. I would have the opportunity to try again, but I would have to watch as my classmates went on to graduate six months later while I was back at ground zero. If you don't make it past Hell Week, you start over. It's like passing a checkpoint in a video game—and I didn't pass it.

I had just washed out of the dream I'd chased since I was a boy. Worse, I had washed out for something entirely beyond my control. I could control quitting, but I couldn't control the structural integrity of my left tibia. *Worse*, I knew that all the suffering I'd been through to get to that point was suffering I'd have to endure *again*. I knew I had the option—and a perfectly acceptable excuse, from the public's point of view—to just opt out of the whole thing.

I didn't opt out. I went back. Why? It wasn't because I was superhumanly gifted or unusually tolerant of pain and suffering. I was able to go back, and succeed, because I availed myself of the tools of a proper mind-set. No Plan B, remember? I never had a choice except to keep going.

I took it ten minutes at a time.

I internalized responsibility without blaming externalities.

I understood the value of doing something hard.

I never gave myself a choice.

Six months later I started up again. "I was blessed with the benefit of additional training," as those of us who were rolled back to another class would quip. Why do Hell Week once when you can do it twice? I determined that I would have to be killed or broken (again) to quit. I began again with Class 264 and I made it. I went on to Second Phase to endure the controlled-drowning experiences that I relayed to you before. I made it through five weeks of isolation on the island of San Clemente, where we did fourteen-mile ruck runs and shot thousands upon thousands of rounds at the range every day. I graduated BUD/S. About eight months later I graduated from the more advanced SEAL Qualification Training. I became a SEAL.

So you're asking me now, "Dan, what did you get out of it?" Good question. I got a lot out of it. I got a profession I loved. I got brothers who will be my friends for the rest of our lives. I got a small group of men I could trust with anything—that's rarer than it ought to be. I got a chance to serve a country that had given me so much. I got the chance to live according to my purpose.

To get all that, I had to earn it. To earn it, I had to suffer.

As a consequence of doing something hard, I was rewarded with *meaning*. It is self-evident that success won through hard work and sacrifice are more appreciated and more meaningful than success simply given. Suffering and hardship, taken on with purposeful intent, lead to a sense of meaning. Finding meaning is what I think Thomas Jefferson meant when he wrote the words "the pursuit of happiness" in the Declaration of Independence. In exchange for the promise that our government shall protect this right, it is expected that our citizenry live responsibly and pursue that which is meaningful. It is rare that something meaningful is found without a degree of hardship.

Professor Scott T. Allison, a psychologist at the University of Richmond, writes that "the search for meaning not only alleviates suffering; the absence of meaning can *cause* suffering."

Meaning is another antidote to outrage culture. Meaning,

purpose, perspective: All these qualities are wrapped up in one another. But they are not gifts conferred; they are earned. The degree of one's hardship is, in the end, a matter of perspective. One man's suffering may be just another easy day for another. When *Dirty Jobs* host Mike Rowe treks across America highlighting the many blue-collar jobs that are backbreaking, dirty, and exhausting, it goes without saying that many white-collar workers would find that work to be simply too hard. I feel sorry for those white-collar workers who have not had the opportunity to experience the spiritual awakening that comes with truly hard physical labor. I can honestly say that some of my most memorable moments of self-fulfillment were after grueling three-day operations in the mountains of Afghanistan, wading through miles of knee-deep snow and sleeping in the dirt. There was meaning within the hardship, and it's difficult to describe that meaning. I can only suggest that you do your best to experience it.

Not everyone can engage in grueling physical labor, of course. Perhaps your doctor won't let you. But there are other ways to challenge yourself. When I majored in international relations at Tufts University, I also minored in physics. It seems at odds, as the two subjects are so distant. There was also no logical reason to add a bunch of challenging physics classes to my already demanding schedule. I knew I wanted to be a SEAL, if you recall, so minoring in physics was arguably pointless.

Or was it? I did it for three reasons. One, because it interests me. Two, because I believed in self-improvement, and while liberal arts classes *expand* the mind, you need science and math to *sharpen* the mind. And three, because I've always believed that there is reward in challenging yourself, even if it's not immediately apparent. The journey itself may be the reward. Doing something hard is the reward. Maybe I did it just so I could fill a small part of this book talking about it. Who knows? I just know I don't regret it.

The way studying physics sharpens the mind, it also turns out that purposeful suffering might actually change your health, your genetic expression, and your brain. The study of neuroplasticity has shown how mental activity—our thoughts—can actually make meaningful changes to your brain. And the study of epigenetics has shown that our thoughts, actions, and habits can influence the way our genes are expressed. This goes against the notion that we are totally captive to our genetic makeup, instead suggesting we have far more power over our physiology than previously thought. As it pertains to the nature-versus-nurture debate, it turns out nurture (meaning our environment) can be very influential on our physiology.

It's widely accepted, for instance, that an exercise routine has a plethora of health benefits—controlling weight, reducing risk of disease, and relieving stress. Epigenetics helps us understand *how* exercise helps prevent disease and dysfunction by signaling to your DNA that it should produce certain proteins with health benefits. One study, for instance, links exercise to the production of brain-derived neurotrophic factor, which enhances memory and the growth of nerve cells.[2] I think it goes without saying that a healthier brain is a tougher brain. So start exercising.

Taking this argument a step further, Dr. Caroline Leaf argues that our *thoughts* can act as the signal switch for our genes in the way that other external stimuli can. After all, our thoughts manifest in electromagnetic and chemical signals, and those react with our DNA. An example is the "CREB gene," which is switched on by merely thinking about it. This results in the production of proteins in the brain's frontal lobe cells, which grow protein branches that hold memories.[3]

---

2   https://www.whatisepigenetics.com/exercise-linked-to-epigenetic-benefits-that-keep-the-brain-healthy/
3   *Switch on Your Brain*, Dr. Caroline Leaf, Baker Books, 2013.

Additionally, the psychological literature suggests that positive changes in character formation can result from traumatic events. M. Elizabeth Lewis Hall, Richard Langer, and Jason McMartin write:

> In fact, positive changes have been reported empirically following chronic illness, heart attacks, breast cancer, bone marrow transplants, HIV and AIDS, rape and sexual assault, military combat, maritime disasters, plane crashes, tornadoes, shootings, bereavement, injury, recovery from substance addiction, and in the parents of children with disabilities (Joseph & Linley, 2005). This type of change is known in the psychological literature by a number of labels: posttraumatic growth, stress-related growth, positive adjustment, positive adaptation, and adversarial growth. The idea is that it is through the process of struggling with adversity that changes may arise that propel the individual to a higher level of functioning than that which existed prior to the event.[4]

This is all a bit scientific, but the broader point is this: You have control over your thoughts, and your thoughts are more powerful than you may realize. Healthy habits create a healthy mind, and a healthy mind creates healthy people. Doing something hard is the habit of building mental calluses so that when life happens, you are better prepared for it.

In prior generations, this lesson would not have been necessary. Life was harder then. Today, the miracle of modernity, relative peace, and the pursuit of creature comforts has made hardship a rarer thing. So how, then, do we embrace this lesson in a society

---

4   Elizabeth Hall, Richard Langer, and Jason McMartin. 2010. "The Role of Suffering in Human Flourishing: Contributions From Positive Psychology, Theology, and Philosophy." *Journal of Psychology and Theology* 38: 117–118.

that seeks to strip hardship away at every opportunity? Well, I'm not saying you should seek out traumatic experiences, attend BUD/S or take classes in quantum physics. Heck, most of the people who attend BUD/S shouldn't attend BUD/S—the dropout rate is high by design. I'm not saying you have to engage in hard labor for a summer (however, if you are physically capable of it, I would strongly suggest it). I'm not saying the challenges you seek must be physical in nature, given that not everyone is physically healthy enough to join a CrossFit class, run a marathon, or hike up a mountain. If you can do these things, I recommend that you do. Physical suffering—with purpose in mind—is a truly transformational path to mental health and meaning.

What you *should* do is scatter challenges throughout your life. The nature and value of those challenges depend upon you. And these aren't singular, big-goal challenges either. The pursuit of meaningful suffering must be *habitual*. It must be a new part of your routine, where you dedicate yourself to occasional bouts of self-imposed suffering because deep down you know you have *become too soft*.

Maybe what challenges you is finally getting that college degree finished.

Maybe it's beginning and sticking with an exercise program.

Maybe it's sleeping on the floor, or even outside, away from the comforts of your home.

Maybe it's running a marathon.

Maybe it's learning a new skill, or finishing a major household project.

Maybe it's embracing and practicing an ethic of forgiveness with people you despise.

Maybe it's devoting yourself to a charity.

Maybe it's walking up the escalator, not riding it.

Maybe it's proving to yourself that you can fast for a full day.

Maybe it's finding out how much you have to sprint before your legs give out.

Maybe it's a polar bear plunge, or taking a cold shower once a week.

Maybe it's making amends with an old friend or family member.

It's valuable to emphasize something here: The challenge must be self-imposed. There are a few reasons for this. The first is that your hardship needs to be habitual. Good habits cannot be forced upon you, at least not in the Aristotelian sense. And the hardening of the mind and body is not something that can be done only once. It must be built upon consistently and with regularity. Those dumbbells aren't going to lift themselves, after all, and the longer you wait the harder they become to lift.

Pain should not be avoided just because it is pain. Voluntary hardship—say, willfully immersing yourself in an ice bath—elicits a totally different psychological response than involuntary hardship— someone forcing you into an ice bath. I think we know this intuitively. Research also suggest that the physiological reaction is different, and more beneficial, when the stress is voluntary and a sense of control over one's fate is present. In *The Truth about Stress*, Angela Patmore writes, "A number of key studies in the stress literature have highlighted the importance of *control* in the vulnerability to illness from distressing experiences."[5]

Stress, at the right dose and frequency, can make you stronger. But the voluntary aspect is important. Voluntary stress is purposeful suffering, and involuntary hardship is just … torture. We cannot expect someone to engage in habitual *involuntary* hardship. While

5   *The Truth about Stress*, Angela Patmore, Atlantic Books, 2014. P. 116.

the same result of "increased mental toughness" might be achieved by, say, an IED exploding in your face, I would not recommend it. No sane leader, teacher, instructor, or coach would advise that you place yourself in an unsafe situation just to see if you can survive an unsafe situation. Arduous swimming is good. Arduous swimming on a beach closed due to shark sightings is bad.

Voluntary hardship builds resiliency so that when the involuntary suffering comes, you are better prepared. The saying "No pain, no gain" gets at the heart of this lesson more clearly. As the BUD/S instructors gleefully remind us, "Pain is weakness leaving your body." The more pain you endure, the stronger you become. Suffering *now* pays off *later*. Carl Jung, the renowned psychologist, summed it up: "The foundation of all mental illness is the avoidance of true suffering."

And this isn't a new idea, by the way.

Ancient Stoic practitioners believed in "practicing misfortune." Seneca, advisor to Nero and one of Rome's greatest minds, suggested that a certain number of days each month should be dedicated to practicing poverty. In other words, removing yourself from your normal comforts. The point of this exercise is to desensitize yourself to the misfortunes that life inevitably confronts you with. It is meant to remove uncertainty from future hardship, and therefore dampen the emotions of fear and anxiety that accompany such uncertainty. In short, you will be ready for it.

During a particularly grueling workout circuit at my local gym in Houston, I was asked by one of the trainers what I was training for. I wasn't training for anything, I thought. So I said, "Life. Training for life." He nodded with approval. Challenging yourself, and engaging in purposeful suffering, delivers a sense of meaning. But there are more practical benefits as well. At the heart of the Stoic's lesson isn't necessarily the pursuit of meaning, but the pursuit of *preparedness* through suffering. Preparedness for what? Life. That's what.

Life happens, and you can't stop it. But you can control how you react to it. If you have already proven to yourself that you can fast for a whole day, then it will be easier to do when you get stranded on a desert island. If you prove to yourself that you can survive a night sleeping on the floor without indoor plumbing or electricity, then that same situation, if forced upon you, will be less shocking and debilitating. All those masochistic weekend warriors running Spartan Races aren't doing it for the T-shirt at the end, they are doing it for the *experience of suffering*. They love it. Not only does it give them meaning, even if temporary, it gives them confidence. Not only does it give them confidence, it gives them a sense of preparedness for the future.

We know this as SEALs. We train as hard as possible so that we are ready, both physically and mentally, for the real thing. In training, we often mimic the worst possible scenarios—ambushed, outnumbered, broken radios, wounded teammates. We watch as our teammates get wounded or killed over and over again—in training. Before Jocko Willink was famous for his public message about extreme ownership and personal discipline, he was famous in the SEAL teams for prescribing training scenarios that simulated killing half the platoon and put us in the worst situations imaginable. It's not morbid; it's real-life-scenario training. And when it happens for real, we aren't paralyzed. We know what to do.

If finding your own hardship is beneficial, then finding it with others is even better. There's a reason CrossFit gyms charge preposterous sums for the privilege of making groups of people come together and do simple exercises until they vomit. People aren't paying for the exercise—though many of them will insist up and down that they are. People are paying for the most precious thing we all yearn for inside: *community*.

When you do something hard, you find meaning. When you do something hard with someone else, you find meaning in community.

The fiercest bonds are forged in the hottest fires. There's a reason that many corporate team-building exercises involve difficult challenges conducted as a team. In fact, some companies pay good money to retired SEALs to send their staff to the Coronado beach, where they are put through a small taste of BUD/S suffering. *People actually pay for this suffering, because it works.* Dr. Allison observes, "Suffering brings people together and is much better than joy at creating bonds among group members.... Misery doesn't just love miserable company; misery helps alleviate the misery in the company."

When you have meaning and community, either or both, then cheap outrage becomes increasingly difficult to generate. It is no accident, I think, that the most vocal members of the outrage mob, the angriest and the most passionate, tend to be those with the easiest lives. Few places on earth are as sheltered, and accommodating, and insulated from adversity as an American college campus. And college campuses are the petri dishes where most outrage and protest and grievances multiply and spread. That doesn't mean I discount individual suffering and challenges—far from it. The utility of suffering should not immunize us from compassion for those who are suffering against their will. Everyone has a story of some hardship that they hide from the world and we should not diminish that. But the reality is that modern outrage culture corresponds with an America and a way of life that is easier than it has ever been. We are wealthier, more connected (albeit superficially), more entertained, more fed, and freer than we have ever been in all of human history.

It is not a coincidence that we are also unhappier.

Our societal unhappiness—increasing suicide rates, increasing rates of depression, decreasing trust in our institutions *and* in one another—has many causes. The declines of religion and the family, and the replacement of community activities with social media, to name a few. But I think it is worth noting that a loss of perspective about suffering also plays a role.

We have liberated ourselves from suffering to an extraordinary degree: A man whose great-great-great grandfather arrived in America an emaciated skeleton and refugee from the Irish potato famine today can have any type of food delivered to his front door twenty-four hours a day, and he has never in his entire life wondered where the next meal is coming from. Moreover, where his ancestor endured a monotonous diet of a few unseasoned root vegetables, he enjoys meats and processed foods of exceptional caloric content, nutritional value, and flavor. The ancestor objectively suffered more, but the descendant finds less meaning in his life, and is decidedly less grateful.

In fact, there is a reasonable chance the descendant spends a decent amount of his time raving on Twitter at the latest controversy, weighing in with uninformed but highly opinionated snark and sass. He doesn't suffer in any real way—and he is outraged. His problems are small but his emotions are not—they are elevated, outsized, and shared across cyberspace. The loss of suffering, this perpetual quest to remove all obstacles and hardships from our paths, has allowed people to find grievance in the small things, or—worse for the mind and soul—find grievance in things they have no ability to change.

This modern descendant may work a dead-end job and believe it is big banks or failed foreign policy that blunts his progress. He rails about foreign aid to Israel and corporate bailouts. He could control the direction of his life, enroll in community college or trade school, work hard, and become a partner worthy of marriage. Instead he focuses on that which he cannot control. Or imagine an affluent Yale undergrad, clothed in expensive designer wear and partaking in thousands of dollars' worth of therapy a month. They are utterly convinced they have been victimized by a sinister patriarchy and capitalist corporate interests, all while conveniently failing to acknowledge the daily comforts they enjoy or the gratitude they should feel for the wonders of modernity and the Western civilization that created it. Alas, they are simply unable to guess why their therapist can't cure their anxiety and anger.

I am not suggesting that the solution for these lost souls is to return to yesteryear with high infant mortality, byzantine medicine, archaic gender roles, and all the deprivation and sorrow that accompanied those challenging times. Romanticizing the past is no way to cure the present. That's not my argument. But I do believe we need to *understand* suffering. And we need to understand what doing hard things did for generations that were happier, less anxious, and less prone to suicide and self-harm than modern America. Then, having understood it, we need to seek those challenges in new and constructive ways.

St. John Paul II said, "Human suffering has reached its culmination in the passion of Christ. And at the same time it has entered into a completely new dimension and a new order: It has been linked to love...to that love which creates good, drawing it out by means of suffering, just as the supreme good of the Redemption of the world was drawn from the cross of Christ, and from that cross constantly takes its beginning. The cross of Christ has become a source from which flow rivers of living water."[6]

For Christians, our faith was founded on the ultimate act of suffering, the example set by Jesus of Nazareth during his passion and crucifixion. Sacrifice to the gods, whether human or animal, was instrumental to most polytheistic faiths and even Judaism prior to Christ's arrival, and His sacrifice—the sacrifice of the Son of God— was so profound, so extraordinary that it made all other sacrifices seem trite and meaningless in comparison. It was a sacrifice, rooted in suffering, done on behalf of the sins of man, to take them upon Himself and offer redemption to mankind. This was, as St. John

---

6   https://todayscatholic.org/meaning-value-suffering/

Paul II had it, the ultimate act of love and mercy. Romans 5:3–4 states, "We glory in our sufferings, because we know that suffering produces perseverance; perseverance, character; and character, hope." In short, *suffering has both moral value and spiritual worth.*

This is not exclusive to Judaism and Christianity, as I've demonstrated with the psychological literature. There is both secular and theological evidence that suffering has an immutable moral value and is indispensable to developing higher consciousness and better character. We know this intuitively also, as every parent will tell you that raising a child is simultaneously the most challenging and the most fulfilling experience of their lives. In the Christian sense, without suffering there can be no redemption, no mercy. In the raw, humanistic sense, without suffering there can be no internal resilience to adversity. No proper preparedness for the future. Suffering, controlled by you and for the right cause, can be a building block for both spiritual health and mental toughness. In a liberty-based nation like the United States, where we are free to fail and to suffer, that fortitude is a welcome and necessary attribute. Rather than trying to erase suffering at every opportunity, we would all be wise to value it and seek it out. So go do something hard.

CHAPTER 9

THE STORIES WE TELL OURSELVES

I recounted in detail how my dream to become a SEAL came to be. I read a book. I internalized it. I made it my goal. I had no Plan B.

But I didn't tell you about the other half of that goal, the part of that goal that never came to be. Becoming a SEAL officer requires a commission as a naval officer. There are only three ways to obtain that commission: the Naval Academy, Naval Reserve Officer Training Corps (NROTC), or Officer Candidate School (OCS). OCS is for candidates who already have a college degree, so this option was out for a guy graduating high school. As you know, I was commissioned through NROTC after graduating Tufts University. But here's the thing: It wasn't my first choice.

My first choice was the Naval Academy. I failed to get in.

My second choice was Rice University. I failed to get in.

If you've been paying attention, you know that wasn't my first failure, nor my first encounter with hardship. I failed to make the cut for my old Houston soccer team, for which I was a shoo-in. In high school, having recovered my confidence and making it as a starting forward on an all-Colombian soccer team, I failed to make the winning goal during a tie-breaking shootout in our most important game against our fiercest rival. I lost my mom to breast cancer when I was ten years old. I failed to get good enough grades in high school to become valedictorian. Maybe if I had, I would have made it into the Naval Academy. I broke my leg in Hell Week, I lost my eye to an IED, and I lost my career to a Navy bureaucracy that no longer had a place for a SEAL with damaged vision. And after all that, with a Harvard master's degree to boot, I still failed to be nominated for a White House Fellowship in 2017. Beyond that, I fail every day in some way. I overreact, I sleep in too late, I don't read that book I promised myself I would finish by the end of the week.

In this chapter I will sometimes use the terms "failure" and "suffering" interchangeably. Not because they are the same thing, but because the point of this chapter is to discover the importance of our *reactions* to those two words. After every failure, after every hardship, we create a personal narrative to account for that moment. We tell ourselves a story. We may not control the event itself (though we probably have more control than we think), but we certainly control the story that comes out of it. The new narrative goes something like this:

I didn't have time to finish that book, or maybe I didn't *make* enough time.

I lost my eye to an IED, or maybe I failed to get out of the way when the bomb went off.

I lost my career in the Navy, or maybe I failed to make my case strongly enough.

I broke my leg in Hell Week, or maybe I failed to do enough strength training so my muscles wouldn't fail.

It's hard to tell a story of failure after my mother's death, but I can certainly take responsibility for my reactions to it. I take on this perspective because it gives me control, accountability, empowerment, and therefore freedom.

Jordan Peterson, a renowned clinical psychologist, writes in *12 Rules for Life*: "If you buy the story that everything terrible just happened on its own, with no personal responsibility on the part of the victim, you deny that person all agency in the past (and, by implication, in the present and future, as well). In this manner, you strip him or her of all power." The wrong story leads to disempowerment.

You could tell the story of my life as a succession of hard times and heavy burdens. You could tell it as an array of kicks to the head interspersed with failures. My mom died, my leg broke, my eye got blown out, my active commission got taken away, my fellowship application got denied. All these things are factually accurate. They happened. I endured them.

That is where a lot of people would leave it. These are things that happened *to* them, *from* forces beyond their control. Leaving it there communicates a handful of ideas about someone. He's unfortunate. He's unlucky. He's beaten. He's a victim.

That is not where people *should* leave it. Stories about burdens borne on their own omit the most important parts: the responsibility of the individual, the reaction of the individual, the growth and maturing of the individual. The world does something to you because it will always do something to you. But once it's done, that share of the story is over.

That's where your share of the story begins. That's the point where the story stops being something done *to* you, and starts being *about* you.

As I've said before, the most devastating mental state I could ever wish upon someone is a sense of helplessness, a sense that they are not in control of themselves or their destiny. To be helpless to change your circumstances is to be totally disempowered, and to be disempowered is to be resentful, depressed, and unable to succeed. It's akin to being a bystander in your own life, watching from the bleachers while others scrimmage on the field below. It is the quickest path to despair and victimhood, a dark hole from which it is increasingly difficult to escape, because the draw of self-pity is so utterly powerful. Self-pity is an easy (and natural) emotion to embrace. The shirking of accountability for your circumstances is easy to do. It feels as if you are unburdening yourself of life, responsibilities, and hardships. But this relief is only temporary and offers no lasting benefit. This is how people in the most prosperous nation on earth, with all their material needs met and a standard of living that is the envy of the world, end up anxious, depressed, and overmedicated.

In a sense, this is the difference between normal citizens and the abnormal outraged: One tells stories about what they've done, and the other tells stories about what was done to them. One is about accomplishment, the other grievance. These narratives matter. We're designed as people to think in narrative, bringing to bear the full range of our God-given reason and emotion both to arrive at an understanding of ourselves and our place in the world. Stories are practice runs for the mind. We hear them, we read them, and we act out our own role within them.

The only way to resist that warm blanket of self-pity is to tell yourself a different story. It can be supremely difficult, because taking responsibility for your circumstances is *always* difficult and often seems unfair. When we fail to achieve a goal, make a timeline, or be there for a friend when they need us, we default to outside forces to explain why. To admit we had control over that outcome would be to admit we failed, to admit we lost. And no one likes losing. We value winners in our culture (and rightfully so), and when we aren't a winner, the last person we want to blame is ourselves.

Maybe you've seen the old 1970 war film *Patton*. It's a great movie—one of Francis Ford Coppola's first big screenplays and a cinematic achievement in every way. The opening monologue, a version of a real address delivered by the real General George Patton to Third Army troops before D-Day, features the titular character before a large American flag, exhorting his soldiers onward. At the very beginning, he says the passage that sticks with me now:

> When you were kids, you all admired the champion marble shooter, the fastest runner, the big league ball players, the toughest boxers. *Americans love a winner and will not tolerate a loser.* Americans play to win all the time. Now, I wouldn't give a hoot in hell for a man who lost and laughed. That's why Americans have never lost and will never lose a war. Because the very thought of losing is hateful to Americans.

The relationship of an American to victory—to *winning*—has never been more perfectly expressed. That goes for great matters of war and peace, and for small matters of personal conduct.

I love to win. My competitive instinct has been sharp and present since I was a young boy giving it my all on the soccer fields of Houston, Quito, and Bogotá. I always had a desire to excel. I decided when I was young to become a SEAL less out of patriotism—though that was there—than a desire to be *the very best*. If you'd told me there was something better than a SEAL, well, I probably would have gone for that instead.

The other side of that coin is obvious: I hate to lose. My father tells me that when I was young and on the soccer field, failure was the one trial that changed my countenance and darkened my demeanor. Nearly anything else could happen: I could get tripped, kicked, badly injured, exhausted, dehydrated, anything. It might tire or hurt me, but none of it would dispirit me.

But failure would.

Losing to a better runner, a superior player, an impenetrable defender, an outstanding goalie: All these things gnawed at me in ways that nothing else did. I never blamed them. They were only doing what I sought to do to them. I blamed myself. I knew I could do better. I knew I *must*.

Worst of all were the moments when defeat came not at the hands of others, but by my own doing. When I didn't work hard enough, when I failed to try, when I quit: Those were the episodes that dug deeply into my soul and psyche. That was *real* failure—because I failed myself.

"Americans love a winner and will not tolerate a loser." True. But that was World War II stuff, the era of the Greatest Generation, when losing wasn't an option. We're in a different generation now, a few removed from Patton and his heroic Third Army. We still love winners, but here's the thing: Eventually we are all going to lose.

Every one of us. Even SEALs. Especially SEALs. In fact, we are so used to failing that it's like second nature. It starts in BUD/S. Our bodies break. The instructors are never happy with our performance. Nothing is ever good enough. The mantra "It pays to be a winner" is true in the deepest sense, because the winner is rewarded in BUD/S. Boat crews who win their races get to rest or sit by the fire. The losers suffer, just as they would in combat. The top five finishers of the two-mile race on Tuesday of Hell Week don't have to run the race a second time. Where there are winners, there are also losers. In training, our scenarios are basically a long string of failures that we must overcome. And then in the debrief, we tell each other how screwed up we are and why we need to train harder. In combat, we sometimes fail to bring all our guys home. The worst failure.

When failure comes, there are a series of questions we have to ask ourselves: "Which actions of mine caused this? What could I have done differently? What will I do when and if it happens again?" Note something important about these three questions: They're all inwardly focused. They're all about personal responsibility. They all accept and face circumstances.

Let's make the questions outward facing and see how they look: "Whose fault was it? What do they need to change? How was I wronged? Why did my boss or professor not set me up for success? They asked too much of me, so why are they blaming me for falling short? How could I be expected to focus on my goal when there is so much injustice in the world?"

You see the difference, I hope. The first set examines self. The second critiques others. Inward questions accept responsibility and open the door to improvement. Outward questions assign blame and seek to pass failure off on others.

The second set of questions is a font of outrage culture. This is what fixation on "institutional" and "systemic" structures, real and imagined, looks like. An injustice occurs, or a wrong is done, or a failure presents itself—and the second set of questions simultaneously externalizes blame to a vague scapegoat and disclaims personal responsibility. The individual is able to concurrently maximize external critique and minimize individual culpability. The burden of injustice is shifted outward; the presumption of innocence is drawn inward.

In *Discrimination and Disparities*, Stanford economist Thomas Sowell spends 223 pages examining in data-driven detail whether the disparities present in our society—hiring, education outcomes, accumulated wealth, wage gaps, etc.—are in fact due to systemic discrimination. Spoiler alert: Discrimination is rarely the primary factor, if a factor at all. "Each fallacy seems plausible on the surface, but that is what makes it worthwhile to scrutinize both their premise and the underlying facts," he writes. For instance, firstborn children have vastly better outcomes than their siblings: They are significantly more likely to be National Merit Scholarship finalists, have higher IQs, achieve higher education, or become a member of Congress. Of the twenty-nine astronauts in the Apollo program, twenty-two were firstborn or an only child. "If there is not equality of outcomes among people born to the same parents and raised under the same roof, why should equality of outcome be expected—or assumed—when conditions are not nearly so comparable?"[1]

It's actually easy to see why people fall prey to this unique form of self-pity and buck-passing. It's seductive, simple, and often yields quick and favorable results. Personal growth is hard work, and self-reflection is frequently unpleasant. It doesn't help that there's a whole industry out there fueled by grievances and propelled by narratives that tell individuals they're victims of forces beyond their control.

Didn't get into the college you wanted?

Sure, you could have studied more—but it's really because you are structurally disadvantaged.

Still paying off your student loans fifteen years later?

Sure, you could have paid more than the minimum each month, and sure, you got a $50K-a-year master's in human services[2] rather than business, law, or medicine—but it's really because the student-loan industry is predatory and it's unfair that the federal government wants to be paid back after lending you money.

Lose your marriage?

Sure, you cheated on her—but it's really because she was so unreasonable that she drove you to another woman.

Didn't get the job you hoped for?

Sure, your résumé had three typos, you had a stain on your shirt when you interviewed, and your handshake is weak—but it's really because there is a societal bias against you.

---

1 *Discrimination and Disparities*, Thomas Sowell, pp. 7–8.
2 https://www.marketwatch.com/story/the-most-worthless-graduate-degree-in-america -is-2017-11-10

Hard times maintaining the household budget?

Sure, you could move to a town with better prospects for yourself and your family—but it's really because capitalism, or
trade, or immigrants, or whatever, are holding you back.

And on, and on, and on, and on.

We have a lot of Americans asking the second set of questions:
"Whose fault was it? What do they need to change? How can I
avoid it next time? *Which politician is going to fix it for me?*"

Let me say as an aside here: I am not at all suggesting that
Americans should ignore real societal, structural, or institutional
problems. They exist, and we should assess and perceive them with
candor and calmness. If a female lawyer with a superior litigation
record is passed over for partner in lieu of the founder's golf buddy,
then the founder better have a damn good explanation—rooted in
performance and results—for why she wasn't promoted. But those
causes are not assumed, they can be examined through evidence
and corroboration, and there are adjudicating bodies—the courts
and company boards—that can determine if discrimination laws
were broken. The shoe can fall on the other foot as well. In Austria,
a man won a €317,368 lawsuit against the transportation ministry
for discrimination, arguing that his application rated higher than
that of the woman hired to the position.[3] He too had empirical
evidence of discrimination to take before the courts, and was
given a fair hearing. The opportunity for *external* review of *external*
factors is a healthy and necessary and indispensable element of a
just society. Bias and prejudice are the rawest forms of injustice,
and I do not advise complacency in the face of injustice. What I
do advise against is the automatic assignment of blame outward at

---

3 https://www.newsweek.com/man-wins-gender-discrimination-lawsuit-after-woman
-gets-promotion-he-wanted-853795

the expense of self-reflection. Most of the time, there is only one cause for failure: yourself and your choices. This is a useful thing to know, considering there is only one thing you can control: yourself and your choices.

Therefore, choose your questions wisely and deliberately. Be the American we need more of, the one asking the right set of questions: "Which actions of mine caused this? What could I have done differently? What will I do when and if it happens again?" This is a necessary exercise, because you will encounter failure at some point in your life. And having a mind properly disciplined to learn from that failure is vital to self-improvement, growth, and earning the respect of your peers.

Let me walk you through some of my failures. Not failures in the sense I have described before—failing to make the team, for instance. I mean failures in the worst sense: The failure to react to hardship appropriately. The failure to ask the right set of questions. The failure to live up to the values that I myself have espoused.

After I was blown up, I went through a lot. The recovery was a lot more arduous than the experience itself. Multiple surgeries, immobilization, six weeks facedown in bed: I thought my limits had been thoroughly tested in BUD/S, but my recovery proved there were new frontiers of endurance to explore.

Before June 2012, I lived most of my life expecting to become a SEAL, or expecting to stay a SEAL. There wasn't a lot of room for alternatives in my mind. When I was wounded, I didn't make room for those alternatives. As I lay on my weird massage-table contraption and faced the floor for six weeks, I told myself that it was all worth it, because soon—*soon*—I would be recovered, and back on my way to SEAL Team Three. My platoon was out there. My brothers needed me.

And, if I admitted it to myself, I needed them. My identity was deeply woven into the SEAL community. Still is.

So, there in the most helpless position I'd been in since I was a baby, I went full-bore into a SEAL and military mind-set. That wasn't so unusual, and there was certainly nothing wrong with it. What went wrong was that I expected the same of others. My wife-to-be was there. My family was there. My friends were there. Physicians doing their best to put me back together were there.

I had no patience for those around me. A slight misstep from anyone was met with seething criticism. I was broken, but I was going to win and keep winning, as I always had. What excuse did anyone else have for doing any less—especially if they could walk, lie on their backs, and use two eyes?

My expectations of others made me a very unpleasant person to the people I loved—and who, despite my best efforts, loved me. My expectations were at bottom a product of the trauma I'd been through and my efforts to cope with it. But that doesn't change the hurt I caused in those days. I was keeping up a façade and expecting everyone to be a SEAL. I demanded perfect planning and execution, the right jokes at the right times, and discouraged any kind of "sensitive" or "emotional" discussions. I berated my closest loved ones who failed these tests. This wasn't unique to the worst days I spent as an inpatient in the hospital; it lasted for months, maybe even years. Our human temperament is like a rubber band, able to be stretched in the face of little annoyances. A patient person has more rubber band to stretch. Mine was taut, already at its limit. Patience was a virtue that I lacked in the most profound sense. I did and said things that I am deeply ashamed of. It was horribly traumatizing for those who cared for me most. Tara stuck by me anyway, something I am deeply grateful for.

That was a failure. I'll ask for a little mercy on it, given the circumstances. But the fact remains: I externalized blame instead of internalizing responsibility. It got better over time, but it took a lot of work. And it took longer than it ever should have. There is no excuse for treating those who love you poorly.

My anger, my impatience at my situation, was not related to my sight, as many might think. It was tied to the fact that the Navy would not give me what I wanted. It infuriated me. It ate at my soul. My hopes of simply rejoining SEAL Team Three and resuming platoon leadership faded as recovery stretched into weeks, and then months, and then years. Miracles happened with my left eye, and vision was restored, but it was highly imperfect and erratic vision. My battered eye was clouded with cataracts, scarring, and debris in the ocular fluid. It always will be. Two and a half years after my first successful surgeries in 2012, I was still grappling with clouded, blurred, and obscured vision in the one eye I had left, constantly testing out new contacts to improve my vision.

While I failed to treat people with the respect they deserved on many occasions, there was one small iota of redemption here: my ability to continue my career in a meaningful way, even if it wasn't leading a SEAL platoon. I did everything I possibly could to get back to my teammates. I was wounded in June 2012, and by October 2012 I was back on the gun. I requested to go to the Mid South Combat Shooting Institute in Mississippi with a platoon from SEAL Team Seven. Platoons go to Mid South (the Kill House, as many know it) every predeployment training cycle to hone their close quarter combat (CQC) skills and shooting techniques. I knew that if I was going to regain my confidence as an operator, and prove to the teams that I was worthy, then this was the place to do it.

Mid South is highly competitive. Every single shooting drill is ranked so that losers can be shamed endlessly. This is exactly how SEALs like it. I was in an especially good position for talking trash to my teammates when it came to competitions. If they beat me, I could simply point to the fact that I could barely see, and I was shooting my rifle left-handed now (I lost my right eye, and I am right-handed). If I beat them, I could berate them viciously for losing to the one-eyed man with blurry vision in the remaining eye. It was a win-win situation for me, and I had the time of my life. I did live-fire house runs on night vision goggles, left-handed and one-eyed. I didn't screw up. I remembered my CQC training, a complex set of rules that dictate how we move silently through an enemy building, taking cues from one another's movements, clearing every angle and ensuring that the enemy never has an advantageous position. The tactics of CQC are far more intricate than the movies would have you believe, where two guys simply burst through a door and split the room. I did it all. I spent extra hours with instructors perfecting my left-handed rifle reloads and weapon transitions. All my years of muscle memory training had to be unlearned and then relearned on my left hand. I worked at it. I put in the extra time. By the end of the training, I was passing the key operator standards tests that determine SEAL shooting competency.

But this wasn't enough. Shooting on the range is one thing, but unique missions, like combat diving, were closed to me—not just because I had no depth perception, but also because the low-light conditions below the surface would render me effectively blind. Land-based patrolling of the sort I knew in Iraq and Afghanistan were out of the question: I would see neither men nor IEDs with sufficient clarity to make the necessary calls in the field. My limited field of view would make it harder to quickly spot movement that might be life-threatening. I had to wear a contact in my remaining eye; what if it got dirt or dust in it? I would be incapacitated.

Two and a half years after the injury, and after many failed attempts at getting a viable contact, the Navy doctors finally referred me to a small firm called BostonSight that specialized in contact lenses for damaged eyes like mine. I went, and behold: Another miracle. The lens gave me 20/20 distance vision for the first time since the blast. Now, 20/20 distance vision isn't full recovery—I still need glasses to read, and my iris doesn't function—but from where I'd been it was a long way toward a more normal existence. I was back. I was ready to rejoin the Navy and get out there with my fellow SEALs.

The Navy tried to make it work. I wasn't going to be out there in the field with a weapon. But I could do the next best thing: lead teams that provide intelligence support to SEALs who were in harm's way. I was assigned to Special Reconnaissance Team One, and in 2014 I returned to the Middle East—this time to Bahrain, where the United States Fifth Fleet is headquartered and a considerable American intelligence and communications apparatus has long been in place. I worked throughout the Persian Gulf and even in Lebanon. In 2016 I was sent to Korea.

It wasn't the same sort of thing I was doing, nor what I had expected to do when I dreamed of the SEAL Teams as a boy. But I was *serving*. I had a mission. And that was what mattered to me.

But in the end, the medical rules and regulations of the Navy could not be overcome. The Navy, years before, had taken me in and made me a SEAL. All the attributes, training, and experience I'd attained were still there, minus a bit of visual acuity. I could see my way to continued service for years to come. The Navy could not.

I want to clarify something important here. I love the Navy still, and I am grateful to have served. Service is a privilege—not a right. There's a scene in the miniseries *Band of Brothers* where one officer says to another, "They took away your platoon?" The response: "It isn't my platoon, it's the Army's platoon." Well, it's the same with my time in the Navy: It wasn't my time, it was the Navy's time.

In late 2016, the Navy decided my time was over. I came home from Korea, and I was given a medical discharge. That was it. That day, when I stopped being a commissioned officer and starting being a civilian, was the day a dream ended that had begun nearly twenty years before, when my dad handed me *Rogue Warrior* by Dick Marcinko and said I might enjoy it.

I failed. And I had to confront it.

I had fought to stay in the Navy and to stay in the fight, literally since the first moments after the IED hit me four and a half years before. I had walked on my own to the evacuation helicopter because I wanted no man carrying me who could be fighting. I had decided I would see again, even when told I probably would not, because I knew I had to see to stay a SEAL. I endured a long and painful recovery with the singular goal in mind of rejoining SEAL Team Three. I accepted assignments around the globe that were outside the ordinary confines of my former profession so I could continue serving. I did all that was asked of me and did it eagerly.

I did all that and the Navy still showed me the door. I tried, and I failed.

It didn't feel good. I would be lying if I said there was not an internal struggle, where I vacillated between accepting defeat gracefully and moving on to the next objective, and wallowing in self-pity while I blamed the shortsightedness of the Navy for not recognizing the value I still brought to the fight. In the end, it wasn't one or the other. It was both. I allowed myself a degree of self-pity. I am not proud of it. I derided the Navy's overly bureaucratic and inflexible methods as wasteful and shortsighted. Why would we simply kick out a perfectly qualified and willing officer, and then put him on retirement and disability for the rest of his life? Do you really need 20/20 vision in two eyes to deploy to noncombat zones? What a waste, I thought. I wasn't necessarily wrong, objectively speaking. As a policy maker now, I think we should be asking these questions. But from a personal perspective, these toxic thoughts were a waste, serving only to focus my mind and anger on the things I could not control. My self-pity was not a useful emotion, and I should have known better.

Fortunately, that self-pity did not totally consume me. From the moment I knew the decision was final, I was looking forward, not backward. Despite my grumblings, I still knew a very important truth: Even if I was not totally responsible for what happened, I was still responsible for what *would* happen. I sought out my next mission.

I completed my master's degree immediately after leaving the Navy and I ran for Congress. My wife and I started an against-all-odds campaign in my parents' game room, competing with candidates who had millions of dollars to spend. We started the campaign with only three months until the first election. I worked for every vote and slid into the run-off by a margin of only 155 votes. Seven months later I won the general election and became a United States congressman for Texas's Second District, a feat which no one had thought possible when we announced in December of 2017.

But even if that had never happened—even if I had ended up with a private-sector job in a Houston-area firm, and stayed anonymous for the rest of my days—I'd still have a mission. My mission is my wife, the home we are creating, the community we serve. My mission is my role as a husband—and my role as a citizen.

Failure, when encountered properly, is often a gateway to a different sort of success. That success can occur only in the context of the right story. What do you call those stories? What are they? They *begin* as a litany of failures, bad luck, misfortunes, and un-deserved suffering. They *end* as redemptive episodes, each obstacle becoming an opportunity, because of the stories we tell.

There are certain statements we make about our hardship to summarize these stories: "I have to" or "I get to." If you *have to* deal with something, then it is being done *to* you. You are not in control. You are powerless. If you *get to* do something, then it is being done *by* you. You are in control. You have power.

I use this storytelling technique in my own life:

I don't have to suffer through Hell Week again.

I get the benefit of double the training.

I don't *have* to suffer the loss of my mother.

I *get* to live a hard experience and grow from the lessons she taught me.

I don't *have* to wear an eye patch.

I *get* to wear an eye patch.

I don't *have* to wake up nearly blind every morning.

I *get* to appreciate the gift of sight—any sight at all.

This applies to all challenges, big and small. It's the difference between failure and growth, or failure and more failure. You don't have to spend hours a day searching for a new job. You get to network and seek out a challenging new experience. You don't have to be depressed about a breakup. You get to explore new relationships. You don't have to pay the bills. You get to live with fiscal responsibility and learn the value of hard work to make a living.

If you're scoffing at some of these statements as unrealistic fantasies, go back and read this chapter again. You weren't paying attention. These statements are not meant to change external reality (of course you *have* to pay your bills); they are meant to change your internal reality. We are changing our perception of reality, not changing reality itself.

And this takes work. Psychologists treat patients with intense regimens of positive psychology therapy in order to create better stories. These stories help us turn the suffering into positive character traits. There is ample evidence that suffering can lead to better character outcomes, so long as our internal narratives serve as the pathway toward growth. At first it may be an internal narrative, but that narrative eventually makes its way into reality. Remember the two-mile run on Tuesday of Hell Week? The one where winners get to sit the next race out? During my first Hell Week, I was dead last, limping through the finish. Six months later, in my second Hell Week, I got first place by a long shot. An internal narrative of perseverance resulted in a tangible outcome of victory.

Going back to Dr. Allison's research at the University of Richmond, he argues that true leaders cannot rise to the occasion if they have not experienced and overcome suffering. He writes:

> For an individual or a group to move forward or to progress, something unpleasant must be endured (suffering) or something pleasant must be given up (sacrifice). Humanity's most effective and inspiring spiritual leaders have sustained immense suffering, made harrowing sacrifices, or both. These leaders' suffering and sacrifice set them apart from ordinary people who deny, decry, or defy these seemingly unsavory experiences.[4]

Suffering must not be avoided, Allison is saying. I agree. In chapter 8, we talked about self-imposed suffering as a way to build resiliency, confidence, perspective, and meaning. But resiliency for what? The involuntary suffering. Life. And when faced with that involuntary suffering, we better be ready to tell the right story. If we do, there are immense benefits. Allison writes, "The paradox here is that if we avoid suffering, we avoid growth."[5]

Pain and suffering can lead to growth, and growth is good. But suffering, failure, or trauma can also be terribly negative if our personal narratives are not in order. The stories we tell ourselves are what ultimately lead to the character growth, not the suffering itself. In the *Journal of Psychology and Theology*, M. Elizabeth Lewis

---

4   *Suffering and Sacrifice: Individual and Collective Benefits, and Implications for Leadership*, Scott T. Allison and Gwendolyn C. Setterberg, 2016. P. 211.
5   P. 203.

Hall, Richard Langer, and Jason McMartin write, "The role of suffering is not to endure it for its own sake, but for the sake of cultivating the flourishing life."[6]

Failure must be handled by taking responsibility for that failure—*even if it is objectively not your fault.*

The military embraces this hyperaccountable philosophy wholly. If a Navy ship runs aground, the captain is almost always fired. But what if the captain was not on duty at the time? What if he or she was sleeping? What if the officer of the deck was clearly to blame, through specific errors made? It doesn't matter. The captain should have trained the crew better. The captain is always accountable.

In BUD/S the entire class is punished for the mistakes of one. Every single time. If one guy overslept, the whole class suffers. Why? Because we should have woken him up. The punishment comes swiftly and decisively to the whole class, and especially class leaders. During my time as a "roll-back," in between BUD/S classes while my broken leg healed, we had a problem. Somehow, the watch schedule (a schedule for students to stand watch at certain duty stations) was not up to the lead instructor's liking. I can't even remember why. It was something small. I hadn't actually committed the error. But it didn't matter because I was in charge. I spent the entire next week, in January, shadowing an active First Phase BUD/S class around, following them to every single evolution, observing. But I was forced to observe while soaking wet. If the instructor—a relatively small but mean SEAL with a multitude of combat deployments—ever saw me without water dripping from my clothes, I would get another day added to my punishment. I

---

6   Elizabeth Hall, Richard Langer, and Jason McMartin. 2010. "The Role of Suffering in Human Flourishing: Contributions From Positive Psychology, Theology, and Philosophy." *Journal of Psychology and Theology* 38: p 111.

shivered violently for a week straight, to the point where even the First Phase students looked at me with sympathy.

In combat, if there is one weak link on a team, we all die. Personal accountability matters greatly. When one person stops taking responsibility for their actions, the unspoken implication is that they are expecting others to take responsibility for them. This is a toxic mentality for a platoon, as responsibility is slowly diffused until there is none at all. It is equally toxic for a society, where more and more people begin to believe that others should bear their burden, that the government is responsible for their happiness, and that personal responsibility is nothing but a nostalgic throwback to a bygone era.

The increasing popularity of an unaccountable existence should worry us. The pinnacle of failure is the refusal to take responsibility for mistakes and transgressions, and instead blame external factors. It has a societal impact, because an increasing number of unaccountable individuals make up an increasingly unaccountable society. Our culture begins to popularize the narrative that we are always victims of circumstance, rather than victims of personal shortcomings.

Outrage culture is built around this sense of victimhood in the face of failure. After the *SNL* moment, I lost count of the number of people who expected me to be outraged, asked if I was angry, or inquired when exactly I was going to put this awful comedian on notice.

As I said, my initial reaction wasn't emotional. I did not actually internalize his words or derive offense from them. I did not let them hurt my feelings. I compartmentalized them as information to reference, not emotions to react to. I didn't worry about what Pete Davidson had said. I worried about what I would say. And I knew that I wasn't going to be outraged. I wasn't going to be the aggrieved victim that our petty outrage culture was expecting me to be. I don't expect accolades for refusing to throw a fit, for refusing to fire off one of those self-righteous tweets or Facebook posts that are so fashionable these days. What I did should be considered the bare minimum, assuming that dignity and respect are still things we value.

We all have the choice to respond to failures in that spirit. When we don't make the grade we want, don't get the raise we want, don't get the recognition we want, don't get the parking spot we want—*don't get what we want*—sure, it can wear you down. But here's the thing: America is depending on us to rise above it.

America is a country of individuals, and together we comprise the American spirit. When one of us refuses to take responsibility, refuses to be accountable, and tells a story of victimhood instead of victory, the American spirit is chipped away. It feeds resentment and despair. And if enough people succumb to victimhood, avoid accountability, and externalize blame, it won't be long before America itself is unrecognizable.

★ ★ ★

Twenty years ago, I received a letter in the mail from Rice University. The letter might as well have been addressed "Dear Failure" because it was indeed a letter informing me that my services were not required at the prestigious school. I had failed to get in. Twenty years later, I became the US congressman who *represents* Rice University.

The path from that failure to present-day success was not an easy one. Many more obstacles and failures would present themselves. Every day, against each small obstacle, I had to tell the right story in order to stay on the path to self-fulfillment. I still do, and believe me it is harder than ever in my current line of work. But it is a habit that we all must engage in regularly and persistently. Failure, like suffering, has intrinsic value and worth, should we choose to confront it properly. Otherwise the ultimate story of success, whatever that may be for you, will never get told.

The stories we tell ourselves ultimately make up our characters and decide our fate. These small stories make up the larger narrative that we build together as Americans. The next chapter is about the *American* story, and what we must tell ourselves if we are going to defeat outrage culture once and for all.

CHAPTER 10

THE STORY OF AMERICA

In the flurry of media activity accompanying the fiftieth anniversary of the Apollo moon landing, the *New York Times* ran a piece that, but for the fact that it was in the *New York Times*, would have read as parody. "How the Soviets Won the Space Race for Equality," went the July 16, 2019, headline. According to the author, Sophie Pinkham:

> The space race was a prime opportunity to signal the U.S.S.R.'s commitment to equality. After putting the first man in space in 1961, the Soviets went on to send the first woman, the first Asian man, and the first black man into orbit—all years before the Americans would follow suit.[1]

The moral? Well, wrote Pinkham, "Under socialism, a person of even the humblest origins could make it all the way up." Setting aside socialism's tendency, *especially* in the Soviet Union, to produce rigidly suffocating class stratifications and the occasional genocide, it's a valid point.

The reaction to the *Times* story was swift and informed with

---

1 https://www.nytimes.com/2019/07/16/us/how-the-soviets-won-the-space-race-for
-equality.html

historical context, and exposed the misleading angle of Pinkham's essay. As one Twitter user wrote:

> USSR and post-Soviet Russia combined? 4 women astronauts since 1963. The USA? Almost 50, including all these firsts: mother, Chinese-born woman, payload specialist, married couple, black woman, hispanic woman, shuttle pilot and commander, ISS commander, and teacher. Also oldest.

So why did Pinkham and the *Times* run this piece? It's possible one or both just really still love the USSR and wanted to say something positive about it. It's also possible—and more likely—that the piece was an implicit critique of the United States. Just another microbattle in the larger culture war that seeks to tell a different story of America, or perhaps wants a different America entirely.

The casualties of outrage culture are many. Careers have been ruined, relationships destroyed, Twitter accounts deleted, and lawsuits filed. Politics has become toxic and vindictive. Therapy visits have increased as depression diagnoses rise. Thoughtful conversations have been substituted by social media snark and insult, where your opponent is assumed to have the worst intentions—simply because they are an opponent. Fairness and due process have been supplanted by self-righteous hysteria and public shaming. The meme has replaced good argument, the tweet has replaced the well-reasoned op-ed, and the op-ed has replaced objective journalism. The result is nothing short of information chaos, a culture of contempt, and a deep sense of unhappiness that is blamed on everyone but ourselves.

There is another casualty: the story of America itself.

The individual stories we tell ourselves—not just about our hardships but about who we are—combine to create our American story. Every one of us adds a small thread to the larger fabric of our culture. And as we change and evolve, so do our cultural norms. The American story itself evolves. This isn't a bad thing, either. It is natural and constant throughout history.

But something *is* changing for the worse. The American story itself is being threatened.

Our cultural fabric has often changed and evolved, but it has never been irreparably torn. The closest we ever came was the Civil War. It's worth remembering that one side in that fight set itself against the Declaration of Independence's core contention—that "all men are created equal"—and the other affirmed and extended it. President Abraham Lincoln so believed in the *right* American story, the one "conceived in liberty," that he was willing to fight a war that left well over half a million Americans dead, and wounds that would remain unhealed over a century and a half later.

I suggest to you that the latest threat to our American story is outrage culture, identity politics, and the victimhood ideology that it elevates. The threat is born of small beginnings, as big threats so often are. It starts with toxic personal narratives wrapped in the cheap cloth of victimhood, always looking to an external culprit to blame for real or perceived injustices. At first, this blame is assigned to an individual—your unfair boss, your neglectful parent, a teacher who refused to see your potential, or just perpetual bad luck. But this isn't enough for the outrage enthusiast. There must be more culprits. More oppressors to be blamed for your misfortune. Those individual culprits become group oppressors, thus expanding the category of oppressors from mere individuals to entire groups of people. The narrative becomes group-on-group oppression as a way to explain any and all misfortune or unhappiness that might occur. These groups may be different—based in skin color, sex, ethnicity, or socioeconomic status—but the story remains consistent. Misfortune or disparity is a result of an oppressive group. Identity politics becomes the new normal, and cultural leaders and politicians take advantage of these stories and even encourage them.

Take, for just one example, the *New York Times'* 1619 Project, explicitly designed to reframe the American Founding around slavery, instead of its actual foundation in 1776 and the promise of liberty. Among many other historical inaccuracies, the *Times* conveniently ignores the fact that America's founding documents were consistently used as the abolitionist movement's primary argument for *ending* slavery. Grievance reaches back a long way to make its case in the pages of the *Times*, even blaming modern traffic jams on the legacy of slavery.[2]

People are told that they are powerless and oppressed, and there is a specific other group to blame for it. The very real injustices that do exist—some individuals are, of course, victims of circumstance—are conflated haphazardly with perceived group injustices. Your misfortune is not the fault of your own decisions, but a consequence of the "1 percent" who ensure the "system is rigged." The phrase "check your privilege" becomes the favorite tactic used to discredit opponents and subvert real discourse. Groups are promised more power over other groups in the form of wealth redistribution, reparations, or wage regulation. The resentment that individuals may have silently felt for one another is encouraged and even elevated as a virtue. Anger is good. Wear your oppression proudly. Resist. Seek revolution. The politics of grievance and resentment become mainstream and arrive in full force.

But it doesn't stop there. The identity groups aren't enough, so the natural next step on the oppression hierarchy is our institutions, whether they be government or cultural institutions. The tax system is rigged and unfair, argue the Democratic Socialists.

---

2   https://www.nytimes.com/interactive/2019/08/14/magazine/traffic-atlanta-segregation
    .html

The very notion of a meritocracy is illusory and unjust, argue an increasing number of journalists and academics. The "establishment" is rigging the system, scream political activists on the left and the right. The Deep State is organizing to overthrow President Trump, conservative talking heads claim. Our legal system shields racists, argues the Center for Human Rights. The fundamental notion of sovereignty, and the stronger border enforcement needed to protect it, is racist and xenophobic, contend many of my Democratic colleagues. The institution of marriage is oppressive, argue many feminist activists. Ordinary religious groups advocating for traditional values are "hate groups," asserts the Southern Poverty Law Center.

The institutions that our society is built upon—law enforcement, religion, the financial system, the government—are labeled as fundamentally oppressive and are shamed and discredited. Other cultural institutions—the media, Hollywood—irresponsibly partake in such labeling and thus become discredited themselves. If not being condemned directly, important institutions such as the Supreme Court come under threat of permanent disfigurement as power-hungry politicians threaten to "pack the court" by adding additional justices. Even the greatest of our institutions, our Constitutional framework, risks ruination as some argue against such vital elements as the Electoral College and the First and Second Amendments. The maniacal desire to *tear it all down* begins to take hold.

Thomas Sowell addresses this problem with characteristic clarity and insight. In his book *A Conflict of Visions*, he discusses "unconstrained vision," and explains, "When Rousseau said that 'man is born free' but 'is everywhere in chains,' he expressed the essence of unconstrained vision, in which the fundamental problem is not nature or man, but institutions." Sowell is describing eighteenth-century French philosopher Jean-Jacques Rousseau's absurd belief that only good things can happen naturally, but that all bad things are a result of our oppressive institutions. In other words, your hardships are not natural, not a part of reality, but instead exist only because of oppressive institutions. The blame for suffering is punted to an external and identifiable culprit. It is no wonder then that Rousseau was a leading voice in the French Revolution, because only tearing down the institutions brick by brick could bring the secular utopia he envisioned. The result was the French Terror, where almost 17,000 death sentences were handed out in the span of a few short years. There's a real and tangible danger in all of this.

If our institutions are always to blame, then the next and ultimate oppressor should be obvious: America itself. In the search for oppressors to target, the identity politicians and outrage specialists have found the ultimate boogeyman: our American founding. In a growing number of circles, cheered on by major publications such as the *New York Times*, America is the vessel and origin of evil, the embodiment of sin against a more enlightened progressive ideal. This is the heart of the new culture war, which is the fundamental question of whether America is inherently good or inherently bad.

The origin of this culture war has many causes. French enlightenment thinking pioneered the idea that there is moral truth to be found in your feelings and passion, thus removing the need for God. When Rousseau declared that it was the institutions to be blamed for our troubles, he opened up the door for a utopian government that could perfect human nature—and the bloody revolutions necessary to implement such a utopia. Marxism, in its crusade against capitalism, was founded on the idea that revolution was a necessary force for good, while the Nazis fully believed in the state's ability to perfect mankind in their vision. The devastating history of the twentieth century in Europe was the result. All of these ideologies were built on a foundation that (1) someone else is to blame, whether it be the owners of capital or another race or religion, (2) that the government existed to perfect human nature, and (3) in light of society's imperfections the only solution is total revolution.

In America, Herbert Marcuse of the 1960s New Left movement championed the idea that only rebellion at all levels—sexual, societal, political—would lead to a respectable version of America. Marcuse advocated not only for rebellion but also for "repressive tolerance," as a way to censor speech that was serving the prevailing institutional constructs. "The objective of tolerance would call for intolerance," he said. The birth of the notion that speech is violence began with Marcuse, when he called to "reexamine the issue of violence and the traditional distinction between violent and nonviolent action." Marcuse argues that the only way to help minority groups and other oppressed people would be to *actively suppress* their "masters," by which he meant "the Right," and "prevailing policies, attitudes, and opinions." As Ben Shapiro writes in his book *The Right Side of History*, Marcuse laid "the roots of sexual liberation, victim politics, and political correctness."

Howard Zinn, a historian and, in his words "something of an anarchist, something of a socialist. Maybe a democratic socialist," took to the mainstream the idea that American history was proof of our country's role as an oppressor. In his influential work *A People's History of the United States*, Zinn portrays America as rigged by elite rulers who have subjugated their own people and peoples abroad. In a 1998 interview, Zinn admitted that the goal of his book was "quiet revolution," where people would begin to take the power back from the corrupted institutions he despised. While one could argue there is value in presenting counternarratives to prevailing historical interpretations, the truth is that these counternarratives have taken on an outsize influence in our current understanding of the American story. Even Zinn might have been surprised by this, since he praised the high-minded ideals of the Declaration of Independence as a thing to be proud of. Nowadays, it seems that many young people are being taught *only* Zinn's version of America and nothing else. The result? A strong and growing desire to tear it all down, include the Founding and the ideals it brought forth.

All of these thinkers, academics, and historians have contributed to this new, toxic story of America. And these are but a few examples. Navigating this labyrinth of blame and alternative histories that define our cultural struggle is worthy of a book unto itself. But what is at *the heart* of it all? I believe it originates from the poisonous psychology of victimhood and the search for oppression that it has fostered. In this twisted view, people are categorized into three groups: the oppressed, the oppressor, and the champion of the oppressed. The social justice warriors are of course the self-appointed champions, and it is usually conservatives who are labeled as the oppressors (though not always). The oppressed—usually a minority group—are designated by the so-called champions and told that their future prosperity depends on the champion's benevolence. But just targeting specific groups as oppressors has become insufficient for the outraged social justice warrior. It is America itself that must be put on trial and indicted as an oppressor. This malevolent group categorization is at the heart of the war against the American story, and outrage is its primary weapon.

I don't think I am exaggerating my case here. The evidence of this new movement—victimhood ideology turned identity politics turned into a hatred of America itself—is plentiful and espoused not just by the left-wing extremists, but by elected officials and mainstream celebrities. It's not just the left, either. While the right is much more likely to view the story of America as overall positive, there is still that festering discontent with America's institutions and our governing elites that has grown in recent years, and traces of victimhood ideology woven in with it. Distrust of government at all levels permeates the right, often justified but sometimes bordering on conspiracy. As a conservative, I too distrust government institutions because they are inherently flawed, overreach at times, and are often inefficient and poor at solving the problems they claim to be solving. But I do not distrust them because I think they are innately malevolent. And victimhood ideology, defined as the tendency to blame external factors for your situation, is a part of that distrust. Many on the right believe their economic prospects have been diminished because of excessive illegal immigration, for instance. Whether it is true or not (sometimes it is, and sometimes it isn't, with respect to the immigration debate) isn't the actual point. The point is that it contributes to a story of deep dissatisfaction, wherein blame is leveled at American institutions and politicians, and our proud and self-reliant American experiment in representative government becomes a story of being beaten down by someone else.

I note with great concern the right's loss of faith in many of our institutions and condemn the "burn it all down" mentality when I can. But the path from victimhood to American self-loathing is uniquely attributable to the modern radical left. A new example of victimhood-as-virtue makes the headlines weekly, tied to an indictment of our very own country and sense of self. Wealthy celebrities in particular are all too eager to jump onto the proverbial bandwagon of oppression, and lecture us about the evils within our country. In *Vogue* magazine, Taylor Swift said, "Rights are being stripped from basically everyone who isn't a straight white cisgender male." Congresswoman Alexandria Ocasio-Cortez, elected to Congress at twenty-nine years old, famously said that her generation "never saw American prosperity." Such overstatements, totally devoid of evidence, only make sense in the context of a culture that has become accustomed to seeking victimhood over self-empowerment. And because we have elevated the aggrieved victim to such a high status, people are actually creating their own stories of oppression, even if they don't exist. The Jussie Smollett hate-crime hoax and many other documented hoaxes are indicative of this desire to be the aggrieved victim. To be oppressed is good for your status, according to the new counterculture.

From victimhood to hatred of the traditional American story has proven to be a very short path. The Pledge of Allegiance and the national anthem are routinely protested. Antifa regularly burns the American flag at its rallies. Last year's Fourth of July celebrations were marred by the *New York Times* video claiming "America is just okay."[3] The *New York Times* felt the need, on the Fourth of July, to put together a video listing a litany of American failures, for no other reason than to push back against patriotism on Independence Day. Activists in Colorado protesting the detention of illegal immigrants at an ICE facility went much further than denouncing immigration policy, and actually tore down the facility's American flag and replaced it with a Mexican flag. Nike was forced to cower to the Twitter mob that didn't like their Betsy Ross flag–themed sneakers on the Fourth of July, even though the flag simply symbolizes the American Revolution. Meanwhile, corporate interests like major sports leagues and video game companies are perfectly willing to express sensitivity to a totalitarian Chinese Communist Party, all while freedom-seeking protestors in Hong Kong wave the American flag as their symbol against *real* oppression.[4] The people of Hong Kong seem to understand our American story better than we do.

---

3 https://www.youtube.com/watch?v=6mjef8NsNfU. The *New York Times* felt the need, on the Fourth of July, to put together a video listing a litany of American failures, for no other reason than to push back against patriotism on Independence Day.

4 Both the NBA and Blizzard Entertainment acquiesced to Chinese demands for censorship that directly violate our American tradition of free speech.

The success of this counternarrative against America is a result of the left's superior understanding of the culture wars, and the need to engage in culture on all battlefronts. The left has conquered academia, pop culture, comedy, and journalism to an exceptional degree. This isn't a controversial statement, just a true one.[5] Self-identified liberals outnumber conservatives in journalism by a ratio of thirteen to one.[6] In 2016, 96 percent of the media's political donations went to Hillary Clinton. Only 9.2 percent of academic faculty members identify as conservative.[7] The late-night shows are almost exclusively dedicated to ridiculing conservatives. Hollywood actors take great pleasure in using their platforms to express their discontent with the opinions of half the country. And should any of these pop-culture icons commit the ultimate sin of engaging in friendly dialogue with the likes of us conservatives, they are viciously ostracized.[8] The elements of culture that we should share—music, movies, comedy, education— have been weaponized against political opponents, and even the American story itself.

We are forgetting how to tell the right American story. We are telling stories of what was done *to* us, and missing the real stories *about* us. We are letting our hardship be blamed on an "other" and

---

5   I will surely be accused of "conservative victimhood" here, but the facts are pretty clear. It is not an opinion or a complaint, but an observation.

6   "Media Bias: Pretty Much All of Journalism Now Leans Left, Study Shows," editorial, *Investor's Business Daily*, November 16, 2018, https://www.investors.com/politics/editorials/media-bias-left-study.

7   Scott Jaschik, "Professors and Politics: What the Research Says," *Inside Higher Ed*, February 27, 2017, https://www.insidehighered.com/news/2017/02/27/re-search-confirms-professors-lean-left-questions-assumptions-about-what-means.

8   Look no further than Chris Evans's Twitter comments after he posted a harmless photo of me and him reacting to my Captain America–themed prosthetic eye. He took on even more criticism after daring to launch a website where politicians, including myself, speak with him about certain issues and allow viewers to decide which one they like best. Justin Ray, "The Problem with Captain America's New 'Both Sides' Website," *Columbia Journalism Review*, April 10, 2019, https://www.cjr.org/criticism/chris-evans-a-starting-point.php.

then quickly indicting the very foundation of our country for any and all grievances.

So what is the *right* story? Is it just blindly assuming that whatever our country does is inherently good and righteous? No, that isn't what I am suggesting. Just because victimhood ideology is toxic *does not mean we have never had victims*. But we must tell the story of America in a way that squares our suffering and injustice within the American identity without holding it in contempt for that injustice.

How might we do that? Let us look to our own history, when the trials and tribulations faced were not microaggressions or offensive tweets, but systemic injustice and persecution.

Meet José de la Luz Sáenz, a fellow from south Texas in the early twentieth century. He was a schoolteacher, a Mexican-American in a time and place where that was a hard thing to be. The years from 1910 through 1920 were exceptionally violent along the southern border. The Mexican Revolution exported anarchy across the frontier, including a 1915 insurrection in south Texas that delivered bloody mayhem to those unlucky enough to be caught up in it. The Texas Rangers responded in kind and then some, waging their own bloody and lawless terror campaign against south Texas Mexican-Americans. Racial tensions ran high. The year 1917 was nearly the rock bottom of the period—and it was the year José de la Luz Sáenz was called to serve the United States as a soldier in the First World War.

Think about what that would look like from the perspective of the modern left. Here's a man from a genuinely oppressed class, whose community endures real terrorization from agents of the state, compelled to go abroad and possibly die on behalf of that same state. Sounds like the basis for a protest movement, doesn't it? Perhaps an opportunity for some civil resistance, maybe an opening for a radical denunciation of an

America that oppresses its minorities and then sends them to be killed? No doubt an illustration of the fundamental racism and injustice that is the very basis of the United States?

You don't have to think very long. It's one of the easiest hypotheticals out there. It would have been very easy for José de la Luz Sáenz to see himself as a victim. It would have been very easy for him to tell that story.

Here is what José de la Luz Sáenz actually did. On receiving his induction notice, he put his personal affairs in order, closed up the one-room schoolhouse where he taught in the small town of Cotulla, Texas, and posted a note on the door including these lines:

> You will soon hear that I am holding a rifle in the very trenches of France and upholding our people's pride for the glory and honor of our flag....
>
> I am not going on an excursion, I know that the life that awaits me will be difficult, the most demanding that I will have experienced, but I do not think it will be as difficult as Washington's crossing of the Delaware and his stay at Valley Forge. If it becomes just as difficult, so much the better, it will be a greater honor for our people. Long live Washington! Long live the star spangled banner! Long live our *raza*!

José de la Luz Sáenz—educator, liberal of his day, eventual cofounder of the venerable League of United Latin American Citizens—did the *exact opposite* of what the modern left prescribes. Though given a story about something done *to* him, a story of injustice in peacetime and enforced servitude in wartime, he didn't stop there. *He continued the story*, making it a story *about* him and his responses to those things.

He knew full well what was happening to his community in

those years. He felt in full the sting of official and de facto racial segregation. He understood that coming across a lynch party of Rangers on the wrong country road at the wrong hour would mean his death. He knew that the preceding eight decades of Anglo domination of his own native Texas had mostly meant a progressive diminishment of his own people's stature and dignity. He knew that the Mexican-American students whom he taught in tiny Cotulla were likely doomed to lower prospects and pay than their Anglo peers, regardless of their talents.

José de la Luz Sáenz knew all this, and here's the important thing: He didn't take injustice and use it to reject America. Instead, he demanded that America live up to its promises. He deliberately and willingly inserted and included himself in the great American story. A Mexican-American schoolteacher in south Texas reminded his students that he was walking in the footsteps of George Washington's men.

And he was no outlier. In that bloody era, the collective response of the Mexican-American community in south Texas to the lynch campaign of the Texas Rangers was not to reject American identity, nor to rebel in still greater numbers against the United States. It was, again, the opposite of the modern left and "progressive" prescription: They embraced American identity tightly, as the best guarantor of their own rights and dignity.

The stories they chose to tell themselves, *about* themselves, was an *American* story.

These men could have easily perceived themselves as victims of an oppressor that was embodied by the entirety of America. The injustices against them were *real*. We cannot escape that fact. Our country's hands are not clean, and we shouldn't pretend they are. But the right story to tell is this: Our country has not always lived up to its ideals, but that does not make the ideals themselves wrong.

No one exemplified this better than Frederick Douglass.

On July 5, 1852, Frederick Douglass addressed precisely this point in his oration, "What to the Slave is the Fourth of July?" Twenty times in the address, in referring to the American Founding, he invokes the phrase "your fathers"—America and the Americans being a thing, he says, from which he and the slaves of America are excluded. "This Fourth [of] July is *yours*, not *mine*." Yet at its close the address takes a turn. Having exposed and excoriated American hypocrisy on Independence Day (and rightfully so), he abruptly situates *himself* and *his story* and *his hope* squarely in the American Founding and its documents.

> Fellow-citizens! there is no matter in respect to which, the people of the North have allowed themselves to be so ruin-ously imposed upon, as that of the pro-slavery character of the Constitution. In that instrument I hold there is neither warrant, license, nor sanction of the hateful thing; but, in-terpreted as it ought to be interpreted, the Constitution is a GLORIOUS LIBERTY DOCUMENT....
>
> I, therefore, leave off where I began, with hope...drawing encouragement from the Declaration of Independence, the great principles it contains, and the genius of American Institutions.

America was not living up to its own ideals, and Douglass was pointing that out in one of the most eloquent and important speeches in American history. The story Frederick Douglass told himself was a story in which he and every other slave were included in the American story. It was an unbelievably brave and inspirational moment, when the gravest injustices did not dim his hope for the American experiment.

Imagine if it were different. Imagine if modern outrage culture and victimhood ideology had had their way. What if the stories

233

stopped with the things done *to* them, a cavalcade of injustices and wrongs piled high with no end in sight?

Imagine José de la Luz Sáenz defying his induction orders, posting on his schoolhouse door in Cotulla an exhortation for his students to join him in *la revolución*, bringing more bloodshed to his homeland and communities.

Imagine if Frederick Douglass had called for an all-out rebellion not against the proslavery Confederacy, but against America itself.

These patriots never did anything like this, of course. But we imagine the counterfactual because it illuminates an alternate history exceptionally well. One is the past we didn't have, specifically because the prescriptions of today's anti-American culture were not present, and therefore not followed. The other is the future we *might* have had, were those modern cultural proclivities present. The result would have been a deep and dark dissolution of America.

Americans who understand the American spirit build communities of affirmation that embrace and encompass their identities in an American framework. Frederick Douglass and Martin Luther King Jr. are in this category. Despite the injustices they faced, the stories they told *about* America enabled us to better live up to the spirit of equality inherent in the Founding, and see the good in our American story.

Americans who do *not* understand the American spirit build communities of dissension and discontent that understand their misfortune as requiring *the destruction of America*. This is the Howard Zinn, Herbert Marcuse legacy. When you see yourself as a victim of America, permanently on the receiving end, then the inevitable outcome is the desire to denounce America in its entirety. Modern politics today swells with this shameless lack of perspective, most prevalently on the left. This phenomenon is even more bewildering when you consider the stark difference in severity of complaints being leveled by the modern left compared to the horrible—and very real—injustices faced by King and Douglass. House Representative Ilhan Omar, one of my own House colleagues, has expressed her disapproval of the American sacrifice on behalf of her own fellow Somalis in 1993, while also claiming "America was founded on genocide." Former presidential candidate Beto O'Rourke took this a step further, proclaiming loudly that "America was founded on white supremacy." *Founded*. Pete Buttigieg, another presidential candidate at the time of this writing, has expressed his belief that Thomas Jefferson was unworthy of public admiration. In early 2019, the city of Arcata, California, removed its statue of President William McKinley, apparently because it implicitly endorsed racism and imperialism. In this mind-set, America becomes an untenable prospect: Instead of Lincoln's "last best hope of man on earth," or Winthrop's "shining city on a hill," our republic becomes a malignance and an object of scorn.

How does all of this affect our modern politics? How does outrage culture, and the underlying victimhood ideology that permeates it, play out in our political present and future? What can we do about it?

On the one hand, I think individuals from both sides of the political spectrum engage in outrage culture, albeit in different ways. The hypersensitivity of left-wing students and activists to any perceived offense or injustice is laughable, to put it mildly. The true injustices faced by heroes like King and Douglass would absolutely break our modern-day outrage enthusiasts. Not only do the slightest of disagreements trigger their emotions, but they see value in being the aggrieved victim. The victim-hierarchy ideology has actually encouraged people to seek out injustices to be proudly worn as badges of honor.

But conservatives are no stalwarts of thoughtful stoicism, either. I watch with disappointment as many of my own supporters are drawn in by the angriest and loudest theatrics on cable and the internet, increasingly susceptible to conspiracy, attracted to a form of anarchy hiding in the cloth of conservativism, and willing to deride anyone who doesn't show total compliance and deference to their ideas as "Republicans in name only (RINOs)" or establishment sell-outs. There are no compelling facts given to substantiate such claims, no coherent arguments made, no room for nuance. Just insulting rhetoric and vapid sloganeering. The outrage on the right is different, but it exists nonetheless, and the overall effect is the same.

These individual tendencies concern me greatly, enough so that I wrote this book. But what concerns me even more is the question of what we do about it. This is where the left and the right diverge dramatically, and it is ultimately why I believe conservatism is a more responsible and enduring political philosophy. Allow me to explain.

There are two major philosophical and existential camps driving our politics today. One of them is, well, mine. I am a conservative. We can define conservatism generally as an approach to governance that values individual freedom, personal responsibility, and moral virtue as a bulwark for that same freedom. We believe in a limited role for government, fiscal discipline, and an understanding that government exists to protect our inalienable rights, among them life, liberty, and the pursuit of happiness. Government does not exist to end your suffering; it exists in order to create the proper structure, based on equality and justice, so that you may pursue your own happiness. It should be noted that this differs from many right-wing libertarians who are aggressively against just about any government role in your life.

The other philosophy is that which goes by the label "progressive." I want to define this term carefully, since I know many people who identify as progressive and yet agree with me about the proper role of government. The word "progressive" has assumed many forms, and taken on many definitions. When I say "progressive," I am not referring to the social norms it may engender. Many young people label themselves as progressive because they support LGBTQ rights, have tattoos, smoke pot, do yoga, and generally live a liberal lifestyle. That is all fine. I can understand all of that. I am not talking about that form of progressivism or liberalism. I am referring to the original ideology of progressivism championed under President Woodrow Wilson. Let's call this *political* progressivism as opposed to *social* progressivism. Wilson's progressivism was, and still is, an aggressively statist philosophy that rejected the Constitution—and the checks and balances it protects—as outdated and no longer suited for a complex modern society. Wilson and his progressive descendants have long believed in powerful central government that is unconstrained by limiting principles, unburdened by states' rights and individual liberties, able to implement a vision for society that is defined as... well... progressive.

I will give my political opponents the benefit of the doubt and say that this is at least mostly well-intentioned (except for the early Wilsonian progressives who targeted journalists, promoted eugenics, and were seething racists). While modern progressives are mostly well-intentioned, I fully reject their ideology as unsustainable, inherently antiliberty, and naïve in its utopian pursuit.

I reject this strain of progressivism for yet another reason, which is that it is a false god. It promises something never before seen in thousands of years of recorded human history: the end of suffering.

But wait, you might ask, what is wrong with trying to end suffering? This seems like a noble and virtuous goal. It is in our nature to relieve our friends and neighbors and (in the Christian sense) our enemies of pain and agony and burden. To do so is not only just but a higher calling. After all, isn't the point of progress to improve the human condition?

Of course it is, but it is one thing to strive for human progress, and quite another to believe that an all-powerful government can enforce that progress or even define what it looks like. This is where progressivism begins to blur the lines of political philosophy and a faith-based belief system. For it relies on the false premise that an all-powerful government can deliver upon the ultimate eradication of suffering. In this sense it imitates Christianity, with a promise to wash away the sins of the world. But there is a very deep and fundamental problem with this: While the sins and expectations of the Bible are well defined—based in thousands of years of wisdom, human experiment, and transcendent truth—the sins that the progressive wishes to eradicate are decidedly not. They are ever-changing, as is the case with any man-made moral structure. It is flawed because, for the progressive, morality can be relative. And when morality is relative, it can be changed according to popular opinion or social whims. The targets, or the sins to be eradicated, become increasingly bizarre, ranging from a boycott of Chick-fil-A to enforcing the ability of biological men to compete in women's sports. The goals of the progressive, whether to end suffering or reform human nature into an imagined utopia, are based on the mortal preferences of a select few, not the universal and transcendent authority of an all-knowing God.

Outside of the spiritual false promises of progressivism, there is also a very practical dishonesty at play. Certain questions quickly arise: Who defines progress? What is considered "good" in this Brave New World? What if we, gasp, disagree? There are obviously certain issues that people of all political stripes agree should be addressed by government: security, protection of property rights, and regulation of interstate and international commerce, to name a few. We often agree on certain social safety nets and antipoverty initiatives as well (though conservatives and progressives tend to disagree sharply on how to implement such efforts). But the modern progressive is far more likely to believe that these basic roles can be expanded indefinitely, so long as enough enlightened policy wonks with sufficiently elite PhDs are there to craft the ultimate solutions for all to live under. While it may be true that unique expertise is required for, say, nuclear power regulation, it is far from obvious that the same can be said of most social or economic policies. This sort of social engineering fails the test of practicality for two basic reasons: knowledge and preference. It is utterly impossible for elite policymakers to have the knowledge necessary to craft such bold proposals, and it is utterly conceited to believe that all Americans have the preferences that those same elites want them to have.

Modern political progressivism has shifted from addressing basic needs to *all* needs. The New Deal of the 1930s is a far cry from the current promises of Medicare for All, free college, free housing, and a job guarantee, to name but a few. This progression is predictable: After all, the ideology of well-intentioned progressivism is based upon promising more government services to constituents. Eventually you run out of basic promises and must come up with newer and bolder promises. As these promises become more extreme, the modern progressive must create societal afflictions to justify such bold action. And it seems that the more just our society becomes, the louder the progressives scream, "Injustice!" This isn't surprising when in fact their entire governing philosophy is predicated on fighting injustice. You're out of a job if the problem begins to disappear.

So they make sure it doesn't. They must make their ideas seem superior to the status quo, to the current system of American government. And since you cannot elevate progressivism above its self-described divine intent, you must bring America down in order to justify change. Look at what progressivism contends against: systemic forces, real and imagined, that bear sole responsibility for the ills and evils afflicting mankind. Capitalism. Racism. Sexism. Everywhere an -ism. The tenets of victimhood ideology become the force by which modern progressives make their case to voters to gain more power.

Give us power, say the progressives, and we will *end human suffering*. We will *end failure*.

But until we do, stay angry. Stay outraged.

It's an approach that does more than diminish the country. Far worse, it diminishes people. That's why you'll never see a happy (or funny) social justice warrior: A system that falsely promises the end of suffering also strips individuals of the capacity to deal with it. It's ontological malpractice. And it's growing.

I should also note that I don't believe it is *only* progressives who have fallen into the trap of endless false promises. We do see it on the populist right as well, where voters are told, "If you elect me, I will make you happier." Voters are promised better jobs, better everything. That being said, in practice the Republicans using this kind of language still implement a far more measured and limited policy approach, thus neutering the danger of excessive government overreach. However, the effect on the psyche of the population is unfortunately the same, because the message is this: Someone else can solve your problems. Someone else can end your suffering.

This is a deeply dishonest trick played on the American public, where politicians boldly produce impossible promises for the sake of votes. When Elizabeth Warren was criticized during the 2020 Democratic primaries for her Medicare for All plan being unrealistic and unaffordable, she responded by asking what the point was of running if she wasn't going to promise bold reforms. Ironically, we always hear that "elections are bought," "votes are bought," and "politicians are bought." The truth is much simpler than that. Votes are bought, yes, but not by some murky corporatist overlord. They are bought with the currency of politicians' false promises.

Adherence to this ideology allows and encourages people to tell the wrong story. Instead of a belief in self-reliance, dependence on government promises becomes normalized in the collective narrative. This replacement of personal responsibility with dependency has the fundamental effect of disempowering people. As I've said, if you aren't personally responsible, you are disempowered. It is completely and utterly self-defeating, and creates the kind of resentment and despair that leads to widespread outrage culture.

It is up to us—all of us—to reverse this trend. As a culture, we have to decide collectively that we will no longer be bought off by false promises. We must decide that our happiness is ours to pursue, not given to us by a supposedly benevolent politician. We will decide that our story—despite all the suffering we may endure—is not the product of an external immovable force, but our own to contend with. We must decide that we will be empowered and in charge of our own destiny. We must decide to tell the story of America that embodies the founding ideals and gave us the miracle of opportunity that we have today. We must tell a story that we are proud of.

This is the path to mending our cultural fabric. We begin to tell the story of America that we should be telling. We should start by recognizing that America is a miracle. A product of the best and most promising ideals that humankind ever had. The founding was the ultimate political and cultural experiment, where the great minds of Jefferson, Madison, Hamilton, Washington, and others could craft the blueprint for a new country using all the lessons from thousands of years of political and philosophical evolution. These ideas—the greatest lessons from the cities of Jerusalem, Athens, Rome, and London—were studied and drawn upon by our Founding Fathers to craft the Declaration of Independence and Constitution. In *The Roots of American Order*, Russell Kirk wrote, "Whatever the failings of America...the American order has been a conspicuous success in the perspective of human history....Under

God, a large measure of justice has been achieved; the state is strong and energetic; personal freedom is protected by laws and customs; and a sense of community endures."

America has been a purveyor of freedom and prosperity throughout its short existence. We can tell the story of our sins—and we should, for greater perspective—but we must also recognize that these sins do not render corrupt the foundational ideals of America. Our imperfections do not define us. What does define us is the greatness that America has generated.

Since the rise of America as a world power, human prosperity has undeniably flourished. It was America that led to the defeat of Nazi Germany and Imperial Japan. It was America that rebuilt a war-torn Europe and Asia. It is America that has underwritten global security for free trade and commerce. It is America that has led the world in innovation—from energy to advanced computing to the internet— and shared that technology with the world. It is American innovation that put a man on the moon, pioneered manned flight, and led to healthcare breakthroughs like the first organ transplant, the MRI, and the Human Genome Map. It was America's unwavering defense of freedom and human rights that prevented the scourge of communism from becoming a global power.

This is our story. Like many stories, it is filled with villains, heroes, dark times, proud victories, sadness, overwhelming joy, failures, and triumphs. It is a human story, after all. It carries with it all the inescapable imperfections of the human condition. But just as your story does not end with your sufferings or your failings, neither does ours. America is a fabric woven from the threads of human history's most noble achievements and greatest ideas. The American system of government—the first to enshrine natural rights, liberty, and equality—is a pinnacle of human enlightenment born from thousands of years of civic experimentation and ancient wisdom. The American spirit is a product of the oldest and most important virtues: self-sacrifice, courage, tolerance, love of country, grace, and passion for human achievement. These foundations have underwritten our great American story.

And it's a story with a consistent and enduring creed: Fortitude.

★   ★   ★

Fortitude remains the common thread in our American story. I wrote this book because I fear we are in danger of losing it. And what might be left if we do? Fragility and cultural decay, a slow demise of a nation that no longer believes in its own greatness, and an unwillingness to be the beacon of freedom and moral truth that we have long embodied. This is an unacceptable future, and we should avoid it at all costs.

The good news is that we can. We can decide right now that American greatness will not be rejected nor squandered. As the American Founding was grounded in individual liberty, so will be our future. Our rediscovery of our own strength must be an endeavor undertaken by each and every one of us. Mahatma Gandhi said, "Man often becomes what he believes himself to be." We believe ourselves to be capable of strength and courage and a purposeful existence, and so it will be. Our heroes guide us.

I told you before about the SEAL Ethos. Perhaps we now need an American Ethos. Perhaps it goes something like this:

I will not quit in the face of danger or pain or self-doubt; I will not justify the easier path before me. I decide that all my actions, not just some, matter. Every small task is a contribution toward a higher purpose. Every day is undertaken with a sense of duty to be better than I was yesterday, even in the smallest of ways. I seek out hardship. I do not run from pain but embrace it, because I derive strength from my suffering. I confront the inevitable trials of life with a smile. I plan to keep my head, to be still, when chaos overwhelms me. I will tell the story of my failures and hardships as a victor, not a victim. I will be grateful. Millions who have gone before me have suffered too much, fought too hard, and been blessed with far too little, for me to squander this life. So I won't. My purpose will be to uphold and protect the spirit of our great republic, knowing that the values we hold dear can be preserved only by a strong people. I will do my part. I will live with Fortitude.

ACKNOWLEDGMENTS

Writing this book was the first time I thought deeply about the lessons I'd derived from the SEAL teams, and life in general. It is quite the challenge to examine your own attributes, your failings, and then attempt to extract the lessons from your past that make you who you are today. This book is largely a product of that journey.

But like every book, it is also a product of many hands. The idea for this book came out of a breakfast meeting with my agent, Keith Urbahn, when we met for the first time in late 2018. I want to thank Keith for his guidance throughout the process, helping me craft the first outline and subsequent drafts, and ensuring I was in good hands with some great writers, editors, and publishers.

I want to thank my editor, Sean Desmond, for his guidance throughout, and for helping me craft something I can be proud of.

I want to thank Josh Trevino for the long hours we spent talking over the concepts in each chapter, helping to organize my thoughts and experiences into coherent lessons that would make lessons from the SEAL teams relatable to a wider audience. I am also very grateful for Josh's encyclopedic knowledge of Texas and American history, which made the research aspect of this book far less time-consuming than it otherwise would have been.

Thank you, Kerry Rom, who worked long nights to see problems in the first draft that no one else noticed. It is a better product because of you.

Thank you, Hannah Anderson, for helping me with the necessary policy research.

Thank you, Dr. Scott Allison, who sent me vital social-science research on heroes and suffering to check my own intuition.

Thank you, Carl and Gigi and the crew. I never would have completed the first draft on time without you.

If anyone deserves credit for this book, it is John Noonan. Back in 2017, John suggested I run for Congress. I did. In 2018, John suggested I write a book and proposed I take a meeting with Keith. I did. I also want to thank John for taking a highly critical approach to editing. His input helped me create a much better final product.

My dad also took it upon himself to spend countless hours reading through the book to give me the feedback I needed. My dad is responsible for giving me the most consequential idea of my entire life: the idea to become a SEAL. Thank you, Dad, for researching our Texas family history and for staying strong for my brother and me after my mother's death. Thank you, Carmen and Luis, for being loving members of our family. Thank you, CJ, for always being a loyal brother. Thank you to my entire amazing family who shaped who I am today—the Crenshaws, the Breckwoldts, the Smiths, the Bartleys, and the Thompsons.

I also want to acknowledge the Americans whose stories and deeds informed my understanding of fortitude and our national spirit. We live by reason, but we learn by examples, and I have been blessed with some very good examples indeed.

I want to thank every warrior I ever served with. The SEAL teams gave me more than I can ever repay. My ten years with the teams was an experience I would not trade for anything. I hope this book makes you proud. LLTB.

Thank you, Nan and Terry, for always being there to support me and Tara. You've always shown us what true generosity and love look like.

Some of the most important edits came from my wife, Tara, who knows me best. She is my rock and is responsible for the confidence I have today. She stuck with me through the worst of times, and she understands the lessons of fortitude better than anyone. She is also the first to tell me when I don't live up to those lessons.

Thank you, Mom, for being the first to show me a true hero. You are the embodiment of fortitude, and my brother and I have spent our lives trying to live up to your memory.

This book is for you.

ABOUT THE AUTHOR

Dan Crenshaw served in the Navy SEALs for a decade, achieving the rank of Lieutenant Commander. After being wounded in the Helmand Province of Afghanistan in 2012, he lost his right eye and required surgery to save the vision in his left. He earned two Bronze Star Medals, the Purple Heart, and the Navy Commendation Medal with Valor. Retiring from the military in 2016, Crenshaw earned a Master of Public Administration from Harvard University's Kennedy School of Government in 2018. He was elected to the United States House of Representatives in November 2018.